D1160717

Additional Books from the
Cross-Cultural Negotiation Project

COUNTRY-SPECIFIC STUDIES

- *How Germans Negotiate: Logical Goals, Practical Solutions* by W. R. Smyser
- *Case Studies in Japanese Negotiating Behavior* by Michael Blaker, Paul Giarra, and Ezra Vogel
- *Chinese Negotiating Behavior: Pursuing Interests through "Old Friends"* by Richard H. Solomon
- *Negotiating on the Edge: North Korean Negotiating Behavior* by Scott Snyder
- *Russian Negotiating Behavior: Continuity and Transition* by Jerrold L. Schecter

FUNCTIONAL STUDIES

- *Culture and Conflict Resolution* by Kevin Avruch
- *Negotiating across Cultures: International Communication in an Interdependent World* by Raymond Cohen
- *Arts of Power: Statecraft and Diplomacy* by Chas. W. Freeman, Jr.

French Negotiating Behavior

French
Negotiating
Behavior

Dealing with
La Grande Nation

C<small>HARLES</small> C<small>OGAN</small>

UNITED STATES INSTITUTE OF PEACE PRESS
Washington, D.C.

The views expressed in this book are those of the author alone. They do not necessarily reflect views of the United States Institute of Peace.

UNITED STATES INSTITUTE OF PEACE
1200 17th Street NW, Suite 200
Washington, DC 20036-3011

First published 2003

Printed in the United States of America

The paper used in this publication meets the minimum requirements of American National Standards for Information Science—Permanence of Paper for Printed Library Materials, ANSI Z39.48-1984.

Library of Congress Cataloging-in-Publication Data
Cogan, Charles.
    French negotiating behavior : dealing with La grande nation / Charles Cogan.
      p. cm.
    Includes bibliographical references and index.
    ISBN 1-929223-53-6 (cloth : alk. paper)—ISBN 1-929223-52-8 (pbk. : alk. paper)
    1. Diplomatic negotiations in international disputes. 2. Negotiation—France. 3. International relations and culture—France. 4. France—Foreign relations—1995— I. Title.

JZ6045.C64 2003
327.2'0944—dc22

2003061296

Contents

Foreword

IN THE SUMMER OF 2000 the United States Institute of Peace first turned the spotlight of its Cross-Cultural Negotiation Project on France as a subject for analysis. One or two voices expressed surprise. "Why," they wondered, "explore the negotiating behavior of a close and old ally? Shouldn't we be focusing on the way that national culture affects the negotiating style of *adversaries?*" Since then, of course, we have all learned that in the post–Cold War, post-9/11 world, historical allies sometimes have very different views of how present and future international challenges should be managed.

The rift between the United States and France over Iraq that developed in 2002–2003 was profound both in its scale and in its likely consequences. France and the United States have hardly become enemies, but previous assumptions about the two countries always coming together in a crisis have had to be thrown overboard. The new U.S. doctrine of preemptive attack, launched with or without UN approval, against perceived threats to U.S. interests conflicts with a longstanding French policy of maintaining cordial relations with the Arab world and of compensating for France's relative weakness vis-à-vis U.S. power by working through multilateral institutions. The two countries are sure to find common cause on a wide range of issues in the future, but equally they also seem set to collide on some fundamental questions regarding preemption, intervention, the use of force, and the role of the United Nations and other international institutions and coalitions.

This book is, thus, remarkably timely. Like the other volumes that have emerged from the Cross-Cultural Negotiation Project, this study is motivated by a desire to make diplomatic negotiations with a given country more fruitful by enhancing awareness of the negotiating behavior characteristic of that country's diplomats, policymakers, and governmental institutions. Such behavior, as the various volumes demonstrate, is shaped not only by the country's political system and history but also by its political culture, a component of its wider national culture. This is not to say that culture is the most important factor in negotiating behavior. To the contrary, the most important determinants of bilateral or multilateral negotiating outcomes are the interests of the countries involved, the foreign policies of their governments, and the specific issues at stake. That said, cultural differences and the negotiating traits that arise from them can and do affect the tenor, process, and results of diplomatic interactions.

In the new, more adversarial climate that surrounds U.S.-French relations, a clearer understanding among American negotiators of the stylistic traits and characteristic approach of their French counterparts will be all the more valuable in preparing for effective negotiations, thereby, one hopes, minimizing disagreement and the possibility of conflict.

Yet, even if the recent quarrel over Iraq played out in the UN Security Council had never occurred, this study would be scarcely less valuable. The United States and France may have been allies for more than two hundred years, but they have never been the easiest of partners, and their relationship has frequently been marked by misunderstanding, and sometimes by ill feeling, on both sides. A book that promises to enhance understanding of how the French approach and conduct negotiations would surely have found a receptive audience among the administrations of such different presidents as Clinton and Reagan, Johnson and FDR, Wilson and, perhaps, Washington. Furthermore, while the issues that animate French-U.S. relations have changed significantly over the years—with the clash between U.S. readiness to exercise its unmatched power and French eagerness to restrain the American *"hyperpuissance"* being only the latest—the most notable elements of French negotiating behavior have remained remarkably constant for decades, even centuries. The assertiveness of de Gaulle and Chirac, which sometimes seems gratuitous in its willingness to challenge American leadership, can be found in the age-old tradition of French diplomacy and the overpowering centrality of the French state in French society

As the reader will discover, author Charles Cogan emphasizes continuity in this broad-ranging and incisive portrait of French diplomats and leaders at the negotiating table. Some facets of the French approach, Cogan argues, can be traced back centuries. For instance, the days of French military conquest under Louis XIV and Napoleon gave rise to an enduring sense of national grandeur and a tendency to impose harsh peace terms on a defeated adversary; the influence of Descartes and the *philosophes* of the Enlightenment fostered an abiding preoccupation with justifying policy positions in the framework of Cartesian logic; and the French Revolution instilled a sense of France as a shining exemplar of republican values, the selfless purveyor of a universally applicable model of a fair and just society.

Other traits, explains the author, are of more recent vintage. For instance, the sorry experience of French diplomatic "tailism" in the 1930s engendered a determination thereafter in Paris to pilot a more independent, less entangling course; de Gaulle's intransigent assertion of French pride and global relevance after France's humiliating occupation by the Nazis has bequeathed to French negotiators a reputation for tenacious nationalism and arrogance; and concern to save Europe from both another world war and from domination by one or another superpower has promoted a readiness to work within multilateral frameworks, the most recent example, of course, being the European Union and the United Nations (where French power is magnified by its veto in the Security Council).

Continuity with the past is by no means the whole story, however, as Cogan makes clear. French negotiators still exhibit a penchant for delivering lengthy, brilliantly argued opening presentations, for aggressively reiterating their government's position throughout the middle game, and for disdaining any agreement that might compromise French principles or long-term interests. In each of these phases of the negotiating process, however, some change has become evident in recent years, and will likely become more marked in the next decade or two. Globalization is broadening the international purview of French diplomats, diminishing their resistance to the use of English, and encouraging them to display greater pragmatism. As a consequence, French negotiators are becoming less wedded to their opening positions, more inclined to show flexibility in the middle phase of a negotiation, and more likely to come to a final agreement.

Cogan's interest in both the past and the future evolution of

French negotiating behavior, his ability to speak both to scholars seeking more detailed analysis and to negotiators focused on practical advice, and his use both of previous academic studies and of numerous interviews with highly placed diplomats and policymakers resonate perfectly with the broader aims of the Institute's Cross-Cultural Negotiation Project. Mandated by Congress to support research into the means by which international conflicts can be managed or resolved peacefully, the Institute has always sought not only to speak both to the policymaking and the scholarly communities, but also to promote the exchange of ideas and perspectives between those groups. Thus, for example, previous publications resulting from the Cross-Cultural Negotiation Project have included wide-ranging studies on the impact of culture on international communication, as well as country-specific studies. The latter category includes Dick Smyser's *How Germans Negotiate*, Scott Snyder's *Negotiating on the Edge: North Korean Negotiating Behavior*, Jerry Schecter's *Russian Negotiating Behavior*, my own *Chinese Negotiating Behavior*, and *Case Studies in Japanese Negotiating Behavior* by Michael Blaker, Paul Giarra, and Ezra Vogel. The former includes Kevin Avruch's *Culture and Conflict Resolution*, Chas Freeman's *Arts of Power: Statecraft and Diplomacy*, and Raymond Cohen's *Negotiating across Cultures: International Communication in an Interdependent World*. Together with a number of shorter reports—one of which, *U.S. Negotiating Behavior*, turns the spotlight on ourselves—this body of work offers both scholars and practitioners a uniquely broad-ranging and unusually penetrating understanding of the dynamic relationship between culture and negotiation.

Extensively researched, engaging, and candid, Charles Cogan's *French Negotiating Behavior* is an excellent addition to this series. It will surely enhance understanding of how the French approach and conduct diplomatic negotiations. It should stimulate consideration of the difficulties, as well as the advantages, of negotiating between allies. And, at this delicate stage in U.S.-French relations, it may do a service to both countries by suggesting how to make their negotiating encounters more productive if not always more pleasant.

RICHARD H. SOLOMON, PRESIDENT
UNITED STATES INSTITUTE OF PEACE

Preface

THIS BOOK IS THE SIXTH IN A SERIES of studies about national negotiating styles published by the United States Institute of Peace Press. The series is part of the Institute's cross-cultural negotiation program, which examines the impact of culture on diplomatic and other negotiations. The congressionally mandated mission of the Institute is to strengthen the U.S. capacity to promote the peaceful resolution of international conflict. The cross-cultural negotiation project is premised on the belief that a richer understanding of the behavior of negotiating counterparts is likely to make diplomatic encounters more productive for everyone involved.

The flagship book in this series was *Chinese Negotiating Behavior*, written by Richard Solomon, the president of the Institute and the animator of the cross-cultural negotiation program. The Institute has since published books on four other countries: Jerrold Schecter's study of Russia, Scott Snyder's analysis of North Korea, Richard Smyser's examination of Germany, and a study of Japan written by Michael Blaker, Paul Giarra, and Ezra Vogel.[1] The Institute has also published works with a broader, non-country-specific perspective on the role of culture in negotiations.[2]

Although the subject of French diplomacy has attracted considerable attention since the heated confrontation over Iraq in the United Nations Security Council in 2002–03, interest in a book on France goes back to July 2000, when the Institute organized a colloquium from which emerged a short report on French negotiating style.[3] Now, as then, the central intention of this study is to examine how French culture writ large affects the way that the French behave in their relations with foreign countries, and in particular the way that they interact with their foreign interlocutors. This book focuses first and foremost on how French-U.S. negotiations are conducted, but it also includes observations on how other foreign interlocutors view French negotiators and on how the French see themselves.

This work examines a wide spectrum of issues as well as interlocutors. Although the emphasis is on French civil servants as negotiators, the book also considers French military officers and French businesspeople, with an eye to discerning both their differences and their similarities. There are, of course, significant variations in the ways that different French individuals approach and conduct negotiations—one need only think of such odd couples as Charles de Gaulle and François Mitterrand or Jacques Chirac and Lionel Jospin to appreciate that holders of the same office can behave in quite distinct fashions. Nonetheless, as the following chapters seek to demonstrate, and as U.S. and other negotiators are ready to attest, there is an identifiable French style. The various elements of that style may be mixed in different proportions in different individuals, but one can still recognize the overall mélange as being distinctly French.

In approaching this work, I have read widely in French history and particularly in French history as it relates to culture, including what is probably the most monumental undertaking of recent decades, the 4,752-page history of France through memory, *Les lieux de mémoire*, edited by Pierre Nora. Other works that examine the intersection of French culture and history are listed in the bibliography at the end of this book. I have also consulted a considerable amount of the literature on negotiations in general, and these works too are listed in the bibliography. A great deal of literature in French looks at the substance of negotiations and the decision-making structures that dictate French approaches to both bilateral relations and relations within the framework of the European Union. However, relatively little work has been done to date in French on the *process* of negotiations.

Because this study is primarily focused on French negotiating behavior since the end of the Cold War, few primary sources are available. Accordingly, I have relied to some degree on secondary material and to a larger extent on in-depth interviews, some of them with U.S.

and French officials and academics but some with representatives from France's major counterparts in Europe, Germany and Great Britain. As far as international institutions are concerned, my interviews centered on the European Union and NATO. Wherever possible, I have identified the interviewees in the body of the text or in endnotes; in some cases, however, interviewees have understandably preferred to remain anonymous. I am extremely thankful to all my interviewees for their frank and insightful opinions and for the rich conversations I enjoyed with them in the United States and Europe.

I am especially grateful to Alain Lempereur for his advice, particularly on chapters 4 and 7, and for the materials he provided me from the course on negotiation that he teaches at the École Nationale d'Administration, the leading French training school for civil servants. I am also indebted to Nicolas Tenzer for making available to me a study, sponsored by the French government, on the organization of French European and international policy.[4] I am also grateful to Max Johnson of NATO, to former White House official Bruce Riedel, and to Roderick Abbott of the European Commission for commenting on the three case studies in chapter 5. Additionally, I wish to thank four people who were invaluable in helping me arrange interviews with a wide variety of negotiators: Stephane Chmelewsky, French consul general in Boston at the time, provided many services for me and was particularly helpful in arranging interviews with French diplomats in Paris, Brussels, Washington, and Ottawa; Christian Hauswedell, then German consul general in Boston, helped set up interviews in Germany; Ambassador Beth Jones, assistant secretary of state for European and Eurasian affairs, arranged introductions for me with U.S. and European diplomats in the United States and in Europe; and Max Johnson, legal adviser at Supreme Headquarters Allied Powers Europe (SHAPE), arranged for me a series of interviews there. I would also like to add a special word of gratitude to Professor Stanley Hoffmann, my guru and friend over the past dozen years at Harvard and the ne plus ultra of U.S. experts on France. Finally, I am greatly indebted to my editor, Nigel Quinney, without whose suggestions this book would not have been so well realized.

French Negotiating Behavior

Marianne, French symbol of liberty and republican pride. In this representation from 2000, Marianne is modeled on the actress Laetitia Casta, who was elected by the mayors of France from among five candidates. *Photograph by Laurent FAU, reprinted with permission of Dexia Crédit Local de France, Association des Maires de France.*

1

Introduction

A PRICKLY RELATIONSHIP

It has long been no secret in Washington that France is considered the most difficult of the United States' major European allies. Beneath the rhetoric about France and the United States being the oldest allies among the major Western powers and the mantra that France, difficult though it is, generally sides with the United States in a major crisis— from the Berlin airlift to the Cuban missile crisis to the attacks of 9/11[1]—there is an almost universal irritation with the French in official Washington. Since the winter of 2002–03, when France refused to back U.S. demands for UN authorization of a war on Iraq, that irritation has spread from the U.S. government to substantial sections of the U.S. public and media, who have indulged in vocal Francophobia. (Witness the popular currency of such phrases as "cheese-eating surrender monkeys," an inane insult but one that strikes the French at that most repressed of their bad memories, the rout by the Germans in 1940.) British writer Timothy Garton Ash, after a tour of Boston, New York, Washington, and the "Bible-belt states of Kansas and Missouri," remarked that he "had not realized how widespread in American popular culture is the old English pastime of French-bashing."[2]

Indeed the mantra of France siding with the United States in a major crisis now has to be revised: the West-West consensus broke apart in March 2003. This was the worst rupture among "the world powers of the West," to use the phrase of General Charles de Gaulle, since World War II.[3] For in 2003, as back then, the issue was a matter of life and death. Here it was a case of two of the major players in the Western defense community taking up arms against Iraq and the two other major players refusing to. This is bound to have a profound effect, especially over the long term.

Garton Ash has also observed that the French "give at least as good as they get."[4] Indeed, in Paris, anti-Americanism has long been practiced as a sort of art form; as French intellectual Philippe Roger, author of *L'Ennemi américain*, notes, "It is almost a professional obligation *(obligation de service)*."[5] And in France as a whole, as in the United States beyond the Beltway, this strain of xenophobia resonates with much of the public, who decry "American imperialism" of both the geopolitical and the cultural kind. Jean Birnbaum, writing in *Le Monde*, notes the "obscure satisfaction" in France to which the events of September 11 gave rise, and he cites another expert on the United States, Denis Lacorne, to prove his point: "There has been a rise in this phenomenon [of anti-Americanism since these events], and even if one rarely dares to put it on paper, you hear it said in words to the effect, 'they had it coming.'"[6]

As Tony Judt, a leading British specialist on France, points out, this disdain and distrust do not date from the moment the United States emerged as a superpower: "America is solidly organized egoism, it is evil made systematic and regular" is a phrase that dates from the 1840s and comes from the pen of French socialist Pierre Buchez.[7] We will return to "egoism" later in this work, as it encompasses a French view of the United States that is ideological as well as moral at its roots. But although anti-Americanism was detectable in France before the middle of the nineteenth century, as Judt and others point out, it did not become firmly anchored in elements of French society until the period between the two world wars.

France and the United States have been dealing with each other for more than two hundred years but not, let us face it, very successfully. The paradox of French-U.S. history is that it began with an alliance that was vital to the creation of the United States and yet it became in the twentieth century the most prickly relationship among the major Western allies. As Alfred Grosser writes, "the most acute transatlantic antagonisms *(malentendus transatlantiques)* were and still are those between the French and the Americans."[8]

The alliance between monarchical France and revolutionary America was an unnatural one from the start and had been preceded by a long period of seething incompatibility between French and English settlers in North America. The French monarchy wanted to take revenge for having lost in 1763, at the end of the Seven Years' War, its possessions in Canada and India; and so it supported the English colonists in their dispute with the Mother Country. French support was key in the victory of the American revolutionaries, although it left the French treasury virtually bankrupt, which in turn helped to stoke the discontent that fired the French Revolution and destroyed the monarchy.

Once the French revolutionaries gained power, relations with the United States began to sour: diplomats from the United States were treated with disdain, and French ships (as well as English ships) began harassing U.S. privateers on the high seas. French-U.S. naval clashes followed, and the United States abrogated its 1778 treaty of alliance with France. However, French-U.S. tensions did not degenerate into war—unlike U.S.-British relations, which collapsed into the War of 1812.

The period from 1790 to 1910 has been described by former U.S. ambassador to Germany John Kornblum as a time when the United States was "working out its destiny."[9] The major U.S. event in this period was the Civil War, which both Britain and France sought to exploit to their advantage, giving some assistance to the Confederacy but never proceeding to the brink of diplomatic recognition. But at the same moment, Napoleon III of France flouted the Monroe Doctrine in an ill-fated attempt to install an Austrian archduke as emperor of Mexico, backed by French troops.

It was not until the twentieth century and the presidency of Theodore Roosevelt that the United States began to be regarded as a power on the world stage along with France, Britain, Germany, Austria-Hungary, Russia, and Japan. With the United States' long-delayed entry into World War I, the French-U.S. alliance was renewed ("Lafayette, we are here!'' was a rallying cry of the American Expeditionary Force), but in the peace that followed, the United States retreated into isolationism, and neither the United States nor Britain would support what they did not see as a greatly weakened France against a still powerful Germany. France's military collapse in 1940 followed, and although Charles de Gaulle resuscitated the nation, France was left at the end of World War II in a state of dependency on the United States.

But while French-U.S. relations have rarely been entirely cordial, they also only rarely degenerate into the utterly intolerable. The United States and France, it should be remembered, have never gone to war against each other. The same cannot be said of the United States and any of the other historic Western powers: Britain, Germany, Italy, and Spain. France was an ally who was "present at the creation" of the United States, and it remains, on paper at least, a member of the U.S.-led Atlantic Alliance, created in 1949 as a defense against the Soviet Union. It is a force to be reckoned with: a permanent member of the UN Security Council with the power of the veto; a possessor of nuclear weapons; a nation with unique though sometimes conflicted ties throughout the Middle East and Africa as part of a legacy of Western expansion and colonialism; and last but not least a country whose message and meaning as a society have a universal appeal not unlike that of the United States.

In short, France is a nation with which the United States will have to continue to reckon, whether Washington likes it or not. Moreover, notwithstanding the deeply divisive struggle over UN policy toward Iraq in the winter of 2002–03, the two countries have a long tradition of working together toward similar ends. This tradition is too often obscured by mutual antagonism, and its value too quickly forgotten in the heat of sudden disagreements. There is on both sides, but particularly on the U.S. side, what we might call a mist of incomprehension, which, if it could be even partly dissipated, would make easier the business of dealing with the other, as it would reveal not only that which divides us but that which unites us as well. As a senior British diplomatic official put it in the spring of 2002, "The French can't help needling the Americans. And on the American side, there are raw nerves constantly and a readiness to take offense. We [the British] have a ringside seat in all this."[10] More recently, however,

Prime Minister Tony Blair stepped down into the arena and joined the U.S. war against Iraq. Still, despite sharp Anglo-French exchanges at the time of the UN debates on entering the war, Britain continues to occupy a unique position: the road to a Franco-American reconciliation appears to go through London.

This book is not a grail-like attempt to find the "secret keys" to successful negotiations with the French. Rather, it is a work, conducted with the goal of objectivity constantly in mind, that seeks to describe and analyze how French officials—including not only diplomats but also policymakers, bureaucrats, politicians, and military officers—approach and conduct negotiations, especially negotiations with their U.S. counterparts. As well as dissecting the bilateral French-U.S. malaise (what the French might characterize as a *méfiance cordiale réciproque* [mutual cordial distrust]), it also suggests for Americans—and others—ways of attenuating it. There are pitfalls here in terms of receptivity, and these have to be acknowledged and accepted at the outset: as the historian and philosopher Theodore Zeldin observes, "No people criticize themselves as much as the French, but it is also true that the French do not like others to criticize them."[11] Resistance to a dispassionate assessment of French negotiating behavior can also be encountered on this side of the Atlantic, especially among those, and they are not just a few, who reflexively regard the French with a mixture of contempt and irritation.

It is also useful to make a study of French negotiating behavior as a way to avoid repeating some of the errors of the past. For example, in the case of the failed return of the French to NATO over the issue of the Southern Command at Naples (see chapter 5), many people on both sides have since regretted that the issue was not resolved, because what happened subsequently changed the future security outlook of Europe. We now have two potentially redundant military organizations in Europe: the NATO Rapid Reaction Force and the European Union's Autonomous Defense Force.

Similarly, as regards the issue of weapons inspections in Iraq (see chapter 5), the high expectation stemming from the unanimous 15-0 Security Council vote on Resolution 1441 of November 8, 2002, on resumption of inspections in Iraq soon dissolved into a mist of misunderstanding and suspicion. As Richard Bernstein of the *New York*

Times observes: "That expectation, as everyone knows, was soon replaced by the coldest chill in trans-Atlantic relations that anyone could remember, and the reason was that Resolution 1441 obscured, but did not resolve, the fundamental fact that the ultimate goals of the two sides of the Iraqi debate were simply irreconcilable."[12]

Between those in Paris who wanted to give peace a chance and those in Washington who wanted to give Saddam Hussein no chance, a clash sooner or later was ineluctable. No amount of "creative ambiguity," so much a part of diplomatic practice, could obscure this fact. To put it in French terms, the United States was proceeding in a "logic of war," while France was proceeding in a "logic of peace." In other words, each side visualized differently the chain of events that was to ensue.

In the debate over Resolution 1441, France considered that it had succeeded in gaining acceptance of the principle that there could be no "automaticity" in going to war without a further meeting of the Security Council. But it was not specified in Resolution 1441 that a second *resolution* had to emerge from this further meeting, and this was the basis for the U.S. claim at the time Resolution 1441 was passed that it did not need a second resolution before proceeding to war.

A further reason why French negotiating behavior is important for Americans is that in dealing with France we are in many ways dealing with Europe, although it must be said that European unity was another victim of the debate over Iraq in 2002–03. At least two Europes emerged in the debate, what Donald Rumsfeld bluntly referred to as "old Europe" and "new Europe." The former, the "anti-war" party, was represented only by France, Germany, Belgium, and Luxembourg. But these seemingly meager numbers were deceiving, because France and Germany are extremely important as the two largest founding members of the European Community, and the publics in two other significant countries were out of step with their right-wing prime ministers: Spain and Italy. "New Europe," of course, was represented by the incoming members of the European Union, still in thrall to the United States as their ultimate protector. Most important, for the issue of European unity, Britain came down on the side of its American cousin.

The European Union, the major development in Western Europe since World War II, has been described as a "French fling" *(une folie française*),[13] which is to say that France has put its stamp on the European Union more than has any other country. While it is true that many Europeans decry French tactics and what they often refer to as French arrogance—a designation that the French freely admit to—there is also something to be said for the notion that, as far as Americans are concerned, the French dare to say out loud what other Europeans are thinking.

Furthermore, France takes the lead in seeking to draw other Europeans over toward the French, as contrasted with the U.S., vision of what Europe should be: a power in its own right, including in defense; independent of the United States, though in association with it in an overall ensemble that is Western society; and part of the capitalist system, though practicing a "capitalism with a social face," that is, in the model of the social welfare state. That many Americans do not understand, much less accept, the fact of French influence in Europe is itself a reflection of an imperfect understanding of the sources of this influence.

A Distinctive Style

This book assumes that there is indeed something resembling an overall French style that can be discerned in the conduct of French diplomacy. At first blush, this may seem an overly bold assumption. After all, when one thinks of some of the most eminent French statesmen of recent decades, one is struck by the very visible differences in their personal styles: the lofty Charles de Gaulle, intent above all on inspiring fear and respect in others, stands in stark contrast to the sibylline François Mitterrand, dubbed by his contemporaries *le Florentin*; the charismatic opportunist Jacques Chirac presents an equally stark contrast to the unbending and rather too "Protestant" (in Chirac's characterization) Lionel Jospin. Given such glaring differences, can one really talk of a common French style?

To this very reasonable question there are at least two answers. The first is to point out that among the numerous diplomats from other countries interviewed for this book, none has doubted that there exists a distinct and identifiable French approach to the conduct of negotiations. To be sure, say these interviewees, different elements of that style are more or less pronounced in different individuals, and some individuals add colorful characteristics all their own to the mix, but the overall mélange of traits is still recognizably French.

The second answer is to explain that while any single negotia-tion—whether with the French or anyone else—is likely to be unique in terms of the subject at issue, the makeup of the negotiating teams, and the circumstances in which the negotiation takes place, the pur-pose of this book is to focus not on evanescent idiosyncrasies, impor-tant though they may be, but on enduring characteristics. This is not to say that the following chapters disregard the impact of personalities, issues, and circumstances; on the contrary, as the reader will discover, a good deal of attention is given to examining not only the short-term political considerations at play but also the broader, longer-term struc-tural factors that shape France's economic, foreign, and security poli-cies—and that accentuate or temper various negotiating traits. Nonetheless, the reader should be in no doubt that the chief aim of this volume is to identify and analyze the elements that together make up the distinctive French negotiating style.

The reader should also bear in mind that the emphasis here is on how French *officials*—chiefly diplomats and members of the gov-ernment bureaucracy, but also military officers and politicians—con-duct negotiations. Those officials usually share a similarly elevated social background and, in the case of the civil servants, mostly undergo the same rigorous process of preparation and training at the École Nationale d'Administration. Inevitably, these shared experiences tend to create and reinforce a common outlook, and the attitudinal and behavioral similarities grow especially pronounced when these officials are entrusted with defending the interests of France against represen-tatives from other countries. In brief, most of the French negotiators who appear in this book belong to the same elite group within French society, which among other things helps to explain the similarities in their negotiating behavior.

A SKETCH OF FRENCH NEGOTIATING BEHAVIOR

What, then, are the key characteristics of this distinctively French approach to negotiations? Subsequent chapters will paint a detailed portrait, but it may be helpful here to sketch the broad lines of our subject.

Fundamentally, French negotiating behavior consists of a mixture of rationalism and nationalism, the former a product of French cultural and intellectual traditions, the latter shaped by both the glories and the miseries of French history.

Schooled in the tradition of rationalism that sprang from René Descartes and was later elaborated by the *philosophes* of the Enlightenment, French officials worship the "goddess of Reason," who demands an emphasis on abstraction and the deductive approach. For the French, it is in the order of things to find a philosophical framework first, to establish a vision of things, before entering into practical matters. This is compounded by the formalism of French syntax and related to the French educational system's emphasis on the art of logical disquisition,[14] or what the French call *dissertation*, and on rhetoric at the expense of dialogue. Moreover, the French are brought up to have an idea on everything and to express it with clarity. In ancient usage, this was known as the tradition of the "honest man." There is a carryover of this tradition in the way France, as a collective identity, is compelled to express an idea on all issues, in the United Nations and elsewhere—a characteristic that Americans often put down to "pretentiousness."

Thus the French approach, as sketched here, stands in stark contrast to the Anglo-American emphasis on pragmatism and inductive reasoning and does much to explain why these opposite mind-sets have a hard time getting through to each other.

Having arrived at a "logical" solution, based on the exercise of reason, the French negotiator is little inclined to change it. As Gérard Araud, director of strategic affairs and security at the Quai d'Orsay and former deputy ambassador to NATO, wryly remarks:

> The French are prisoners of their Cartesian obsession. They believe, in the religious sense of the term, in reason, and they do not see in their position the defense of their interests but [rather] the expression of a transcendent reason of which they have the monopoly. They sincerely do not see that, as if by chance, this reason justifies their interests precisely.
>
> Once the goddess of Reason has been satisfied, they do not understand it when a "rational" position does not meet with unanimity.

When a French position, ergo logical, is refused or countered, the French
are taken aback by what they consider to be bad faith or stupidity. When
one "is right" one doesn't compromise.[15]

Such an attitude inspires not only a reluctance to compromise
but also a disinclination to prepare a backup plan in case France fails
to persuade its negotiating counterpart with its opening arguments. As
the French themselves recognize, they often pay a price—in terms primarily of a failure to anticipate—for believing that the intelligence of
their elites will by itself suffice for the development of a strategy and
its pursuit over the long term.[16]

French fidelity to the goddess of Reason is not always absolute,
however. In the first place, aggressive intransigence is sometimes leavened by a sense of realism, which the French possess, although they are
loath to admit it. A French ambassador posted to Brussels attributed this
to France's long-standing peasant tradition, which stands in contrast to
rationalism. In his words, "The peasant good sense is never very far
off,"[17] whence the widely prevalent notion—not always borne out, as we
saw in the Iraq imbroglio—that eventually, at the eleventh hour, and
despite the rhetoric dispensed, the French will come around to a compromise.

In the second place, it is often the case that—to quote the same
French ambassador—"reason clothes interest."[18] Certainly, many foreign interlocutors see the French approach not so much as an exercise in abstract reasoning as an aggressive pursuit of the national
interest. To the Germans, generally intent on harmony and thus
acceptance in the Western community, this unabashed French
approach is greeted with resignation, if not resentment. Speaking of
EU negotiations, one German diplomat has remarked, "If all were as
confrontational as the French, Europe would be in a mess."[19] A
German editorialist, evoking Carl von Clausewitz, had this disabused
observation on the French at the time of their wrangle with the
Germans at the December 2000 Nice summit meeting over voting
weights in the European Union: "Europe is the continuation of France
by other means."[20]

The notoriously aggressive, even harsh, manner in which French
negotiators defend their national interest springs in large part from
two contradictory but coexisting attitudes toward France's status in the

world. On one side of this dialectic is the tradition of what I have chosen to call *la Grande Nation*, which in its strict meaning is a term that applied to France's expansion in the revolutionary period (1789–99), as contained in the expression, "A Great Nation, carrier of the revolutionary ideal" *(une Grande Nation porteuse de l'idéal révolutionnaire)*,[21] but which foreigners used in an ironically pejorative sense based on the smugness *(suffisance)* of the French conquerors.[22] In this work, I have given an extended meaning to the term *la Grande Nation*, to connote the military and cultural glories of the French past, the centuries-old history of a centralized state radiating from Paris, and an almost corporeal notion of the entity that is France. In the words of Anne-Line Roccati, "It is doubtless in this ancestral conception of [the] State as the founder of the entire life of the nation that resides that French 'specificity,' of which the Anglo-Saxon countries are unaware."[23] In France the state is seen not as an intruder but as a fair arbiter; public service is highly esteemed; and there is a tradition of secrecy and discipline in what is a hierarchical bureaucracy. The French negotiator always assigns primary importance to defending the position of the state; reaching agreement with one's counterpart may be welcome, but it is of secondary concern.

France, the inventor of *la raison d'État*, is a nation that was built over the course of centuries chiefly by wars followed by harsh terms of peace, giving it in international relations what Alain Lempereur has called a "culture of war,"[24] or what we might call a "culture of authority" in dealing with others. This culture of authority, buttressed by a hegemonic past that is reflected in the awe-inspiring traditions and the ponderousness of the French state structure, helps to produce a comportment that sometimes comes across to others as condescension and arrogance, as in Jacques Chirac's veiled threat to the candidate countries of Eastern Europe for having supported the U.S. position over Iraq: "they lost a good opportunity to keep their mouths shut" (a liberal translation of *"ils ont perdu une bonne occasion de se taire"*).

On the other side of the dialectic is a "culture of the underdog," born of the defeats, interspersed with moments of glory, that France has endured, culminating in the worst defeat of all—the collapse of the French army in 1940. This has developed into a mind-set of what has been described as a "culture of opposition to the dominant norms." This recalls the phrase of Philippe Burrin concerning the French: "a people that celebrates its conquered as heroes—Vercingétorix, Jeanne d'Arc."[25]

This side of French culture is reflected in what can be called the "little Frenchman syndrome," as exemplified by the persistent notion of Charles de Gaulle that the French give in too easily to foreigners. De Gaulle himself, who remains a sort of mystical role model for the way he projected France onto the center of the world stage, was constantly on the defensive in operating from a weak hand. "I am too poor to be able to bow," he told Winston Churchill during World War II.[26] The general's "formidable capacity to say no"[27] cannot have been far from the mind of his Gaullist heir, Jacques Chirac, in challenging the Anglo-American war policy on Iraq in 2003.

Drawing on the example of Charles de Gaulle's solitary intransigence, French negotiators still fiercely contest, with some success, this turn of the historical wheel that, for almost a century and a half, has left France without the means to match its continuing, if unquenched, ambitions. In negotiating terms, this culture of the underdog is reflected, among other things, in an acute sensitivity to slights, in not being treated on the same plane as the stronger negotiating partner (read the United States), and in sometimes confronting the stronger partner in public rather than suffering a negotiation in private—as when Dominique de Villepin "sandbagged" Colin Powell on January 20, 2003, with a public statement attacking U.S. war policy on Iraq after persuading Powell to attend a meeting at the United Nations on terrorism. Unfair though de Villepin's tactic was, it could hardly be argued by the U.S. side that Iraq was not a fit subject for a discussion on terrorism.

More generally the French, caught between the tradition of *la Grande Nation* and the culture of the underdog, alternate, as the historian René Rémond writes, "[b]etween the fear of decline and the hope of redressment . . . We move, almost without transition, from an inferiority complex that is denied by our unquestionable successes, to a superiority complex that sometimes makes us unbearable to our partners. We go back and forth between moroseness and self-importance."[28]

The fact that France still has many of the pretensions of *la Grande Nation* but often not the means to match its ambitions can irritate its negotiating counterparts, especially the United States. In the words of former White House official Nancy Soderberg, "The French are fundamentally driven by a desire to be treated as a world power, which they no longer are."[29] This desire is perceived by many in official Washington, among them Henry Kissinger, who remarks of the French, "they want from the U.S. to be recognized as a major power. Nixon and I were fully conscious of this." In Kissinger's view, given the large cultural differences between the two countries, there is a reflex of the United States to "personalize" things: "There is a tendency to man battle stations. We let the French get under our skin excessively."[30] There is also a tendency within Washington toward a back-of-the-hand treatment of the French, which only confirms for the French that Americans are ignorant of the central role France has played in Europe and particularly in the European Union.

Where once Great Britain was France's greatest rival and philosophical antithesis, today it is the United States that occupies that role. It has become, in French eyes, the major part of an ever-encroaching Anglo-Saxon world of which Britain has become a much smaller, and tamer, element. France has come to find itself, in relatively recent times, in a changed situation with the United States: defeated (in 1940), dependent, and deficient. That this was not always the case makes it all the more exasperating. In their study of the U.S. relationship with the world since the end of the Cold War, Pierre Mélandri and Justin Vaïsse point out that the *flambées* of anti-Americanism in France are inversely proportional to the degree of power and independence that France feels in itself.[31]

Anti-Americanism has deepened since the end of the Cold War and the disappearance of the threat posed by the Soviet Union. A study conducted by the French institute Sofrès and the French-American Foundation in July 2000 showed that the French have an extraordinarily negative image of the United States.[32] Two years later, on the anniversary of the September 11 attacks, the Chicago Council on Foreign Relations and the German Marshall Fund of the United States published results of a poll conducted in six European countries (Britain, France, Germany, Italy, the Netherlands, and Poland) and found that the French were the most critical of U.S. foreign policy, with 63 percent saying that this policy was partly to blame for the attacks.[33] The growth of such animosity is in part a reflection of the contest between France and

the United States to each spread its own "universal" model of the ideal
republic, a contest that involved three players until the demise of the
Soviet Union but now features only two. Today, as Stanley Hoffmann
observes:

> [t]he United States and France are the only nations that present their
> values as universal, and they offer them as models to the rest of the
> world. The conflicts which, since 1945, have seen the two countries
> opposed in foreign policy have often been struggles between interests
> (economic, strategic, or diplomatic), but the rivalry of the univer-
> salisms has at times given them overtones of passion.[34]

As Hoffmann indicates, the idea of *nation* is closely associated
with both French and American universalisms, in contrast to other
universalist movements of the twentieth century, notably communism,
which claimed to transcend the nation-state. But the idea of nation
has a particular meaning for the French, as Dominique Schnapper
points out. France is a democratic community of citizens, united
around a common bond of principles and a common language. The
French model represents a dual rejection: It rejects the particularisms
of ethnicity, race, and religion in favor of a single community of citizens. Multiculturalism is seen as an American disease and not a
French one (although this assertion is sometimes contradicted by the
facts on the ground—for example, there are certain sections of
Marseilles that are de facto off-limits to non-Maghrebians). And, as
Schnapper notes, the French model also rejects the idea of a
"productivist-hedonist" society, namely, a collection of individuals pursuing their own material or other aims.[35] Thus in the French lexicon,
as can be seen in the light of what the French model rejects, the nation
represents a *political* project rather than an *economic* contract among
citizens, whence the perennial call for the supremacy of the political
over the economic, which has a puzzling ring to Anglo-American ears.

At the same time, the French are eager in private negotiations no
less than in public statements to demonstrate what is so clearly to
them the superiority of the their model, a model that is sometimes
subsumed under the notion of a distinctly European "humanism."
Witness Jacques Chirac's elliptical criticism of "the primacy of the sole
law of the market, oblivious of this culture of humanism, whose very
essence is to rally around ethical principles."[36]

As Europe and the United States continue to draw apart politically, France is at the forefront of those Europeans who want to assert policies that are independent of the United States. Of all the critiques of President Bush's "axis of evil" speech of January 29, 2002, it was France's, delivered by former foreign minister Hubert Védrine, that stung the most:

> We are threatened today with a new simplism, which is to reduce all the problems of the world to a struggle against terrorism. This is not serious. We cannot accept this idea. . . . If we are not in agreement with American policy we must say it. We can say it and we must say it.[37]

Although other European leaders, such as the European Union's Chris Patten and German foreign minister Joschka Fischer, made equally serious criticisms, none implied that the U.S. president was personally "simplistic." On this as on many other occasions, Védrine, or so the *New York Times* claimed, "seemed to relish any opportunity to criticize the United States."[38] According to a senior State Department official, what was particularly irritating about Védrine's tenure as foreign minister was his pattern, after a seemingly amicable meeting with U.S. counterparts, of then choosing to make an acerbic comment about U.S. policy in a public statement.[39]

Védrine's readiness to deliver sharp criticism publicly, which the consensus-seeking Americans find so hard to take, reflects two aspects of French negotiating behavior. First, the French judge issues on their own merits, according to the mandate of "reason"—they are not tied to a particular ideological line and will say what they think. Second, given the imbalance in the power position between France and the United States, it may be easier for the French to get across what they want to say in a public statement rather than in a head-to-head confrontation, as in the incident between Védrine's successor, Dominique de Villepin, and Colin Powell referred to earlier.

CHANGES AND CONTINUITIES

Each of the traits sketched in the preceding pages—devotion to logical disquisition and rhetoric, an overriding concern to defend the French position rather than to reach agreement, an aggressive and often arrogant nationalism, an often passionate assertion of France's "universal" message, resentment at Anglo-Saxon and especially U.S. power and influence, a readiness to use the media to deliver sharp criticism—inevitably varies in extent from negotiator to negotiator and from negotiation to negotiation. Changing circumstances also produce variations over time. The advent of globalization, for instance, has intensified anti-Americanism while also spurring recognition of the need for France to make some accommodation to the non-Francophone world. At the École Nationale d'Administration (ENA), proficiency in *two* foreign languages is now necessary, and spending some time abroad is now required as part of the training. Furthermore, the ENA curriculum and elitist student profile have been heavily criticized, and enrollment at ENA went down noticeably in the 1990s, as the private sector began to have more of an attraction in France than before. Today, the younger generation of French technocrats and business elites is generally characterized by flawless English. France has even witnessed the development of a U.S.-style entrepreneurial business culture in the past several decades.

The France of today is hardly the same as the France of fifty years ago, trapped as it was in the Cold War and uncertain of its and Europe's future. What may have seemed in the past unshakable affirmations are changing with time and the pressures of globalization. Who could have foreseen, back at the end of the Cold War, that a French president would have advocated extending NATO to the three Baltic states, as Jacques Chirac did during a visit to the region in July 2001? And who could have foreseen the internationalization of business in France such as has taken place in recent decades. Foreign ownership of French firms increased from 10 percent in the mid-1980s to more than 40 percent at the beginning of the twenty-first century.[40] Also, the past several years have seen a wave of global acquisitions by French companies.[41] These points of change, reflecting, note Philip Gordon and Sophie Meunier, a certain French adaptation to globalization,[42] continue to be by and large belied by French official rhetoric.

Yet France as a country, and France as a nation, perdures. In what can be called the second loss of an overseas empire (1945–62)—the first having been in 1763 with the loss principally of its possessions in Canada and India—France has rid itself of its colonial incubus, though not the ghosts of its colonial past. It is, as Védrine among others has commented, a very homogeneous country,[43] albeit an e pluribus unum society not very different from that of the United States. For example, France has five million Muslims and Islam has become its second religion. Perhaps less well known is the fact that France is the only European country that has experienced massive immigration since the beginning of the nineteenth century.[44] Citizenship is open, based on location (jus soli) rather than on blood (jus sanguinis).

Despite its diversity, and unlike in countries such as Germany and Russia, there is no identity crisis surrounding the notion of being French. France has long had a centralizing machine—notably its public-sector educational system, described as "a political instrument at the service of the construction of the nation."[45] Aggressively secular (and rigorous), the French public school system, founded in the 1880s, was given a consciously "republican" and nonabsolutist stamp. (To extol "republican" virtues in France is a civilized way of expressing acceptance of the French Revolution.) This is a process of conditioning that Eugen Weber describes under the term "[turning] peasants into Frenchmen."[46]

France has its own way of learning, its own approach to moral and social questions, and its own ineffable way of life, summed up in the notion of *la douce France*, calling forth the image of the beauty and timelessness of the French landscape and weekends spent in second homes in the countryside enjoying delicious food and wines—as a German proverb has it, "Living like God in France."

In short, despite globalization and a host of other profound alterations in the international political, economic, and security environment, and despite, too, the real political and cultural adjustments that these changes have elicited in France, the nation remains recognizably different from the other major players in the Western world. As this volume will show, this continuing difference is reflected in the very distinctive behavior of French negotiators.

THE STRUCTURE OF THIS BOOK

The following chapters begin by examining the sources of French negotiating behavior and then move on to dissect its defining characteristics, illustrate those characteristics in three specific cases, offer France's negotiating counterparts suggestions on how to make diplomatic encounters more fruitful, and conclude by looking to likely future developments.

As noted earlier, this book argues that the French style of negotiation can be understood only in light of the country's culture—especially the political and intellectual culture of its elite—and history. (This argument, it should be noted, is hardly unique. Henry Kissinger, for example, contends that French behavior is explainable by the country's "cultural past" and by its "historical past.")[47] Like two strands that make up a common thread, French culture and history are sometimes intertwined and sometimes distinct. To the extent possible, and to enhance analytical clarity, chapters 2 and 3 seek to disentangle them.

Chapter 2 begins by emphasizing the long-standing existence of the state apparatus in France and then looks in turn at France's democratic culture and how it differs from the Anglo-Saxon model; at France's pronounced anti-Americanism, which in part derives from the difference between these models; at the French "Latin" temperament and a taste for panache and audacious actions, at the influence of Cartesianism; and finally at the educational system through which members of the French elite pass.

Chapter 3 explores the main elements of French history: the construction of France through a process of military conquests followed by draconian peace settlements, culminating in the reign of Louis XIV, when France was the hegemon of Europe; and the decline of France in the eighteenth century and its rise again during the French Revolution and the Napoleonic conquests. Throughout, and in the backdrop to these changing fortunes, lies what Henry Kissinger and others see as a consistent French policy of weakening the dominant power in Europe.[48] More often than not this policy involved France in a struggle against empires, from the Holy Roman Empire of the Germanic Peoples, to the British Empire, the German Reich, and more recently the Soviet and U.S. empires. Though the French preference was for the "nation" over "empire," as illustrated in the phrase, "The king is an emperor in his own country,"[49] this did not prevent France itself from succumbing to the temptations of empire, whether it was Napoleonic in Europe or colonial in the Third World. This chapter also describes the decline of France as a great power, its abasement in 1940, its efforts to reassert its former status under de Gaulle, its changing relationship toward NATO, and its continuing effort to build and dominate a European Union that can keep German power in check and U.S. hegemony at bay.

In chapter 4 attention shifts from an examination of the sources of the French approach toward negotiation to a detailed analysis of the key elements of that approach. The chapter begins by discussing a French lack of interest in the negotiating process per se and the French preoccupation with a logical, eloquent, and uncompromising expression of the French position and French interests. Next, the chapter examines a number of prominent aspects of the French style: a superiority/inferiority complex, a concern with form over content, the pyramidal shape of key decision-making structures, a clear sense of one's final position, and an aggressive and emotional approach, à la de Gaulle. The French use of time, of the media, of back channels, and of entertainment is also analyzed.

The case studies in chapter 5 illustrate in very concrete terms the problems and pitfalls of dealing with France. Each of the three cases dates from the post–Cold War period and features sharp points of disagreement between France and the United States. The first concerns the public and acrimonious dispute in 1996–97 over the French attempt to secure for itself NATO's Southern Command at Naples as the price of France's full return to NATO. The second examines the growing differences that emerged following the Persian Gulf War between the French and the Anglo-Americans concerning policy toward Iraq. The case focuses on negotiations in 1999 for a new weapons inspection regime (UNMOVIC) for Iraq, on the negotiation in 2002 that led to Resolution 1441 and the return of the inspectors to Iraq, and on French resistance to the U.S.-led war to overthrow Saddam Hussein. The third case treats France's stubborn defense of its agricultural, commercial, and cultural interests in the later stages of the Uruguay Round of the GATT negotiations in 1993; these were conducted not by France directly but by the European Union. This case was chosen partly to illustrate the different negotiating cultures of those French officials who work through the European Union and those who deal in classic bilateral negotiations. With some exceptions as regards the trade and culture negotiations, access to archival material from the 1990s has been extremely limited. Thus, the case studies rely very heavily on recent firsthand memoirs, on open source material, and on interviews.

The final two chapters are shorter, offering prescriptive and predictive analyses aimed in particular at those who must deal with the French across the negotiating table. Chapter 6 offers a variety of practical suggestions that are likely to make such negotiations more productive encounters. Chapter 7 looks to the near and midterm future with an eye to predicting how the French negotiating style might change. As the reader will discover, the chapter anticipates that French officials, faced with advancing globalization and more reliant on multilateral institutions, will demonstrate greater flexibility in the years ahead and will shift from positional negotiation to process-based negotiation. Even so, the defining characteristics of French negotiating behavior will endure, and the portrait of the French negotiator presented in this volume will continue to be readily recognizable.

2

The Cultural Context

TOGETHER, CULTURE AND HISTORY PROFOUNDLY INFLUENCE the behavior of French negotiators. Determining the exact nature of that influence, however, is no easy task. In the first place, culture and history are like two strands in a common thread, intertwined to such an extent that it is hard to know where one ends and the other begins. In the second place, to the extent that they can be separated, it is difficult to define the elements of one or another strand without being accused of indulging in unhelpful or unreliable generalities. And in the third place, there is the problem of deciding which of the many elements that make up something as multifaceted and complex as "culture" are most influential.

Fortunately, while each of these difficulties is real, none is fatal. As for the first, culture and history are indeed difficult to disentangle perfectly, but there is no need to do so perfectly. The aim of chapters 2 and 3 is to describe the general context within which French negotiators work, not to demonstrate surgical precision in distinguishing between culture and history. Each chapter can fairly claim to focus chiefly on one or the other, thereby enhancing analytical clarity, but to the extent that culture and history overlap, they only point up the interrelatedness of their subject matter.

The second difficulty referred to above—the danger of overgeneralizing—is inescapable. Recognizing the hazardous nature of such a venture, we can nevertheless point to the view of Samuel P. Huntington, as in this passage from Robert D. Kaplan's profile of him:

> On the one hand, Huntington conceded that "actual personalities, institutions and beliefs do not fit into neat, logical categories." But on the other, he argued passionately that "neat logical categories are necessary if man is to think profitably about the real world." . . . A scholar, in order to say anything significant, is "forced to generalize." . . . Without abstraction and simplification there can be no understanding, Huntington maintained.[1]

It is hard to paint culture and history without using broad strokes that ignore innumerable nuances and individual idiosyncrasies. Yet the alternative to depicting every peculiarity is impracticable—one would need an impossibly large canvas—and decidedly unhelpful—it would yield vast confusion rather than recognizable patterns. Furthermore, the danger of overgeneralizing is necessarily limited in this chapter by the fact that the focus is not on the entire French population, past and present, but on a relatively small segment of contemporary France, namely, the elite groups that produce French diplomats, bureaucrats, and politicians. To be sure, much of what is said in this and subsequent chapters applies to some degree to the French as a whole; even so, the focus remains on these elite groups. Moreover, when we refer to "culture," we are concerned chiefly with political and intellectual culture, not with the myriad other categories.

The third difficulty—deciding which facets to spotlight—is perhaps the easiest to address. A nation's culture and history are unquestionably complex structures composed of numerous elements, but the elements featured here are those that both French negotiators and their counterparts have identified as being most germane. They are grouped together in this chapter under six categories: the tradition of the state, the hallmarks of French political culture, anti-Americanism, the French temperament, the influence of Cartesianism, and the impact of the French educational system.

This chapter begins by emphasizing the long-standing existence of the state apparatus in France. The state was formed long before the nation itself emerged and has survived every convulsion in France's history, including the French Revolution, which developed in part in reaction to the authority of the state but which sought to transform it, not abolish it. The leading revolutionary party, the Jacobins, had the aim of establishing a centralized, unitary state. The primacy of the state continues today, evoked in the grandiose trappings of government offices and aggressively defended by politicians and diplomats alike.

The importance accorded to the state helps to shape the distinctively French version of democratic political culture, one that significantly differs from the Anglo-American model in important respects. The second section of this chapter examines these distinctive hallmarks of French political culture, including Jean-Jacques Rousseau's concept of the "general will" and the supremacy of laws over rights, a disdain for untrammeled individualism, the legacy of the French Revolution and the evolution of today's presidential political system, a strong current of anticapitalism, at least in French rhetoric, and a pronounced secularism in public life.

These characteristics form a backdrop to a phenomenon that is more marked in France than in any other Western country: anti-Americanism. The third section briefly outlines the sources and varieties of anti-Americanism in France, and we will return to this subject in chapter 3. The French regard Americans with a mixture of envy—not least for U.S. power—and repulsion—especially for manifestations of U.S. cultural and economic imperialism. Yet the French and the Americans are more alike than both might care to admit; they are, for example, the only countries that believe that their own model of society should be universally adopted.

The chapter next turns to the rather spongy, but nonetheless much-remarked, subject of the French temperament. Many observers have declared that the French are temperamentally closer to their Latin cousins to the south than to their Anglo-Saxon neighbors to the north. The fourth section briefly assesses the influence of such geography on French adherence to the concept of "common ground" or "common good" and, allied with this, the French preference for collectivism over individualism. This section also focuses on the high value the French place on elegance, eloquence, and panache, the latter manifesting itself in the political and diplomatic arena in audacious, sometimes precipitous, actions.

A quite different and yet distinctly French trait is what has been termed the "Cartesian obsession"—the notion that the exercise of reason can change the world. The fifth section of the chapter analyzes this abiding national affair with René Descartes but also notes that this rationalist tradition is leavened by a strong sense of realism, attributable in no small part to an enduring peasant tradition.

The chapter concludes by examining the French educational system, and more particularly the manner by which this system fashions and trains the French elites. As we shall see, the education of future French negotiators is rigorous, designed to produce a cohesive corps of extremely well-informed, highly patriotic individuals.

THE TRADITION OF THE STATE

The French state is personalized—by a well-endowed Marianne[2] (see the photograph on page 2)—and deified to a degree unequaled elsewhere in the contemporary Western world. Many of his compatriots would concur with the late Paul Delouvrier, one of France's most renowned civil servants, who declared: "For me, the State in its constitutive organs is the incarnation of the nation: it is the ensemble of institutions by which the society functions."[3] The almost obsessional way in which French negotiators defend the interests of the state is a characteristic universally recognized by others who have observed them in action.

The French, whose language is not known for capitalization, spell their word for "state" this way: *État*. France has had a functioning state apparatus for the conduct of foreign and military policy for four centuries. As the historian Jacques Bainville wrote, "[Cardinal] Richelieu [1585–1642] left [behind] a doctrine of the State, and to fulfill it, an administration, an organization, a battle-hardened army, [and] experienced generals."[4] Indeed, the creation of the state preceded the creation of the nation. "The state had existed for a thousand years," remarks a former French ambassador, Alain Plantey. "First there was conquest, then there was an administration, justice, bridges and roadways, postal service, finance, *intendants*. The state was above everything. It could not be done away with. The Revolution made the nation, but the state remained."[5] The French state has also survived every convulsion in France's history since the Revolution, including not only the

Napoleonic Wars but also France's defeat by Germany in 1940. And just as in 1940 the advent of the Vichy regime proceeded more or less smoothly, so in 1945 did Charles de Gaulle rapidly reestablish state authority throughout France. In fact, de Gaulle, at the moment of the liberation of Paris, returned to the very building, the Ministry of Defense on the rue St.-Dominique, that he had been forced to vacate in June 1940. Nothing in the office appeared to have changed.

The tradition of *la raison d'État*—defined in traditional French terms as the invocation of the public interest to justify a political action that may be illegal or unjust,[6] or what today would be called, in the words of Henry Kissinger, "a national security interest"[7]—was born with Richelieu in the seventeenth century and is stronger in France than in any other European country. Whereas in the United States many people share Abraham Lincoln's faith that "right makes might," in France it is the state that makes right. This tradition, and with it a reflex of secrecy, is deeply ingrained in French officialdom and in French society in general. Transparency comes harder in France than in any other Western democracy. Delouvrier noted that "France is a country of secrets, in that anything that involves money or sex comes under a category that is carefully concealed. In the civil service, one can say as a general rule that all the work of a senior official is secret: it is destined for the minister, that is, for the elected officials, and cannot be made public without their authority."[8] State secrets are also kept longer in France than in many other Western countries. Most official documents are not declassified for thirty years, and defense-related papers are not released for sixty years. Furthermore, a document can be designated as related to defense by an administrative decision that is without recourse.

Another consequence of the deification of the state is that the trappings of government office—cars, chauffeurs, waiters, honor guards, messengers, cleaning personnel—are omnipresent. "This is the eternal vanity of the French," commented Delouvrier, "which they have never modified, and which [so] exasperates foreigners. Their title—especially if it is published in the *Journal Officiel*—is more important in their eyes than the mission that is conferred on them. When pride in belonging to the civil service is mixed with vanity, this becomes intolerable."[9]

But looked at from another angle, these trappings and traditions are emblematic of the strength and continuity of the French state, and they reinforce the French sense of national identity. Witness this description of former prime minister Lionel Jospin's office building by his cabinet director, Olivier Schrameck:

> [L']Hôtel de Matignon from the time it came into use as a national building, has never been anything but a republican locale par excellence, the only exception being the sinister parenthesis of occupied Paris. However, the entire setting remains very ancien régime, down to the last detail, often [executed] with exquisite taste and elegance.[10]

Jacques Revel, a specialist in the social history of France in the sixteenth and seventeenth centuries, sees vestiges of the court culture of the ancien régime throughout contemporary French political culture:

> The court has founded a lasting memory in the history of France. In the case of all strong executives, of all centralized authority, one has the sense that they must be accompanied by a renaissance of this curial phenomenon even in the midst of our democratic society. The political culture of the Fifth Republic presents the best example of this. The regime is affected by a monarchical coloration that owes much to the conceptions and the practice of its founder [Charles de Gaulle] but which has not disappeared after him. The institutional role of the president is underpinned by a symbolic apparatus whose scale and ponderousness probably have no equivalent in political systems [that are] comparable.[11]

The continuity and the grandeur of the state sustain France, allowing it to sweep under the rug such unpleasant parentheses as Vichy and the Algerian War. They also help to explain the remark by German foreign minister Joschka Fischer that "France is politically stronger than Germany for historical reasons [and] will remain so."[12]

This is not to say that the state is sacrosanct. On another level, there is a tradition of satirical criticism in France that has its origins in the court jesters (les fous du roi) and is carried on by the merciless weekly Le Canard Enchaîné (founded in 1917) and, more recently, by puppet shows on television that mock the country's leaders. On a more profound level, the discipline of the state is contested by a revolutionary tradition, a tradition born of a reaction to the authority of the state and the hierarchical nature of French society. This curious phenomenon is well described by Pierre Nora, French historian and editor of the monumental study *Les lieux de mémoire:*

> France, by its history and its civilization, has developed a reflex of revolt, linked to the formalistic and hierarchical style inherited from the "divine right" monarchy, maintained by a statist and bureaucratic centralization, which has invaded from top to bottom the institutions, the army, education, business and which has impregnated all social relations down to couples and families. France: the land of command. There has resulted from this a latent anarchism, a dialectic of order and subversion which is at the base of France's political as well as intellectual history.[13]

In the same vein, British historians Andrew Knapp and Vincent Wright identify a "domination-crisis model" in France. Central to their formulation is the fact that

> French political culture is characterized by both "limited authoritarianism" and "potential insurrection against authority," and the French oscillate between a normal servility towards authority and sporadic rebellions against it. Closely associated with this idea is the Tocquevillian view . . . that "France is a profoundly conservative country which dreams of revolution but rejects reform."[14]

The enduring potency of the French state is reflected in the fact that even France's revolutionaries have sought not to abolish the state but to use it. A central theme of Alexis de Tocqueville's *L'Ancien régime et la Révolution* is that there *was* continuity between these two phases of French history, particularly in terms of the progressive centralization of the institutions of the government in the capital. Today, despite centuries of challenges from abroad and within, and despite the more recent onslaught of globalization, the state remains the single most powerful force in France, both symbolically and in very concrete terms. No less than 54 percent of France's gross domestic product is controlled by the state. Some 25 percent of French workers are paid by the state, in contrast to 17 percent overall in the other countries of the euro currency zone and 15 percent in the United States.[15] Even though privatization is reducing the state's role, certain key activities remain public, such as electricity, railroads, and postal services.

THE DISTINCTIVE HALLMARKS
OF FRENCH POLITICAL CULTURE

Law, Legitimacy, and the General Will

It is both reassuring and misleading to think in terms of a family of Western democracies. To be sure, Western democracies possess many similarities—free elections, free speech, freedom of the press, government by representatives, rule of law, and so forth—but these shared characteristics do not translate into a common outlook and set of values. It is necessary to point up the differing origins of the Western democracies if one wants to understand why the worldview is so different between, in particular, France and the United States. As Jacques Andréani, author and former French ambassador to the United States, observes:

> It is said that we are in agreement with the United States regarding democracy. But are we all that much? The two countries do not regard in the same way the respective roles of the state and the individual, of the law and of the contract, of the citizen and of the communities. Another difference: there subsists in the United States traces of prejudice toward Catholic culture, in which American WASPs have long discerned dogmatism and authoritarianism, and which they believe to be akin, at the other extreme, to communism; while at the same time the French do not understand American Protestantism, with its combination of the horror of sin and the justification of enrichment, a mélange which is not familiar to them and in which they cannot help but see hypocrisy.[16]

One of the fundamental differences between the French and American conceptions of democracy concerns individual rights versus the common good. The rights of man are the same in the Bill of Rights and other American documents, on the one hand, and in the French declaration of 1789, on the other hand.[17] But the French proclamation is entitled Declaration of the Rights of Man and of the Citizen, the latter term implying a constraining authority above the individual. The U.S. model of democracy, argues the historian Stanley Hoffmann, is that of liberalism, based on the thought of John Locke and other English and Scottish philosophers:

> The word "rights" is at the heart of [the American tradition]. These individual rights should permit those that have them to resist the

pressures of society and of the state. . . . [The French] conception is completely different and owes much to Rousseau. Liberalism is at the opposite [pole] from absolute monarchy; the Rousseauist conception . . . is in a sense a sort of reverse absolutism that substitutes the nation for the monarch. Here the key word is "law" [as] the expression of [national] sovereignty . . . in the French conception law is superior to rights, and individual rights can be restricted or suspended by the general will.[18]

Jean-Jacques Rousseau's conception of the general will (*la volonté générale*, a perception of the common good of society as divined by an enlightened legislator) leads the French to think in terms of "legitimacy" rather than "constitutionality" or even "legality." In the political culture inherited from the French Revolution, there is nothing above the sovereignty of the people, as prescribed by the legislators. Article 4 of the Declaration of the Rights of Man and of the Citizen of August 26, 1789, which is still in effect as it is in the preamble to the French Constitution, states, "Liberty consists in being able to do anything that does not harm others: thus, the exercise of the natural rights of each man has no limits other than that which assures other members of society the enjoyment of the same rights. *These limits can be determined only by the law*" (emphasis added).[19]

The supremacy of laws over rights and the indivisibility of the general will have had a host of implications for France's political culture, notably that the state has to be unitary, not federal, and that the law of the legislators is supreme. As Alain Lempereur puts it, "In the U.S., the court says what the law is *(Marbury v. Madison)*, whereas in France, the legislator says what the law is, and the courts are the 'mouth of the law.' However, in many ways the judicial authority in France is getting closer over the years to a real judicial power."[20] Nevertheless, the case remains that in France the executive and legislative branches of government are "powers," whereas the judiciary is considered only an "authority."

The general will is not the same as the sum of individual wills in the French view, because the latter would lead to hedonism and anarchy. The concept of society as a market where the individual lives for himself and his own happiness, and where the state intrudes as little as possible into civil society—in short, the model of U.S.-style liberalism (in the European sense of the term "liberal")—has never been to the liking of a majority of Frenchmen.

In the U.S. Declaration of Independence, whereas all men are created equal, whether they achieve equality is dependent on individual effort. All are entitled to life, liberty, and the pursuit of happiness, but the latter, it is clear, can be achieved only by the individual himself. In contrast, France's "republican virtues" are not life, liberty, and the pursuit of happiness. To the French there is more than individualism; there is liberty, equality, and fraternity. The late François Furet summed up this point of view in speaking of "modern individualism, with its inevitable civic deficit, which contains the moral detour that it introduces: the absence of the common good."[21]

The same disdain (at least at the theoretical level) for individualism and its lack of collective spirit is contained in Hubert Védrine's sweeping philippic on globalization, which he defined in the following terms: "the ultra-liberal market economy, mistrust of the state, individualism removed from the republican tradition, the inevitable reinforcement of the universal and 'indispensable' role of the United States, common law, the English language, Anglo-Saxon norms, and Protestant—more than Catholic—concepts."[22] Védrine contrasted this with the French tradition: "Historically French identity has been defined by and built upon a strong central state, first monarchical, and then republican. It was painstakingly built by jurists, and based on the idea that France had a specific political, legal, and cultural role to play in the world."[23]

"Republican" and "republican virtues"—meaning acceptance of the values of the French Revolution and the Enlightenment, and their incorporation within a strong, unitary state—have become the watchwords of French political culture, just as "democracy" and the "democratic way of life" have come to form the American mantra. Whereas in the United States "republican" does not have the same connotation of the public good that "democratic" does, in France the situation is almost the inverse, because historically, "democratic" has a narrower meaning, referring to the nineteenth-century parties of the Left, which considered themselves heirs to the Jacobins.[24] Raymond Aron, the leading noncommunist thinker in France during the Cold War, limned this distinction in French political terminology:

Some groups have claimed to represent the will of the people in order to abolish personal freedoms and representative institutions. . . . Too often the democrats proclaimed, No freedom for the enemies of freedom—which is the justification for all despotisms. Too often the defenders of personal freedoms were not democrats, in that they were more interested in limiting the power of the people. . . . Democracy and freedom, inseparable in the minds of the founding fathers of the American republic, have been dissociated many times in France.[25]

The Legacy of the French Revolution

With the disappearance of the Soviet Union, European history is left with a sole revolutionary heritage, that of France. This fact is not lost on the French. Why one of these revolutions succeeded and the other did not finds various explanations, including this one from French sociologist Edgar Morin: "It is humanism and the French Revolution that beat the Russian Revolution hands down."[26]

The French Revolution has proved not easy to explain. What was then the most developed political system in continental Europe was swept away by a revolution that declared it was starting over. François Furet, one of the leading twentieth-century experts on the French Revolution, characterized this extraordinary, and puzzling, phenomenon in the following terms:

How is it that the French were seized with this almost insane ambition to say that ten centuries, fourteen centuries do not matter at all. The social contract, the body politic is going to be remade: the *tabula rasa*. For thirty years I have been studying this, and it is more obscure than ever.[27]

Although the French may disagree on the why the Revolution endured—and on why it began—there is almost universal pride in the Revolution itself, in the principles it espoused, and in the republic it brought into existence. Nevertheless, there is a tendency, as in other things in France, to sweep under the rug the later phase of the French Revolution, which culminated in the Terror.

Rousseau's notion of the general will, as identified by enlightened legislators, apt for a small space such as Rousseau's native Geneva, becomes unworkable in a large country like France. During the

Revolution, the Jacobin members of the French National Assembly, arrogating to themselves the definition of the general will, created for a time a bloody dictatorship. Afterward, Rousseau was largely, if unjustly, blamed for the excesses of the Revolution. As Napoleon remarked on a visit to Rousseau's grave at Ermenonville in 1800, "it was this man who brought us to the state we are in!"[28]

The humanistic élan of the French Revolution did not last long, falling prey first to the bloody quarrels and excesses of the Terror and then to the imperial ambitions of Napoleon. For almost a century thereafter, the Democrats of the Left battled the parties of the Right— the Monarchists (Bourbons or Orléanists), the Bonapartists, and the Liberals—over France's ideological destiny. France settled into its permanent mold of republican government in the late 1800s, when a consensus formed around the formula of Adolph Thiers, leader of the Party of Order (i.e., the Liberals), that "a Republic is the regime that divides us the least."[29]

Still, the Left-Right political struggle continued and at times burst out with surprising intensity, as in the Dreyfus affair of the 1890s, when a Jewish army captain from Alsace, Alfred Dreyfus, was accused, falsely, of spying for Germany, while the real spy, Major Ferdinand Esterhazy, went ignored for years, even though evidence pointed to him, including the fact that he had written openly that he longed to lead a unit of German *Uhlans* in an attack on the "degenerate" city of Paris.

The moment of great unity of World War I *(l'union sacrée)* gave way to a renewed Left-Right polarization in the 1930s, in reaction to the rise of communism in the Soviet Union and of fascism in Germany and Italy. In 1940, with the French defeat, Vichy became the last counterrevolutionary government in France. The Left-Right struggle continues on today, although in a more muted vein than was the case during most of the twentieth century. Political habits appear to have softened and divisions lessened, and the drift of political parties toward the center may signal the fading away of the murderous game in France known as "the verbal civil war" *(la guerre civile verbale)*. Pierre Nora notes an "exhaustion of the classic oppositions [that have existed] since the Revolution: new France against ancient France, secular France against religious France, the France of the Left against the

France of the Right. . . . [This exhaustion] has not brought the disappearance of relationships and loyalties and, at least as regards the latter cleavage, it has not prevented the divisions necessary for democratic organization."[30] The latter phrase is an apparent reference to the fact that the Left-Right divide remains in the parties' representation in the French National Assembly, as it has since the Revolution. There is a left side and a right side in the hemicycle. There is nothing in between.

In sum, France is a divided country.[31] There is even a common expression that expresses this division: "a French-French quarrel" (une querelle franco-française). Although "a unitary, nonfederal state with a national education system, paradoxically France is divided, socially and politically. First and foremost, it is divided on the basic principles and methods of government. The Right, as the heir, though not always admittedly so, of the monarchist tradition, has tended to favor a strong executive. The Left has long been the champion of parliamentary supremacy, inherited from the Revolution's doctrine that nothing was above the will of the people, as expressed through their representatives.

What François Furet referred to as the "legicentrism" of the French, which in part is historically a reaction against the powers of the sovereign courts (parlements) of the ancien régime, has produced a less than independent judiciary.[32] This situation, however, is beginning to evolve. For example, starting in the 1970s the French Conseil Constitutionnel came to rule on the constitutionality of French laws. And more recently, the aggressive tactics of examining magistrates (juges d'instruction) in investigating cases of public corruption have conveyed the point that the rule of law should be applied to high officials as well as to the general public.

The revolutionary tradition of a dominant parliament was later to bring in its train a weak executive in Paris, which represented a counter-model both to the ancien régime and to the various monarchist and Bonapartist recrudescences in the nineteenth century. This weak political leadership was to become the bane of French existence under the Third and Fourth Republics in the twentieth century. Parliamentary supremacy acquired a bad name, associated as it was with the defeat in 1940 and the later loss of the French Empire.

De Gaulle put an end to the "revolving-door" governments of the 1950s and the consequent irresolute international image of France by introducing a strong presidency into the Constitution of the Fifth Republic, promulgated in 1958 and amended in 1962 with the provision for election of the president by universal suffrage.

Furet described what has emerged as a "Monarchy of the Republic."[33] It is a system that is more presidential than parliamentary, in that the president is the only person in the country elected by all the people. Although there is a representative National Assembly, the president holds the upper hand over it. In very recent years, support has grown for the idea of giving the National Assembly a stronger voice and thus constraining the power of the president. Whether this shift in opinion will produce significant changes remains to be seen, but it would appear doubtful.

Still, in at least one respect, the Constitution of the Fifth Republic is flawed, and this may eventually increase pressures for it to be amended. Not only does it divide power, and therefore spread confusion, between the president and the prime minister (reflecting the differences between the two main sponsors of the document, the executive-oriented de Gaulle and his parliamentary-oriented prime minister, Michel Debré), but also its authors failed to anticipate fully a situation whereby the president would be from one party and the prime minister from another—what is now called "cohabitation" and which occurred in 1986–88, 1993–95, and 1997–2002.

The problem of the role of the president compared with that of the prime minister rests in the ambiguity created by Article 20 of the Constitution, which states that "the government decides and directs the policy of the nation. It has at its disposal the administration and the armed forces."[34] Although this article would seem to give full powers to the prime minister as head of the government, it is contradicted by three other articles. Article 5 states that the president ensures respect for the Constitution and provides for the functioning of public authorities and the continuity of the state.[35] Article 15 states that the president is head of the armed forces and presides over the higher councils and committees of national defense. And Article 16 confers special powers on the president in the event of a national emergency.[36]

The upshot is that France is hydra-headed at most international conferences, with both the president and the prime minister in attendance. During periods of cohabitation this can be especially problematic. Even so, a custom has developed over the forty-plus years of the Fifth Republic that the president has primacy in defense and foreign affairs—the so-called reserved domain of the president—and the prime minister must take a backseat, both literally and metaphorically. Most palpably, it is the president who controls France's nuclear arsenal.

An "Implicit Anticapitalism"

Whereas the culture of the United States' founding fathers had no place for economic and social rights, Jacobin egalitarianism promoted strong state intervention in the economic and social domains as a means of compensating for the inequality of conditions.[37] In this context Hoffmann notes "the implicit anti-capitalism of French universalism and the explicit pro-capitalism of American [universalism]."[38]

There is, indeed, a widespread and sincere resistance in France to *capitalisme sauvage*. France provides its citizens with a significantly more secure and higher social safety net than does the United States,[39] and although the gulf between rich and poor is rising in France, it is not nearly as drastic as in the United States.[40] While the Jacobin ideal of the equality of all French citizens is undermined by the reality of unequal levels of French schooling, nevertheless, there is room for a small but not insignificant meritocracy, in part through the system of scholarship holders *(boursiers)*. This system, it should be noted, is all the more necessary because of the rigidities of what Furet called France's "vertical" and "aristocratic" society, which limits opportunities for social mobility far more than is the case in the "horizontal" and "contractual" society of the United States.[41]

The U.S. fascination with the self-made man has little resonance in France. According to the ancient tradition of the French nobility, one should not engage in moneymaking pursuits; if one did, one suffered the *dérogeance*, the removal of one's noble status. State service has traditionally been regarded as "cleaner" than moneymaking. President François Mitterrand's objurgations against "money that corrupts, money that kills" *("l'argent qui corrompt, l'argent qui tue")* struck a chord, especially in rural France.[42] (The fact that Mitterrand's considerable holdings were largely in land excused them or caused them to be ignored. They were not the result of "commerce.")

France's traditional opposition to laissez-faire capitalism has now transmogrified into an opposition to globalization, which is seen as an "Anglo-Saxon" and an exploitative phenomenon, and as capitalism in its most extreme form. This opposition is not limited to the Left but is also seen on the Right in France. Furet probably best summed up this French-U.S. divide with the observation that U.S. civilization "is in reality both too mixed in with the Christian faith and too confident about the idea of free enterprise to attract all those who cannot think of the future of democracy except as separated from Christianity and from capitalism: the innumerable children of the French Revolution."[43]

Yet it would be wrong to exaggerate the degree of anticapitalism. Notwithstanding widespread criticism of unrestrained capitalism, a vibrant entrepreneurial class has arisen in France in recent decades. And all the carping against the selfish *individualism* of liberalism belies the fact that the French are among the most individualistic and refractory peoples of the West. As Charles de Gaulle famously remarked, "How can one govern a country that has 246 varieties of cheese?"[44]

Freedom from Religion

France was the first Western country to "de-Christianize" itself, which it did through the Revolution. To be sure, a significant residue of Catholic values remains in this country of emptying churches[45]—most notably, perhaps, the traditional Catholic aversion to commercial exploitation, rooted in the medieval proscription against usury, which resonates with contemporary critiques of unrestrained capitalism. The Protestant ethic evoked by German philosopher Max Weber—hard work of the individual, including and especially through commerce— is foreign to the French tradition. As U.S. political scientist Ezra Suleiman puts it, "Being a Catholic country, France lacked the Protestant 'profit ethic.'"[46] Even so, the French are sincere in their support for the separation of church and state, and there is considerable resistance to the idea of the Catholic Church—or any other religion—reentering the temporal sphere.

As French diplomat and author Dominique Decherf points out,

in the United States importance is attached to the idea of freedom *of* religion; in France, it is freedom *from* religion that is valued, and especially from the Catholic Church.

> The French have, since the end of the religious wars of the sixteenth and seventeenth centuries, known only one large majoritarian religion. Either one was within the Catholic Church, or one was a freethinker outside of it. In the tradition of French *laïcité* [secularism] that emerged from this context, freedom of conscience is still understood by the French as a freedom *from* the moral authority of a single dominant religion.[47]

The principle of religiosity was never contested in the United States; though the practice of religion has worn off, it is still considerably greater than in Europe. In France, however, antireligiosity was at the foundation of the revolutionary state, even to the extent of doing away, for a time, with the Christian calendar.

At the origin of the United States, a deeply religious people, of varying degrees of largely dissident Protestant persuasion, wanted to guarantee religious liberty within an essentially Protestant world, without the institution of an established church. What happened subsequently was that the constitutional principle of religious freedom was applied to immigrants arriving en masse, many of whom were not Protestants but Catholics and Jews and, more recently, Muslims, Hindus, and others. Without an established church, and with religious expression encouraged from the outset, the growth in religious diversity within the United States has both prompted and paralleled a growing multiculturalism. France, in contrast, with its model of a uniform citizenry imbued with republican values, as inculcated by a national educational system, remains resistant to multiculturalism, despite the particularistic tendencies among France's large, and growing, Muslim community.

Anti-Americanism in France

Anti-Americanism in France has many sources—competing "universal" models, asymmetries in power but not in self-esteem, specific historical grievances, to name but a few—and several varieties. Hoffmann identifies two basic types:

One, on the Right, dislikes the equalitarian and multicultural melting pot of the United States (France's melting pot is seen as hierarchical and based on the prevalence of a single model of integration through assimilation); it dislikes American mass culture, "excessive" social and geographical mobility, and a social ethos based on "savage" competition, the central role of money, individual success and profit, and the frenzied quest of what is new at the expense of tradition. Here nostalgia for a feudal and peasant past leads to distaste for democracy and capitalism. On the Left, there is another kind of anti-Americanism, which deplores American mistreatment of the "natives" and other minorities, the lack of social conscience of American capitalism both in the United States and abroad, and the manifestations of American imperialism abroad. The various French Catholic currents of thought and feelings have contributed to both forms of rejection.[48]

François Mitterrand, whose thinking contained elements of both the Right and the Left—the former a product of his rural origins, the latter of his political itinerary—publicly rejected "any comparison between France and the American 'conservative society.'"[49] In private, Mitterrand could be even more severe:

We are at war against America. Yes, a permanent war, a vital war, an economic war, a war without deaths. . . . [T]hey are very hard, the Americans. They are voracious. They don't want to share power anywhere in the world. . . . You saw, after the Gulf War, that they wanted to control everything in that part of the world. They left nothing for their allies. . . . Remember everything they've done for the past thirty years against the Concorde. . . . Their propaganda. . . . Their manipulations. . . . Their lies.[50]

Here we are confronted with what Hoffmann identifies as the rise of a third kind of anti-Americanism, an *antiaméricanisme d'État*, in which "the universe of values [is] one thing; the universe of power and interests [is] quite another."[51] As Pierre Mélandri and Justin Vaïsse observe: "Down deep, America is reproached for defending its economic interests with the means that its preeminent position gives it; [for an] attitude that brings forth an instinctive mistrust and a desire for countervailing power; [and for an] attitude that many decipher as the result of a vast plot organized out of Washington and aimed at world hegemony."[52]

The rise of this *antiaméricanisme d'État* can be traced to the emergence of the United States as a world power in the early twentieth century and specifically to the moment when Woodrow Wilson intruded in a major way into the negotiations for the Treaty of Versailles at the end of World War I. As will be developed in chapter 3, the triangular alliance among equals at Versailles—Britain, France, and the United States—was never to be significantly replicated after that. A string of grievances was to follow: the disdainful treatment of Charles de Gaulle by Franklin Roosevelt, the U.S. "special relationship" with Britain that excluded France, the dependent situation that France found itself in inside NATO, France's exclusion from the Israeli-Palestinian peace process—all this culminating in 2003 with the so-called Anglosphere (i.e., the United States, the United Kingdom, and Australia) conducting a war against Iraq, with France and its former enemy, Germany, along with Russia, protesting the action. It was, in a manner of speaking, Versailles turned upside down.[53]

Anti-Americanism in France is also in part a carryover of the thousand-year rivalry between France and the first "Anglo-Saxon" power, Britain. But Britain's ties are closer to France, in both human and geographic terms, and the British model is seen as less noxious than that of the United States. If there is a residual reproach of the British by the French, it is the continued tendency of the former to prefer *"le grand large,"*[54] that is, the United States, to Europe, or, as some put it more pejoratively, to play the *"béni-oui-oui"*[55] to America. The French know that they can never replace Britain as the United States' foremost ally, and indeed they would not want to be in the position of America's first lieutenant; they wish, however, that Britain were less tied to America, as this constitutes an impediment to the goal of an independent European political identity.

"France has a particular way of looking at relations with the United States," comments Hubert Védrine:

> It can't be said that the instinctive approach of most of our European partners is identical to our own. But this is a fundamental matter for France, because the question of relations with the United States is at the heart of international relations today. It will be a long time before you'll see all the other Europeans sharing our vision on this matter, except in the area of trade. Should we therefore give it up? No. France

cannot force others to adopt all of its positions, but others cannot ask France to renounce them either. We've got to seek convergence, but it will take time.[56]

There are at least two notable elements in this extraordinary passage: first, the fixation of the French on their relations with the United States; and second, their confidence that eventually it will be their view of the United States that prevails in Europe. This is consistent with the almost unshakable conviction of the French that they are right—what a recent study called the French "burden of being right"[57]—and their concentration on long-range outcomes. In turn, it is indicative of the formula heard in the corridors of the State Department in the aftermath of the Cologne European Union summit in June 2000, when the European Defense Force was set on the rails: "The thing is, the French think they're winning!"

In a special dossier entitled "Unloved America" ("L'Amérique mal-aimé"), *Le Monde* notes the "formidable symbolic charge" that references to the United States encounter in France and suggests that the secret lies in the will of both countries "to play a universal role." Tony Judt supports this observation:

> It is fascinating that no European country is obsessed by the United States as France is. And if anti-Americanism is more irrational there than elsewhere, it is because, down deep, America represents, to a degree, the twin brother that has gone bad: the two countries speak the same language, meaning the language of the universal; both act in the name of moralizing abstractions, like the rights of man or democracy; both in particular have the pretension of describing the world as a universalist project. But America has turned its back on the French republican model, and its own liberal model has sunk into hubris.[58]

It should be noted that if a deep-seated anti-Americanism is a hallmark of French society, an unremitting disdain for French attitudes seems embedded in U.S. popular culture. When the subject of the French comes up, the frequent American reaction is that of a knowing laugh that bespeaks an unwritten code that everyone is supposed to know, but no one explains, as to why the French are so different—and difficult. To the average American, the French are seen as unfathomable, inhospitable, and vain. At the same time, the French way of life is seen as enviable and even superior in many ways, because of its presumption of high culture in art, decor, and cuisine, and because of its intellectualism. Significantly, unlike many other European countries, France is not a country of emigration, and thus there is no mass presence of French origin in the United States, other than a spillover of French Canadians in northern New England and a Cajun presence in Louisiana. There are small claques of Francophiles in some major U.S. cities, but in effect France has no "constituency" in the United States, unlike, for example, Italy or Poland. In this respect, it is interesting to reflect on the sudden and irrational swings of U.S. opinion against the French, as, for example, over the French refusal to allow U.S. overflights for the raid against Libya in 1986. Could this issue have produced such intensity with any other Western European country except France? (Largely unnoticed was the fact that Spain also refused overflight rights for the raid.) And the differences in 2003 over going to war against Iraq raised anti-French sentiments to an unprecedented pitch at the popular level and produced mutterings in neoconservative chat rooms about the need to remove France from the UN Security Council. In sum, a latent rejection of France seems to be a constant among U.S. attitudes projected outward toward the world.

THE FRENCH TEMPERAMENT

The Influence of Geography

The great divide in Europe (if we take the present membership of the European Union as a yardstick of Europe) is between Anglo-Saxon and Germanic Northern Europe, predominantly Protestant, and Latin Southern Europe, predominantly Catholic. France falls into the general category of a Latin country with at its base a Catholic tradition. It is, however, a tradition that was deeply contested by the French Revolution. Furthermore, though Calvinist Protestantism failed to gain control in France, it made a very strong effort to do so before it was subdued and many of its adherents were forced into exile.

 At the same time, France has a great diversity of origins: Celtic in the west, Flemish in the north, German in the east, Italian in the southeast, Spanish in the southwest—not to speak of the waves of immigration from Poland, Italy, and Portugal, and more recently from Spain, the Caribbean, and Africa, especially Arab North Africa. It should also be noted that France is uniquely situated: it is the only European country that extends from the North Sea to the Mediterranean Sea. In light of this ethnic diversity and geographical breadth, France resists easy categorization as a *southern* or a *Latin* European country. Indeed, there is a traditional cultural divide in France itself between the north and the south *(Le Midi)* that is sometimes described as a line between St. Malo and Geneva,[59] below which the "Latin" temperament is more manifest.

And yet many observers claim that the French as a whole do seem to be temperamentally closer to their Latin cousins than to their British and German neighbors. In the words of a senior U.S. diplomat, "At bottom, the French are southern Europeans. They make light of the Spanish and the Italians, but they are more of a piece [with them]."[60]

What, exactly, are the aspects of the French outlook that inspire such comparisons with Latin countries? In the view of Jean-Marie Guéhenno, author, senior French civil servant, and UN undersecretary for peacekeeping operations, one such aspect lies in the domain of affectivity and relates to what he describes as the notion of the "common ground":

> In the United States, there is an emphasis on a detailed written contract, an urge to get something down on paper, so that there will not be any misunderstandings. The French approach is less founded on the idea of a written contract; it is more implicit and is based on the notion of good faith between the parties. This is referred to as the "common ground," which is considered above the contract and even above the negotiation. This is a very Latin notion, that is, that there is a common ground that should not be put in danger and which is based not so much on "contract" but on a "common memory." The American approach, on the other hand, tends to rupture this common ground.[61]

A related trait is an avowed preference for collectivism over individualism. According to a study by Fons Trompenaars, a management expert, "Latin Catholic cultures, along with the Asian cultures of the

Pacific Rim, score lower on individualism than the Protestant West, for instance, the UK, Scandinavia (as a rule), The Netherlands, Germany, America and Canada."[62] Furthermore, like the people of other Catholic and Latin countries, the French regard Protestant and Anglo-Saxon culture as cold, unemotional, and preoccupied with money. However, we must be careful not to overplay the Latin influence, for the origins of this French perception surely owe as much to France's revolutionary tradition, with its collectivist slogan of liberty, equality, and fraternity, as to a common Latin outlook.

The collectivist orientation is in keeping with the concept of honor, another notion that is highly prized in France. Correspondingly, according to Raymond Cohen, professor of international relations at Hebrew University, "Collectivistic cultures attach to the issues of sovereignty and national pride the same importance that they associate with questions of honor and status at the individual level." In Cohen's view, "Relations between the United States [and these cultures] have often threatened to run aground on the twin rocks of pride and sovereignty. . . . Status consciousness and historical grievance have produced an acute sensitivity on the part of these societies to any issue perceived to encroach on their sovereign rights and possessions."[63]

Audacity and Elegance

Conceptions of honor are closely associated in France with the highly esteemed notion of glory *(la gloire)*, which in turn is seen as a close companion to such French concepts as *élan, panache*, and *cran* (guts)— all of which stand in contrast to the (nevertheless secretly admired) British "phlegm." This grouping of ideas may be seen to some degree in the wider Latin world, but it is certainly highly visible in France, where its roots can be traced to the court culture of the ancien régime.

Highly influenced by women, as David Bell observes,[64] the French court culture of the ancien régime emphasized conversational ability, wit, and elegance of expression. This panoply of styles is well captured by Jacques Revel: "A whole gamut of exercises, conversation, dance, horsemanship, games, techniques of the body, the use of words, permit[ted] a verification of the adaptation of comportments to the rules of the arts of the court."[65] Eloquence and wit, especially cutting wit, are still expected of the French elites, and they can generally be found among the students at the *grandes écoles* that prepare France's future leaders.[66] Former minister of finance Wilfrid Baumgartner was in the habit of telling young *inspecteurs de finances,* "1) it is indispensable to be eloquent; 2) it is useful to be intelligent; and 3) it is not at all bad to have good contacts."[67] The power of an argument lies not only in its logical force but also in the elegance of its presentation.[68] This is also evident in the world of manners, where not only eloquence but also charm is prized. French is replete with phrases the English equivalents of which seem affected to Anglo-American ears. For example, the French word *séduire* has a wider connotation than the pejorative "seduce" in English. *Séduire* connotes an obligation to charm, to entertain, to attract, and *un grand séducteur* (a great seducer) usually refers to a man of the world who knows how to charm his audience.

Where Americans celebrate myths of the Wild West and particularly the image of the virtuous and individualistic gun-toting cowboy or sheriff (like Gary Cooper in *High Noon*), the French mythologize heroes from the days of grandeur of the ancien régime, figures such as D'Artagnan and the Three Musketeers, whose swordplay and gallantry fill the novels of Alexandre Dumas. And just as the U.S. obsession with gun culture endures, so in the France of today fencing *(escrime)* is more widely practiced than in any other European country, with French teams excelling in international competition. Jochen Thies, foreign and security correspondent for German National Radio, sees fencing as a quintessentially French sport: "It is elegant and it is a way of escaping from direct confrontation. It is the way they live; it is the way they negotiate. Form and style are more important than content."[69]

Slogans such as *toujours de l'audace* (always be bold) and *impossible n'est pas français* (impossible is not French) feed into a taste for audacious actions and audacious gestures. François Mitterrand's sudden, risky (and unilateral) visit to Sarajevo airport on June 28, 1992—right after he left a European Council meeting in Lisbon without saying a word to his counterparts—was seen by many outside observers as another example of the French "going it alone" and as an essentially meaningless gesture. However, from Mitterrand's point of view, the visit demonstrated in a highly symbolic way that Western Europe had something to say about the destiny of the former Yugoslavia. Moreover, the dispatch of a French battalion to Sarajevo in July 1992 and the establishment of a French military presence there followed up the visit.[70]

The French tendency toward audacity is well described by Admiral Jacques Lanxade, chief of staff of the French armed forces, at a moment of high tension in Paris, in the wake of the Bosnian Serbs taking three hundred UNPROFOR soldiers hostage at the end of May 1995. Half of the soldiers were French. During a restricted meeting of the National Defense Council, the new president, Jacques Chirac, who had served in the army during the Algerian War and was known for his hussar's temperament, demanded to know how the French army had allowed itself to get into such a position. To Chirac, it was an intolerable affront to France's military honor that its soldiers should be tied up by Serb irregulars. To little avail, Lanxade explained that the situation stemmed from the fact that the French soldiers were there not as an intervention force but as part of a UN humanitarian mission. At the end of a tense meeting, Lanxade, who was a holdover from the previous administration, offered his resignation. In his memoir, Lanxade presents the following commentary:

> The honor of the Army was not at stake nor was that of the other countries involved. I was afraid of the momentary seductiveness of a certain "go-for-broke" [jusqu'au-boutiste] mythology in the [French] Army, that of bravura actions in hopeless circumstances. With a tragic result assured, the picture would be grim, and the aftermath would be even more so, [as] for all the forces involved, [it] would be adventurous. It seemed to me that, in the face of this Bosnian Serb provocation, the response in no way should be to strike a blow that had nothing more than symbolic utility.[71]

Lanxade's reference to "bravura actions in hopeless circumstances" recalls the phrase of French military historian Jérôme Hélie: "A taste for ill-fated courage seems to be a French military specificity."[72] Anyone who has visited the battlefield at Verdun (a manner of victory for the French but at a terrible cost) can hardly not have imagined the dreadful spectacle of wave after wave of French soldiers charging uphill, only to be mowed down by German gunners.

Chirac's natural impulse was that a French soldier should shoot back rather than be taken hostage, and he had a similar reaction when

Dutch soldiers did not put up resistance to the Bosnian Serb attack on the UN-declared "safe haven" of Srebrenica in July 1995. Later that summer, French soldiers holding a bridge position repulsed a Serbian attack with live fire.[73]

A taste for precipitation, audacity, and panache seems in part a manifestation of what others, from Cardinal Richelieu to Charles de Gaulle, have referred to as the French "inconstancy." In the former's words, "the complexity of our interests and our natural inconstancy often carry us close to dangerous precipices."[74] This can be perceived across a gamut of behaviors, from the military sphere, as indicated in Admiral Lanxade's account, to a flare-up in an international conference that can lead to a sudden walkout.

CARTESIANISM

The passion that French representatives bring to international gatherings—as when Dominique de Villepin's stirring speech on February 15, 2003, against going to war in Iraq elicited an unheard-of ovation from the UN galleries—contrasts, like the strophe/antistrophe of a Greek chorus, with a devotion to the goddess of Reason in the distinctively French form of Cartesianism: an emphasis on logic and reason, shaped by the manners of the French court and the art of conversation developed there and in the salons of the Enlightenment.

In any discussion of the French style of argument—and thus of negotiation—it is important to stress the centrality of the figure of the philosopher, mathematician, and physicist René Descartes (1596–1650), both for his work and for the myth that surrounds him. Descartes is regarded as a national symbol of clarity, rationality, and reasonableness; during a long historical process in which the Left and parts of the Right have sought to claim him, Descartes has become fused with the image of France itself. As Roger-Pol Droit remarks:

> One does not say of the Germans as a whole, that they are Kantians or Hegelians. Neither does anyone assert that the English are Shakespeareans or the Italians Dantesque. On the other hand, one never stops repeating, from generation to generation, that the French are Cartesians.[75]

Although scholars from later centuries have highlighted flaws in his philosophy, Descartes is still hailed as a precursor of the Enlightenment in at least two respects: in his emphasis on rationality to the point of abstraction, and in his emphasis on liberty of thought that earned him a place on the Catholic Church's list of forbidden works (the *Index*). He is regarded as one of the founders of scientific thought who cast off the mists of scholasticism in favor of a logical and clear approach to issues.

The Cartesian mode of deductive reasoning, named after Descartes, is at the antipodes of the empirically based, inductive style of reasoning found in Anglo-American culture. As Guéhenno explains, "The French and the Anglo-Americans do not start out from the same base. The French prefer to define the principles and then deduce the content. The French approach is 'top down'—to move from the general to the particular. The Anglo-American approach is 'bottom up'—to move from the particular to the general."[76]

The influence of this Cartesian approach can be clearly seen in the French legal system, which consists, says Alain Lempereur, of statutes applied by justices, or what can be called "legislative positivism." In more general terms, the method is deductive: one starts with a general rule and then one applies the particulars. In the Anglo-American system, the approach is empirical: one starts with the particulars and then the principles are built. The U.S. legal system is built around cases and the evolution that cases present; there is little reference to the Constitution or to legislation in this system of "judicial positivism."[77] The U.S. style of presenting arguments in bullet points, in which there may or may not be a link between the points, is quite at variance with the French habit of reasoning, just as French jurists have a horror of Anglo-Saxon law and its way of proceeding by enumeration.[78]

The effect of Descartes and the *philosophes* of the Enlightenment, particularly Voltaire, on the style of French thinking is evident in diplomatic negotiations. The French put great emphasis on the logical and clear presentation of an argument. They pursue their aims with great tenacity. This sense of logic as a rationale for policy positions gives the French the feeling that they are right, even when many others around the table may not be in agreement. The French do not mind the position of being right and being alone at the same time.

They are used to it, and it plays to their sense of national pride—what sometimes appears to foreigners as vanity.

The tradition of French rationalism, or Cartesianism, was characterized in the following way by one French ambassador:

> The cult of Descartes represents a national passion. The teaching dispensed by the Republic [since the Franco-Prussian War] . . . and the insistence on teaching philosophy in the last year at the *lycée*, has a definite effect on the French style of negotiation. This has been for both good and bad. For good in the sense of a capacity to raise the level of the debate, to identify the stakes, and to formulate positions clearly. For bad in the sense of making ideas prevail over facts and sometimes giving over to dogmatism or an excessive importance accorded to language or symbols. . . . The rationalist upbringing [can] lead to a frozen theoretical vision.[79]

Jean-David Levitte, French ambassador to the United States and former ambassador to the United Nations, echoes this view. In his opinion, the French negotiator deserves the reproach of not being attentive enough to the viewpoint of the other:

> [Instead] we often try to lock them up in our reasoning, and we are capable of putting together a reasoning that is quite irreproachable, [yet] also profoundly irritating. The mode of education has a lot of influence over the way one expresses oneself, over the way one presents things. It is fascinating to see, for example, in the Security Council, among the fifteen member countries, what are the approaches, what are the national temperaments, and also the personalities. [80]

While French negotiators try to lock up their negotiating counterpart in their reasoning, they also run the risk of imprisoning themselves in their own logic. Conscious of this danger, French diplomats will usually leave themselves escape routes. According to Guéhenno, "The French like to fix the principles at the beginning, but in so doing leave an element of ambiguity which permits one to escape from them."[81] Pierre Vimont, former French ambassador to the European Union and subsequently cabinet director of the French foreign minister, shares this view: "We prefer our Cartesian approach, one that is theoretical and conceptual. But we can pass from one concept to another. It consists of an intellectual game."[82]

The risk of French negotiators becoming trapped in their own arguments and shackled by their insistence on their own logical infallibility is also reduced by a sense of realism that springs from the strong peasant tradition in France. France for a long time was considered, and considered itself, a nation of peasants. This had some basis in fact. From 1870 until 1940, the country had zero population growth, precious little social mobility, and a tenacious attachment to the land. In 1914, on the eve of World War I, more than 50 percent of the active population worked in agriculture, and this figure did not fall below 10 percent until 1970.[83] Even today, thanks to a successful conversion to agribusiness, France is the second-largest exporter of finished agricultural products in the world. Those French farmers who remain enjoy political influence—especially with the parties of the Right—out of all proportion to their limited numbers, as seen in France's steadfast attachment to the European Union's Common Agricultural Policy (CAP), which is heavily skewed to favor French farmers.

Although France is no longer a "peasant country," the "peasant nostalgia" remains powerful:

> With some rare exceptions, each French family plunges the roots of its genealogical tree into peasant land. This quasi-immediate lineage, in terms of the sweep of history, is not found in the same way in the Anglo-Saxon countries or in Germany, which were affected more strongly and earlier by industrialization and urbanization. In France the peasant tradition remained very vivid until the years that followed the Second World War, even in the cities.[84]

"One must remember," commented a French ambassador posted to Brussels, "to what extent we were for a long time a nation of peasants and how, at least until very recently, this has weighed on our psychology."[85] He saw this heritage influencing French negotiating behavior:

> From the peasant, French diplomats have perhaps a fierceness in the defense of the national interest which contrasts with the greater flexibility of representatives of maritime or commercial nations (who are also at the service of their national interests). From the peasant, our country has also retained a fundamental realism without which

we would not have been able to survive a certain number of historical disasters.

    The peasant good sense is never very far off. French history
and the history of French negotiations demonstrate that the French
are often less ideological than is generally thought, and more reasonable than they themselves think. The little-known cult of mod-
eration in the French tradition, for example, that of the "honest
man," means that the sense of measure corrects many of the faults
of the French nation.[86]

A number of other French officials agree with this observation, including Guéhenno: "The French are realists—but they don't like to admit it."[87]

THE EDUCATION OF THE ELITES

The "vertical" nature of French society is reflected in the complex and
highly sophisticated French higher educational system: a two-tiered
structure consisting of the *grandes écoles*—state institutions, the leading
ones of which train the state elites[88]—and a university system that edu-
cates vast numbers but guarantees neither job security nor success. The
entire system is free to students, being funded by the state.

    The pipeline through which the elites pass is long and daunt-
ing: a student will be selected for entry when he or she is nineteen or
twenty and will not emerge from the pipeline until the age of twenty-
seven or so. For these elites, there is a seamless transition from school
to career. The best graduates of the leading *grandes écoles* are admitted to one of the *grands corps*—the elite corporative bodies whose
recruits come almost exclusively from the *grandes écoles*. Once this
takes place, an individual is set for life as a member of a privileged
caste. He or she may enter one of the ministries or go into politics,
and at the end of his or her career may be rewarded with a high position in a public- or private-sector company. As Ezra Suleiman
observes, "France has one of the most clearly established mechanisms for the creation of its elites of any Western country. This is
principally due to the fact that the state takes it upon itself to form
the nation's elites."[89] "No discussion of the distribution of power, of
social mobility, and opportunities, and even of the policy-making
process can ignore the structure of higher education in France,"

writes Suleiman. "Without this system, we would not find the elite organizations that exist in France."[90]

When foreign diplomats negotiate with France, they almost invariably deal with the graduates of this elite system. And more often than not, they are impressed by what they find. A senior U.S. diplomat cited in a book by Gilles Delafon and Thomas Sancton declared, "French diplomats and the French diplomatic structure are the best that I have encountered in negotiations. They have the training and the capability that allows them to obtain the best for their country, with a clearly defined objective: their national interest. All this in an aggressive manner."[91] In a similar vein, Henry Kissinger rates French diplomatic officials as "extremely able. I never met a French official who was not very bright. Sometimes they maneuver to establilsh superior intelligence." Kissinger attributes the quality of French diplomats to the "terrific" French educational system: "There are two things about education: practical education and the training of the mind. It is life that produces practical education. The French emphasize the training of the mind."[92]

The *grandes écoles* were built over the course of the past two hundred years to create a group of officials and military officers who could ensure internal stability in France and defend the interests of the state. Napoleon, by a decree of 1804, turned the École Polytechnique, which had been formed during the revolutionary period, into a school for the training of military officers.[93] Similarly, the École Normale Supérieure (informally known as "Normale Sup"), created during the revolutionary era, was reconstituted in 1808 as an institution for the training of teachers.[94]

Later in the nineteenth century, in the wake of the Franco-Prussian War, which was seen as a failure not only of French arms but of French diplomacy as well, the École Libre des Sciences Politiques was created under the impulsion of Ernest Renan and other academics profoundly dissatisfied with the French university system. The purpose was to stimulate a *culture générale* and to train students in subjects not covered in the faculties of the university, such as economics, diplomatic history, and politics.[95]

In 1945 the École Libre was nationalized and became the Institut d'Études Politiques ("Sciences Po"). In the same year, the provisional government of Charles de Gaulle created a civil service school based on the École Polytechnique model, the École Nationale d'Administration (ENA).[96] The École Polytechnique (known for short as "X") and ENA have since become the main pipelines into the elite state service and, to a lesser extent, into elite service in the private sector.[97]

Suleiman characterizes the two-tiered French educational system in the following way:

> Two systems of higher education have come to coexist in France. One (the *grandes écoles*) is oriented almost exclusively toward providing a technical or professional training, while the other (the universities) is more preoccupied with theoretical and intellectual concerns. This is, to be sure, an oversimplification because the universities have always provided their share of professional training. Doctors, lawyers, and pharmacists have always received their training in faculties that were attached to universities. On the other side, the *École Normale Supérieure*, one of the more illustrious of the *grandes écoles*, has been solely concerned with intellectual matters, its primary function having been to train teachers for secondary and higher education. Nevertheless, the contrast between the universities and the *grandes écoles* is striking.[98]

The university system was intended to fulfill the ideal of *laïcité* (secularism) by creating a mass public-sector institution that locked in the separation of church and state and was free for everyone. Inevitably, however, some universities have decidedly more prestige than others. Furthermore, only about 20 percent of the entrants to the university system stay on beyond their first year of classes. All that is required to enter a university is to have passed the *baccalauréat* ("*bac*") exam at the end of three years at a *lycée* (high school). The *bac* is roughly the counterpart to the U.S. Scholastic Aptitude Test (SAT). The government's goal, not yet quite achieved, is that 80 percent of those taking the *bac* exam should pass it.

Entry into the *grandes écoles* is much harder to attain. For the École Normale Supérieure, two preparatory courses are required: the so-called *hypokhâgne* (for one year) and the *khâgne* (for an additional year). Likewise, in the case of Polytechnique, stiff preparatory courses are required for entrance. In the case of ENA, passage beforehand through one or more of the *grandes écoles* is generally the rule. *Énarques*, as entrants to ENA are called, are usually graduates from

Sciences Po or from a business school such as the École des Hautes
Études Commerciales (HEC) or the École Supérieure des Sciences
Économiques et Commerciales (ESSEC), or from both. (The various
business schools and scientific schools are also classified as *grandes
écoles*, but unlike ENA and the École Polytechnique, they do not give
rise to an elite.)

The selection system for ENA is designed in such a way that candidates are "formatted" from their first years of study to take the ENA
exam, and not another, which has the consequence of virtually
excluding young students coming out of the universities from passing
it.[99] Moreover, there is an oral exam for entry into ENA, the *grand
oral*, a challenging experience in which the candidate faces a battery
of examiners.

ENA training lasts two years, one of which is spent in the class-
room, the other of which consists of two six-month internships in different government offices. Upon graduation from ENA, the *énarque* is
ready for permanent assignment to the public sector. To gain access to
what are referred to as the generalist *grands corps*—the Inspection des
Finances,[100] the Cour des Comptes,[101] and the Conseil d'État[102]—one
must graduate within the top 20 percent of one's class at ENA.[103]
There are two other *grands corps*, and these are known as the scientific *grands corps*—the Corps des Mines and the Corps des Ponts et
Chaussées, most of whose entrants, again on the basis of strict selection, come from the École Polytechnique. Those who gain entry into
the *grands corps* are immediately pegged as members of an elite,
because it is known that they come from the top of their class in the
grandes écoles.

Other public-sector assignments open to leading ENA graduates
include the Quai d'Orsay (the Foreign Ministry)[104] and the Prefectoral
Corps.[105] The former is considered particularly prestigious, and some
ENA graduates elect to go into the Quai rather than one of the *grands
corps*, as did Lionel Jospin. All diplomats at the Quai d'Orsay do not
come from ENA, however. The Quai has actually retained its own
entrance examinations, the most notable one being the Concours
d'Orient, which allows the ministry to recruit young people with more
specific language skills and area specialization than would be the case
through ENA. These civil servants are often graduates from the

Institut des Langues Orientales (for example, the present ambassador to Washington, Jean-David Levitte) and may or may not have studied in Sciences Po (some are historians or jurists, trained in the university system).[106]

The Quai d'Orsay is at the center of France's relations with the world, unlike the situation that has developed in the United States, where the Department of Defense vies with the State Department for such a role. (As noted elsewhere in this study, the Quai has the lead over the military in foreign negotiations.) In addition to the normal diplomatic function, administered by a Department of Political and Security Affairs, there are separate departments for international cooperation and development, for dealing with the European Union, and for economic and financial affairs. The minister for foreign affairs is assisted at the top by two minister-delegates, one for European affairs and one for cooperation and *francophonie*.

Those who enter the *grands corps* retain their corporate affiliation throughout their careers. In fact, they continue to be paid by their corps even though their activities for the *corps* may be nominal or short-lived.[107] It is commonly said that it is a struggle to get into a *grands corps* and a struggle to get out of it;[108] that is, the entrant normally works for several years in a *grands corps* and then leaves it, often obtaining a position in the cabinet of a minister.

When an *énarque* enters the cabinet of a minister, he or she gradually comes to be associated with the minister's political affiliation. Indeed, the *énarque* may come to play an active role in political party activity while continuing to be paid by his or her parent *grand corps*. When the government changes hands and the minister leaves, the *énarque* has to find another job, in the public or private sector, and sometimes he or she returns to his parent *grand corps*. Thus, as Suleiman observes, "the state in effect subsidizes the political activities, both on the Left and the Right, of the elite. Is the elite, whether its political sympathies lean toward the Left or the Right, likely to abandon a privileged situation that has no parallel in the Western world?"[109]

On the surface, the educational system might appear purely meritocratic. In reality, however, admission to the *grandes écoles* is easier to achieve for students who have attended the best of the public-sector *lycées*, which prepare students for the *bac*. The prestigious *lycées* of the wealthier *arrondissements* (districts) of Paris—for example, Henri IV—are far superior to those of the underprivileged *banlieue* (suburb) areas. In the last year *(la terminale)* in these elite *lycées*, the student curriculum includes eight hours of philosophy and seven hours of science each week.

Thus, despite the competitiveness of French school exams, the fairness with which they are administered, and the underlying principle of meritocracy, the system serves to perpetuate an elite caste coming out of the middle and upper classes. As Knapp and Wright note:

> The uniformity of *background* is certainly striking. Members of the civil service elite come mostly, and increasingly, from comfortable upper middle-class families (often including several generations of senior civil servants). They are frequently products of the top Parisian *lycées*, and almost all of one or another of the *grandes écoles*—the highly selective higher education institutions that channel the ablest students away from France's democratic and under-funded university system.[110]

Still, many parents of *énarques* have "intellectual" jobs *(professions intellectuelles supérieures)* and are not necessarily well off. Joining a *grande école* is as much a matter of cultural capital as it is of wealth. The typical example of this is the École Normale Supérieure, where students are, more often than not, sons and daughters of high school teachers.[111]

Another assignment for those coming out of ENA is that of *administrateur civil*. This is usually not the choice of the top performers at ENA (except for assignments in the Ministry of Economy and Finance), since *administrateurs civils* represent those excluded from the *grands corps*, the Prefectoral Corps, or the Quai. Their careers are as a consequence much different, which is a cause of deep bitterness for those who have not come out in the top 20 percent of ENA graduates.[112] In this regard, a proposal has been advanced to do away with rank-ordering ENA graduates. According to a study on ENA reforms undertaken under the chairmanship of former European commissioner Yves-Thibault de Silguy, the main stumbling block to a profound reform of ENA is "the famous ranking at graduation *(classement de sortie)* which allows a handful of students to gain access to the *grands corps* of the State (the Conseil d'État, the Cour des Comptes, and the Inspection des Finances)."[113]

The study, made public on April 22, 2003, recommends that the rank ordering be done away with because it gives a preponderant weight to scholastic achievement and does not take into account the particular individual. It reverses the normal relationship between the employer and the applicant in the labor market by compelling the former to take on the latter without being able to measure the value of the applicant with regard to the demands of the position. The study also recommends that, without doing away with direct access to the *grands corps*, a number of places in the upper civil service should be opened up by a parallel competitive exam for university graduates and others from outside ENA.

The French educational system is not unchanging; to the contrary, it is in a constant state of evolution, as indicated by the recommendations in the de Silguy report. The *grandes écoles* are making efforts to respond to the pressures of modernization and globalization in two ways: by putting greater emphasis on understanding foreign cultures and on teaching foreign languages, and by what might be called "democratization." This democratization has several aspects. One is an effort to admit more students from less privileged backgrounds. A second aspect is an attempt to modify the traditional values of the *grandes écoles*, where the emphasis has been on authority and rationality, by giving greater attention to interpersonal communication and negotiation skills—this has been termed a transition from "rational intelligence" to "relational intelligence."[114] More generally, in the French school system as whole, greater emphasis is now being given to mathematics at the expense of the former concentration on *culture générale*, in which students coming from a privileged social milieu enjoy a distinct advantage.

To date, however, such efforts have not significantly changed the social makeup and the professional outlook of the men and women who occupy the leading positions within the French state. Thus, today, as in past decades, the typical French negotiator will hail from the middle and upper classes and will be highly educated, wedded to Cartesian argumentation, fiercely protective of the French state, and passionately and eloquently assertive of French interests and values.

3

The Historical Context

T HE FRENCH ARE VERY CONSCIOUS OF HISTORY, *their* history. It is not merely a subject of academic endeavor—though historians are indeed highly esteemed in France—but an omnipresent influence shaping French attitudes to all manner of issues, not least France's place in the contemporary world. As François Furet put it, the French focus on history to such an extent that they have difficulty reconciling the nation's present with its past.[1]

Thus, when U.S. diplomats tell their French counterparts that they should not be involved in the Middle East peace process because they have been absent from it since the start, the French see U.S. ignorance of France's long-standing position in the Levant. To Americans, such an attitude may seem preposterous or ridiculous, but to the French it only confirms their suspicions that Americans are profoundly ignorant of history. In the spring of 1996 Dennis Ross, then the leading U.S. negotiator in the Middle East, was reported to have disdained the mission of the French foreign minister, Hervé de Charette, to the Middle East in the following terms: "He doesn't know the history; he wasn't involved in it. He knows nothing about what was decided in 1993 . . . and what we did at that time."[2] For the French, history begins long before 1993.

Similarly, during the wars in the former Yugoslavia in the 1990s, some U.S. officials and military officers found it puzzling and disquieting that many French officers seemed sympathetic to the Serbs. This French-Serbian amity, however, predated not only the breakup of Yugoslavia but also its creation; it extended back to the experience of the military alliance in World War I.

This fixation on history can give the French a keen awareness of the origins, depths, and complexities of long-running conflicts, but it can also blind them to new departures. As Gérard Araud notes:

> The French are the victims of their knowledge of History, which leads them to miss making a break with things. Everything repeats itself; therefore, nothing is new. In *Verbatim*, Jacques Attali recounts that Mitterrand said that German reunification would not take place because the Prussians would never accept submitting to the Bavarians. For de Gaulle, the USSR was only the avatar of eternal Russia, which led him to neglect the communist factor. This also leads the French to be faithful to their friendships (Serbia, Rumania) and faithful to causes (Lebanon, Cambodia) when they do not have any interest, or not anymore.[3]

This chapter explores the master themes of French history that, together with the cultural predispositions described in chapter 2, help shape the singular comportment of French negotiators. Prominent among these themes are two related but almost contradictory elements: that of France as *la Grande Nation* and that of France as the struggling underdog. The idea of *la Grande Nation* was born with the conquests of revolutionary France at the end of the eighteenth century, but I have extended the term as a metaphor for the expansion of France in history, as it constructed itself around military conquests followed by draconian settlements, and as it celebrated its achievements in a swell of pride. Although the days of French hegemony have long since passed, the sense of pride in what France represents has not gone away, and French negotiators often assert a degree of national importance that cannot be justified purely in terms of present political and military realities. The term *la Grande Nation* is not well known in contemporary France, but it is frequently used in the German press as a critique of French pretensions.

The second element sees France as a nation fighting against the dominant power in Europe. Often this turned out to be an empire—from the Holy Roman Empire of the Germanic Peoples to the British Empire, the German Reich, and, in the Cold War, the Soviet and U.S. "empires." This struggle against the dominant power has produced a culture of the underdog or, to put it another way, a "culture of opposition to the dominant norms."[4]

In addition to exploring these and other prominent themes that shape the contemporary French sense of history, this chapter charts the rise and decline of France. Such an account could reasonably begin in A.D. 987 with the coronation of Hugues Capet, the first of the French monarchs, or with the accession of Charlemagne as emperor of all the Franks in 800, or even earlier, but for present purposes we can start in the Middle Ages and then move swiftly on to the nineteenth and twentieth centuries.[5] The focus is on the years after 1940, when French fortunes reached their nadir with the swift capitulation of French forces to the German army. Since then, successive French leaders, from Charles de Gaulle to François Mitterrand to Jacques Chirac, have sought to rebuild France's power and image. Those leaders and the negotiators who have served them have typically projected a tough, intransigent, and independent foreign policy, but at the same time they have worked bilaterally and multilaterally to shape a strong European community, strong enough to contain German aspirations and resist U.S. domination.

Woven into this chapter is also an analysis of how France stands on some of the crucial issues of the day: the future of Europe, including European defense; relations with the United States; the future of the Franco-German "couple"; and the position of France in the world. How France stands on those issues constitutes an important background for those engaging, or about to engage, in negotiations with the French.

LA GRANDE NATION: FRANCE AS VICTOR

As noted, the phrase *la Grande Nation* was coined during the French Revolution. Later it became briefly *le Grand Empire* under Napoleon, whose Grande Armée rampaged through Europe. But the origins of

French greatness were laid centuries earlier. The classic French school textbook, referred to as the "Malet-Isaac," paints this picture of France at the end of the fifteenth century: "Internal unity almost completely achieved, royal authority obeyed everywhere, a very strong army, a permanent tax system, a rich country where national consciousness was already very developed."[6] Although the country had yet to acquire its present dimensions,[7] it was the most populous state in Europe, with perhaps fifteen million inhabitants. England, in contrast, had only 3.5 million and at the time included neither Scotland nor most of Ireland. France and England had fought the Hundred Years' War, which ended in 1453 without a treaty. Although the English won the three major battles (Crécy in 1346, Poitiers in 1356, and Agincourt in 1415), the war ended with the French, spurred on by the figure of Joan of Arc, having driven their opponents out of all of France except the city of Calais.[8] The war effectively ended English attempts to control substantial parts of France—although it certainly did not signal the end of conflict between the two countries, which was to erupt on numerous occasions until the end of the nineteenth century.

Although wealthy and populous, France was not peaceful. Religious strife between Catholics and Protestants plagued the country through the last half of the sixteenth century, and the seventeenth century witnessed a revolt (La Fronde) of the bourgeoisie and the nobles that prefigured the French Revolution at the end of the eighteenth century. The country was also torn by the emergence in the seventeenth century of the highly influential Catholic sect of Jansenism and its fierce persecution by the Roman church and French state in the eighteenth century.

The peace of France was continually broken not only by internal challenges but also by confrontations between France and its neighbors. For centuries France strived for but in the end was never able to secure its so-called natural borders. These were, in the north, the English Channel; in the west, the Atlantic; in the south, the Pyrénées and the Mediterranean; and in the southeast, the Alps. In the northeast, this would have meant bringing the border up along the Rhine and over toward the Scheldt. The principal objective here would have been to acquire the Spanish Netherlands (what is today Belgium), or at least its French-speaking southern part. French aims remained unrealized, because of the opposition of the German populations in the Saar and the Ruhr, and because of the opposition of Britain. France's long rivalry with Britain, more often than not over present-day Belgium, found France usually coming out second best, largely because of Britain's dominance of the seas. And insular Britain, in the process of nation building, did not have the same problem that France had—of foreign armies almost continually harassing it along its vulnerable northeast border.

Even so, France grew into a formidable force in European affairs. Particularly during the premierships of Cardinal Richelieu (1624–42) and of his successor, Cardinal Mazarin (1643–61), France enjoyed considerable success in overcoming its enemies and expanding its territory. With the Peace of Westphalia (1648), which ended the Thirty Years' War that was fought between Protestants and Catholics in what is present-day Germany, France removed the threat presented by the German populations to the east, acquired oversight (together with Sweden) of developments in the Holy Roman Empire, and confirmed its possession of most of Alsace. This brought France to the Rhine for the first time since the Treaty of Verdun in 843, when Charlemagne's empire, comprising large areas of present-day Germany and France, had been divided into three north-south parts. The treaties of Westphalia also ushered in the long reign of Louis XIV, the "Sun King," who ruled from 1654 to 1715, when France emerged as the leading power on the Continent. Even today, French officials study the Westphalian peace as a salient triumph of French diplomacy, and the seventeenth century is known as *le Grand Siècle* (the Great Century).

For a time, without the sure hands of the previous prime ministers, Cardinals Richelieu and Mazarin, Louis XIV was able to continue a policy of aggrandizement of France. This meant, however, leading France into a series of wars that gradually sapped the energy of the regime. The high point was reached with the Treaty of Nimegen (1678), in which Louis XIV gained Franche-Comté as well as some territories in the northeast, but in 1697, after another war, these gains were largely erased with the Treaty of Ryswick. With the turn of the eighteenth century, the rise of England served as a check on the advances of the French monarchy and also on Spain, in the Treaties of Utrecht (1713)

and Rastadt (1714), which ended the War of the Spanish Succession.
Louis XIV died in the following year, 1715. As Alain Lempereur
describes it, these two treaties were "the ultimate signs of the failure of
an expansionist policy, based primarily on campaigns of war and ending up, as a consequence, confronted by alliances that were progres-
sively larger and well organized."[9] This is what Lempereur has described
as France's "culture of war."[10]

Under Louis XIV's successor, Louis XV, French diplomacy
became less effective, as in the unnecessary renunciation of French
gains in the northeast and in Savoy in the Treaty of Aix-la-Chapelle at
the end of the War of the Austrian Succession (1740–48). In this and
the next conflict, the Seven Years' War (1756–63), the principal beneficiaries were England, supreme on the seas, and Prussia, now
emerging as a powerful land-army state under Frederick II. In the
Seven Years' War, France lost two hundred thousand men fighting—in
a change of alliances—with Austria against Prussia while losing its
colonies in America and India to England for want of men to defend
them. From that point until the French Revolution in 1789, France
did not play a very active role in European power politics.[11]

But though the reign of the Sun King was over, France was still
used to considering itself—in Charles de Gaulle's words—the "mas-
todon of Europe." It had 26.5 million people when the Revolution
broke out in 1789,[12] far more than twice the number who lived in
Britain.[13] Germany was still a collection of some three hundred
states, some important, some insignificant, loosely grouped together
in the Holy Roman Empire, which Napoleon would abolish in 1806
and replace with the far less numerous grouping known as the
Germanic Confederation. Germany would not attain full nation-state
status until later in the nineteenth century. Russia and the United
States had yet to complete their colonizing destinies and therefore
acquire their full dimensions.

Given the huge demographic advantage that France enjoyed in
the eighteenth century, conditions were still there for a national resus-
citation—if only Louis XIV's habit of provoking other European countries to ally against him could be overcome, and if only the profligacy of
the French monarchy could be held in check. On the eve of the
French Revolution, the royal treasury was exhausted, in part owing to

the regime's significant military contribution to the success of the American Revolutionary War against England.

The moment of French resurgence came with the Revolution, which was directed against both the monarchy and the Catholic Church that had supported it, and which henceforth made France a threat to both the monarchical order and the ecclesiastical order in much of Europe. France's revolutionary ideology held that the people were the supreme authority, with their power exercised through the "general will." Thus, as Furet put it, the Revolution

> invaded the religious domain by substituting its terrestrial offer for that of God. Inversely, the Catholic tradition constitutes the pillar of the Counter-Revolution. It is this philosophical radicalism that constitutes the most profound character of the French Revolution and its most distinctive mark in relation to the English and American Revolutions.[14]

With the entire nation mobilized by the *levée en masse* (an act of 1793 that conscripted all French men between eighteen and twenty-five to create the first mass army), France, bursting with revolutionary energy and its new republican message, was able to quell revolts at home, repulse invading royalist forces, and advance into present-day Belgium. In 1795 three of its opponents, Prussia, Spain, and Holland, sued for peace. England and Austria remained opposed. Here the military genius of France's rising general, Napoleon Bonaparte, came into play in a brilliant campaign in Italy, forcing the Holy Roman Emperor to sign a peace treaty at Campoformio in 1797. Four satellite republics under French protection were set up in Italy and two others were established in Switzerland and Holland.

La Grande Nation was on the move, inspiring downtrodden nationalists throughout Europe. The French historian Jacques Godechot recounts:

> The Grande Nation was in the minds of "patriots" everywhere, who saw the French Republic bringing to them that which, in the optic of the Enlightenment, appeared utopian, and which now took on reality. "We observe with joy the spectacle of your *Grande Nation* bringing liberty to Europe . . ." wrote the Irish "patriots" to the French Convention in November 1792.[15]

But there was a reverse side to the medal: instead of liberty, a protectorate; instead of equality, discrimination; and beyond that, forced contributions, requisitions, pillages, and even atrocities at times.[16]

For a time, the only check on Napoleon's immeasurable ambition was England, first with the defeat of the French fleet at Aboukir in 1798, in the midst of Napoleon's expedition to Egypt. In December 1799 Napoleon staged a coup d'état and proceeded to attain full power, taking the title of emperor in 1804. In eight years, from 1804 to 1812, Napoleon conquered much of continental Europe. At the service of a revolutionary message, in the interests of the French state, and to fulfill his own demented ambition, Napoleon marshaled his troops from Lisbon to Moscow, and from Rome to Hamburg.[17] The Napoleonic Wars represented an attempt, and a unique one, to impose French control and French political ideas on Europe as a whole.

At the zenith of Napoleon's power, aside from Sweden, Denmark (which included Norway), Prussia, and the three empires—Austria, Russia, and Turkey—all of continental Europe was under his sway. This territory was divided into two parts: the French Empire, which included France itself and which had a population of 44 million; and the vassal states, with a population of some 38 million.[18]

Napoleon's achievements were considerable. He had the political will to conduct an expedition into Egypt that had archaeological as well as military aims. He was the driving force behind the creation of the legal corpus known appropriately enough as the Napoleonic Code (it is now known as the "civil code"), which spread through much of Europe and even into Egypt. It was a liberalizing code, in keeping with the gains of the Revolution, allowing, for example, divorce. At the same time Napoleon made peace with the Catholic Church in the Concordat of 1801. On the social plane Napoleon was able to forge a new elite based on a rehabilitation of the former landowning class and a meritocracy emerging from the ranks of military officers.[19] Napoleon strengthened the position of the centralized state in France and created the institutions to train the elites who would run the state.

But Napoleon's experiment foundered on the shoals of his reckless ambition and in the end, similar to the experience of Louis XIV but on a grander scale, the whole of Europe coalesced against him and brought down the Napoleonic structure. France lost the lands it had won during the revolutionary period and was cut back to the dimensions of a French-speaking territory, with three main exceptions: parts of Switzerland, parts of present-day Belgium, and Savoy.[20]

Under Napoleon, as under Louis XIV, the sense of French grandeur was palpable. In Paris, perhaps the most enduring example of Louis XIV's reign is Les Invalides, a huge edifice inspired by the king's wish to have a hospital for the treatment of wounded military personnel. Behind Les Invalides a church and dome arose, to which Napoleon's remains were brought back from St. Helena in 1840. In front of Les Invalides is a vast grass esplanade leading to the Seine and the stateliest of its bridges, the Pont Alexander III. Outside Paris, Louis oversaw the construction of the extravagant palace, buildings, and grounds of Versailles. The most enduring monument inspired by Napoleon is the towering Arc de Triomphe de l'Étoile, which stands at the head of the Champs-Élysées. Started in 1806, it was completed in 1836 and contains the tomb of the Unknown Soldier. (During the German occupation in World War II, Parisians had to suffer the daily humiliation of a noontime march by German troops from the Arc de Triomphe down the Champs-Élysées.)

Paris today is still bejeweled with architectural evocations of past glories. Besides Les Invalides and the Arc de Triomphe, for example, there is the Palais de Louvre, begun under Henry IV, continued under Louis XIV and later the two Napoleons, and completed under François Mitterrand with a towering glass pyramid in its courtyard, under which is a vast underground display of many of France's art treasures. The Eiffel Tower, built on the occasion of the Universal Exhibition in Paris in 1889, and festooned with lights at the turn of the twenty-first century, is another example of France's extravagant ambition. Grandiose architecture and statuary throughout Paris remind French civil servants, military officers, and ordinary citizens that their history has been one of grandeur and enlightenment. In a similar vein, street and place names in towns throughout France recall great victories, from Bouvines to Valmy, from Iéna to Marengo to Austerlitz.

As it had during the previous eight centuries, so during the Napoleonic period France expanded its boundaries through the medium of war. As was the pattern with Napoleon, and with Louis XIV and other kings, France concluded its victories by imposing draconian but ultimately self-defeating settlements on its conquered foes. After the defeat of the Austrian army at Austerlitz in 1805, Charles Maurice de Talleyrand Périgord advised Napoleon:

> Your Majesty can now either break the Austrian monarchy or revive it. Once broken, it will not be in the power of Your Majesty to put together the scattered debris. . . . But the existence of this mass is necessary. It is indispensable for the future salvation of the civilized nations.[21]

But Napoleon ignored his foreign minister's advice and dissolved the Austrian-led Holy Roman Empire in 1806. Talleyrand would be proved right, and France would pay dearly later in the century, when Prussia pushed Austria aside and became France's principal enemy.

Talleyrand's lesson went unheeded into the next century. "In 1918," as Alain Lempereur points out, "the Treaty of Versailles, with its exorbitant terms vis-à-vis Germany, renewed the principle of the diplomatic humiliation of the losers and, once again, we know what followed. The route of arms, followed by a harsh treaty, remain[ed] the preferred instrument of the international policy of France."[22]

Old habits die hard. According to Lempereur, "a long history of conquests and imposition by force has left traces in the way [the French] negotiate." For example, the "empty chair" crisis of the 1960s, provoked by the French to counter the decisions of the other members of the European Economic Community, "illustrates perfectly the failure to listen and the refusal to communicate with others; it confirms [the French] difficulty in accepting negotiation itself as a political tool."[23] The origins of this attitude, in Lempereur's view, can be found in what he calls a "culture of war, translated into vindictive, ironic, and Voltairian speech, [which] is reflected in the intellectual debates which France so fancies and which remain marked by a Gallic taste for confrontation and exclusivity."[24] Or, to put it another way, as a senior French diplomat says, "The French are a quarrelsome and individualistic people."[25]

THE ENEMY OF THE DOMINANT POWER IN EUROPE: FRANCE AS UNDERDOG

The idea of France as a *nation* has historically carried with it the theme of the country struggling against the dominant power in Europe. Often this meant fighting empires. The first and foremost of these imperial adversaries was the Holy Roman Empire, founded in 962 by Otto the Great and lasting until 1806. At its founding, the Holy Roman Empire represented a reiteration of the attempt by Charlemagne to re-create the Roman Empire with Christianity at its base. It became known in French as the Sainte-Empire Romain et Germanique or the Sainte-Empire Romain de Nationalité Germanique because it comprised mainly Germanic territories and as of 1250 had ceased to include Italy.

In 1440 the vast and loosely structured Holy Roman Empire came under the rule of a German princely family, the Hapsburgs, who acquired Austria and established themselves at Vienna. From 1519 until 1556 a Spanish Hapsburg, Charles V, ruled both Spain and the empire (1519–56), giving him theoretical control over a vast swath of territories that virtually encircled France. Much of the story of sixteenth-century France centers on a series of wars between Charles V and the French monarchy, a conflict that ended in 1559 with France losing its presence in Italy but keeping three cities in the north of France—Toul, Metz, and Verdun—which had been offered to the French by German Protestant princes opposed to the Hapsburgs.

A constant of French continental diplomacy from the beginning of the sixteenth century was that the Hapsburg House of Austria was France's principal menace. This was sometimes the subject of dispute in France, since it meant that France would at times ally itself with non-Catholic powers against Catholic Austria. A pendant of this policy was the illusion that Prussia, under the rule of Frederick the Great from 1740 to 1786, could become a long-term ally of France, as Frederick was an admirer of the French Enlightenment and a sometime patron of Voltaire. (An exception to the anti-Hapsburg policy was the Seven Years' War, during which France paid a high price for allying itself with Austria against Prussia and England.)

For Régis Debray, who fought as a guerrilla for Che Guevara and later served as an adviser to President Mitterrand, the theme of France struggling against empires has been the key to its survival and emergence as a nation:

> Kingdom or Republic, France was built in opposition to the idea of
> empire and its successive incarnations. If France, since the eleventh
> century, had always sided with the winner, she would have been an
> English, German or Spanish province. She owes her existence to

having allied with the weak power against the strong power of the
moment. When she did the contrary [a reference, it seems, to Vichy's
support of Adolf Hitler's Third Reich], she betrayed her own history
as well as her interests and her future.[26]

Debray's formula is similar to that of Henry Kissinger, who sees
a consistency in French national interest dating from the days of
Cardinal Richelieu, namely, "a policy of weakening the dominant
power in Europe which was then Austria. Now this applies to the
United States."[27] After Austria was defeated by Prussia in the middle
of the nineteenth century, France turned its strategic attention to the
new continental power, Prussia, with disastrous results: the war of
1870–71, resulting in the formation of the German Reich.

After World War II and the demise of Germany, France was
caught between two "empires," as Debray describes in *Les empires contre l'Europe*.[28] The French opposition to the superpowers took the form
of rallying opposition to both Soviet and U.S. domination. But during
the Cold War, there was never any doubt about where France's ultimate
allegiance lay, as was proved in the Berlin and Cuban missile crises.
With the end of the Cold War and the breakup of the Soviet Union,
France turned its attention, as Henry Kissinger observes, to limiting the
unilateralism of the "hyperpower"–the United States–by means of
actions undertaken mainly through multilateral institutions.[29]

Not a continental power, but continually interested in the balance
of power on the Continent, England–in Charles de Gaulle's words,
"our greatest hereditary enemy"–stood always ready to thwart French
ambitions. "From the Hundred Years War to Fashoda," de Gaulle said
to his information minister and amanuensis, Alain Peyrefitte, in 1962,
"she has scarcely ceased struggling against us. And since then, she has
had difficulty in not opposing our interests. . . . She continually forms
a bloc with America. . . . She wants to prevent us from making the
Common Market a success. It is true that she was our ally during the
two wars, but she is not naturally inclined to wish us well."[30]

"Fashoda" is a reference to rival British and French colonial
aims in Africa, which may be said to have intersected at Fashoda,
Sudan, lying between French west and north Africa and British east
Africa. France's thrust into Africa followed the Franco-Prussian War,
in part in compensation for that defeat. In 1898 two rival colonial

expeditions nearly came to blows at Fashoda, and the last British-French war scare occurred at that time. War was averted, and both countries, fearing the rise of Germany, turned to form what was called the Entente Cordiale, agreed to in 1904.

Notwithstanding Debray's contention that "France was built in opposition to the idea of empire and its successive incarnations," France too has had its flings at empire—sometimes in Europe, sometimes in the Third World. In 1804 Napoleon declared himself emperor and ruled, almost without interruption, until 1815. Hoping to duplicate the feat, his less brilliant nephew, Napoleon III, proclaimed himself emperor in 1852 and ruled over the self-styled Second Empire for the next eighteen years, until he surrendered and was taken into custody by the Germans in the Battle of Sedan.

The imperial expansion of the first Napoleon was justified in part as a legacy of the French Revolution: it was France's "universalist" duty to liberate by force the peoples of Europe from monarchical rule. Both Napoleon I and Napoleon III called the regime an empire, which was a way of asserting that France was not restoring its traditional monarchy. Even so, France itself has on occasion seemed to recognize the contradiction between its republican values and its imperial and colonial activities. In 1946, for example, the new French constitution designated France and its possessions overseas as the "French Union," not the "French Empire."

As noted earlier, the consistent idea of France struggling against the dominant power in Europe has engendered a long-standing "culture of opposition to the dominant norms," which views France as an underdog fighting against the odds to defend itself and its values against the tyranny of the moment, whether Austrian or German or British or American.

According to one French ambassador, France took on the status of underdog in 1763, when it lost the Seven Years' War to England, and has kept that status ever since. In keeping with this view, the ambassador maintained that the Napoleonic period represents an "aberration."[31] "The Napoleonic parenthesis—so little French in its hubris—is only an exception," he contended.[32] He extended his argument on the underdog to modern times:

> France was nearly crushed by Germany. Hence the German "obsession" of the French. And for a long time she has the obscure feeling

of being submerged by the outside "Anglo-Saxon" world. . . . French negotiators perceive themselves as representatives of a small country. And this historical memory leads them to sympathize with other underdogs.[33]

The culture of the underdog is reinforced by and reflected in the gap between French ambitions and French power. As noted in chapter 2, the mismatch is particularly conspicuous today, but it began to be felt in the nineteenth century, if not earlier. Assessing France's emerging predicament in the aftermath of the Franco-Prussian War, Henry Kissinger comments: "In the end, international politics came to be based on raw power. And in such a world, there was an inherent gap between France's image of itself as the dominant nation of Europe and its capacity to live up to it—a gap that has blighted French policy to this day."[34]

The French, observes John Kornblum, "mask their sense of inferiority in a cloak of greatness."[35] But the French also look upon their disadvantaged position as something to be exploited, and in this they seek to live up to a master principle of Gaullist thought, as expressed by historian Maurice Vaïsse: "To be credible, France must exert an influence out of proportion to its material means."[36]

THE DECLINE OF FRANCE

The Napoleonic structure was finally brought down in 1815 by a coalition of European monarchies—Britain, Prussia, Austria, and Russia—known as the Quadruple Alliance and dedicated to keeping the peace by containing France. In September 1815 the latter three monarchies formed a separate grouping called the Holy Alliance (Sainte-Alliance), which sought to stifle the nationalist and democratic movements that the French Revolution had spawned across Europe. To this day, French statesmen evoke the bugbear of the Sainte-Alliance to criticize the invocation of religion in carrying out foreign policy. In a modern tropism, French spokespeople, particularly on the Left, use the term as a means of denigrating certain U.S. collective security initiatives that are perceived to have moral undertones, such as the attack on "godless communism" during the Cold War.

The Napoleonic Wars and their aftermath spelled the end of

France's attempt to expand its territories farther to the northeast, to "where the boundary markers of Holland are placed."[37] Britain, enjoying more or less continual maritime superiority over France, had always stood by to thwart this French ambition in the northeast. With the creation of the independent state of Belgium in 1830, Britain's aim was finally secured. Throughout the rest of the nineteenth century, Britain and France would alternately ally (as in the Crimean War of 1853–55) and spar (as during the Fashoda incident in 1898), but then they buried their thousand-year rivalry with the Entente Cordiale.

France's position in Europe began to erode permanently not with the downfall of Napoleon and the wise peace of Vienna that followed, in which France was returned to the concert of European nations, but by the shocking defeat of Napoleon III at the hands of the upstart Prussia—sometimes described as "an army in possession of a state"—in 1870–71. When, four years earlier, Prussian forces had crushed the Austrian army at the Battle of Sadowa, it had become evident that Prussia was on the way to unifying Germany and that the French policy of keeping Germany divided by opposing Austria and by allying with the German ministates in the west had failed. The French had not expected the Austrians to lose and thus had not acted to check Prussia. As Charles de Gaulle wrote in his memoirs, "With how much blood and tears did we pay for the error of the Second Empire in letting Sadowa happen without moving the Army to the Rhine?"[38]

Following its triumphant victory over France at the Battle of Sedan in 1870, the new Germany humiliated France. By the terms of the peace signed in 1871, Germany proceeded to "take back" Alsace, which had been part of France since the treaties of Westphalia (1648), and also seized Lorraine, which had been annexed by France in 1766.[39] Wilhelm I, the king of Prussia, declared himself emperor of the Second Reich in the symbolic heart of French grandeur, the Hall of Mirrors in Versailles.[40] And the German chancellor, Otto von Bismarck, insisted that Prussian forces march down the Champs-Élysées in Paris, a supremely offensive gesture that helped provoke the left-wing uprising of the Paris Commune.

From that moment on, France's attitude toward its position in the world became defensive. It has never changed. As Max Beloff wrote, "The creation of the new German Empire was one of the fruits of the

Franco-Prussian War of 1870–71—the first of what some would see as
the three Franco-German wars that formed much of the substance of
European history between that date and 1945."[41]

In 1918, at the end of the second of those Franco-German wars,
World War I, France reclaimed Alsace-Lorraine, but only at a terrible
price. France had contributed 1,385,000 of its young men to World
War I's funeral pyre; by comparison, the United States lost 115,000
and Britain 947,000.[42] Germany suffered more fatalities than France—
1,808,000[43]—but Germany's population was considerably larger; furthermore, a large swath of territory in the northeast of France had
been devastated by four years of war, whereas German territory had
not been invaded.

Europe had nearly bled itself to death in World War I, and the
France that emerged from it had won but a hollow victory. After the
losses of World War I, the country was afflicted with what Stanley
Hoffmann characterizes as "deep battle fatigue." There was "general
horror at the thought of more casualties and a retreat into defensiveness."[44] Henry Kissinger describes France's position at the end of
World War I in poignant terms:

> France . . . now found itself in a truly tragic position. For two cen-
> turies it had struggled to achieve the mastery of Europe, but, in the
> war's aftermath, it no longer had confidence in its ability to protect
> even its own frontiers against a defeated enemy. French leaders felt
> instinctively that containing Germany was beyond the capacity of
> their ravaged society. War had exhausted France, and the peace
> seemed to induce premonitions of further catastrophe.[45]

Moreover, the victory of the Allies was damaged by the vindictive Treaty of Versailles, as well as by the U.S. Senate's refusal to
ratify the treaty and to join the League of Nations. The Senate's non-
ratification voided the security guarantee that France had expected
to receive from Britain and the United States through the treaty.
Although France recovered Alsace-Lorraine, its objectives east of the
Rhine in the Saar and the Rhineland were not met, except for a temporary occupation and a demilitarization of the latter. Also unsatisfied
on German reparations payments, France sought to force the issue by
occupying the Ruhr in 1923 but had to accept in the following year a

scaled-down schedule of payments in the Dawes Plan. In the latter part of the decade, under Foreign Minister Aristide Briand, France began to pursue a policy of reconciliation with Weimar Germany, notably in the Locarno Pact, in which Germany recognized its western frontiers, and Britain and Italy guaranteed the accord.

Through the doleful decade of the 1930s, France was tailing after its allies, particularly Britain. Unable to persuade either Britain or the United States to adopt a stronger stance against Adolf Hitler, and ambivalent about approaching the Russians, France stood helplessly by as Hitler denounced the Treaty of Versailles in 1935, unilaterally remilitarized the Rhineland in 1936, and then took over Austria, the Sudetenland, and in March 1939 all of Czechoslovakia. In that month, France entered into a pact with Britain in which the parties agreed not to withdraw unilaterally from a war in which they both might become involved. In the same month the British extended a unilateral guarantee to Poland, reformulated in April in a bilateral treaty. This disastrous chain of circumstances, which saw France first fail to obtain an Anglo-American security guarantee and then allow itself to become indirectly linked to a British pledge to defend Poland, has since inspired a French determination to opt out of, or refrain from, entangling arrangements that France cannot control.[46]

The swiftness of France's defeat in May and June 1940 by German forces, and French acceptance of a relatively benign armistice that was in fact a surrender, destroyed the prominent rank among nations that France had held for centuries. If the decline of France had become a chronic fact of French history since the Franco-Prussian War in the nineteenth century, the debacle of 1940 made it palpably acute.

France's history is marked by heights of glory and depths of abasement. At no time did the pendulum sweep so low as it did in 1940, when France broke its pact with Britain not to withdraw unilaterally from the war and instead concluded an armistice with Hitler. "We the French," wrote Charles de Gaulle, "had in the course of time endured many disasters, lost provinces, paid indemnities, but the state had never accepted the domination of a foreign power."[47]

What would have been justified, in de Gaulle's opinion, was a military cease-fire between the Alps and the Atlantic, carried out by a military commander under the orders of the government, which would have repaired to Algiers, "taking with it the treasure of French sovereignty, which for fourteen centuries had never been surrendered, continuing the battle, keeping its word to the Allies."[48] The Vichy government's unforgivable sin, in de Gaulle's view, was

> to have retired from the war with the empire intact, the fleet untouched, the air force largely undamaged; to have withdrawn our African and Levantine troops without a single soldier lost; to have abandoned all those forces which, in France itself, could be transported elsewhere; to have broken our alliances; above all, to have submitted the state to the Reich's discretion.[49]

Virtually alone, the haughty and clairvoyant de Gaulle realized that if someone did not act in June 1940 to challenge the course of events, France would be written off as a long-term mediocrity. In de Gaulle's own words:

> I thought, in fact, that it would be the end of honor, unity and independence if it were to be admitted that, in this world war, only France had capitulated and that she had let the matter rest there. For in that case, whatever might be the issue of the conflict . . . [the country's] self-disgust and the disgust it would inspire in others would poison its soul and its life for many generations.[50]

De Gaulle left for London to continue the struggle. In France four years of German occupation followed.

FRANCE AT THE END OF WORLD WAR II

Until World War II, relations between France and the United States had ranged from cordial to curt but had typically featured a good deal of mutual respect. France, of course, had assisted the American colonists struggling against their British colonial masters. Such support had begun under the ancien régime, and the alliance continued, for a time, after the Revolution in France. Although the French Revolution was partly inspired by the American example, it was both more far reaching and considerably more immoderate, and before long Americans and French came to see themselves as champions of distinctly different models of republican societies. Ideological differences were compounded by differing national interests, and by the turn of the century, the infant American republic was struggling not only with the former colonial power, Great Britain, but also with France, for its freedom of navigation on the seas. Later in the nineteenth century, as tensions with the mother country wore off and the Anglo-Saxon world seemed set on a course of irresistible global ascendancy, a permanent Anglo-American alliance began to develop, marking the United States off even further from its "oldest ally," France.

Although between the middle of the nineteenth century and 1940, the United States and France had some difficult moments, as in French meddling in the New World during the American Civil War and in the perceived U.S. leniency toward the Germans over the reparations issue following World War I, nevertheless the bilateral relationship was tolerable.

In 1940, however, a gulf opened up not just between the U.S. administration and Charles de Gaulle but between the United States and France.[51] The swift French military defeat convinced many in the administration of Franklin D. Roosevelt that France was finished as a great power. At the same time, Roosevelt developed an almost pathological aversion to de Gaulle, which filtered down through the administration. Roosevelt's refusal to accept de Gaulle's attempt to delegitimize France's surrender and establish a substitute center of power that could emerge in the postwar period turned out to be the key event that was to set the United States and France profoundly at odds.

In French eyes, the Roosevelt administration denied the legitimacy of the Gaullist myth that wartime France was a country of resistance and only incidentally a regime of collaboration. Even with the liberation of Paris, when de Gaulle quickly assumed control of the levers of power, Roosevelt still withheld full recognition. It was only on October 23, 1944, that the United States, followed immediately by Britain and the USSR, recognized de Gaulle's provisional government de jure. "The recognition of the provisional government . . . in itself was a minor episode," later wrote Jean Monnet, one of the great French statesmen to emerge from World War II, "but like a recurrent fever it has troubled Franco-American relations for the past thirty years. Many of the attitudes would be inexplicable, were it not for the illusions born of wounded pride in a memory that never forgot."[52]

France came out of the war better than anyone could have expected from a country that had left the war in 1940. Resuscitated almost single-handedly by de Gaulle, the French by the end of the war had 1,300,000 men under arms, earning themselves a place at the surrender ceremonies, to the astonishment and chagrin of the Germans. Thanks to de Gaulle (and to Winston Churchill, who saw the need for a strong postwar France), France could also boast a series of prized positions: permanent membership in the UN Security Council; an occupation zone in Germany; and membership in the Control Commission at Berlin, which was supposed to decide the future of Germany.

But, as Furet noted, France had "recovered more the appearances of its 'rank' than the reality of its influence":[53]

> In 1945 [France was] in a unique situation: neither victorious nor defeated or, rather, both victorious and defeated. . . . She had been able to obtain—painfully and in extremis—a stool at the table of the conquerors. . . . But she was present neither at Yalta nor at Potsdam. No one had really forgotten that she had capitulated in 1940, and that she had contributed only marginally to the final victory.[54]

Indeed, the contrast between the endings of the two world wars was striking, as Furet noted, quoting a passage from Raymond Aron's *Le spectateur engagé:*

> November 1918. . . . What Paris was on the day of the Armistice, on the day after the Armistice, no one can imagine it; it had to be seen. The people embraced in the streets. Everyone: the bourgeois, the laborers, the office workers, the young, the old. It was a madness of the people, but a joyful madness. . . . By contrast, in the month of May 1945, Paris was mortally sad, such as I saw it. I remember having a conversation with Jules Roy at that moment. He was struck, as I was, by that sadness, by the absence of hope. It was the victory of the Allies more than that of France. Nothing comparable to the transports of enthusiasm of the days of November 1918.[55]

After World War II, France was economically prostrate and still fearful (though unreasonably so) of Germany. Moreover, it had the unenviable distinction of being the only major Western democracy to have been occupied in modern times. The shame and the shock felt by the French were profound, and those sentiments endure, albeit in diminished form, beneath the surface of contemporary France. It is difficult to overemphasize the traumatic effect of World War II on the French psyche and how much it affects the way the French think—and negotiate—today. Charles de Gaulle, who did his best to sublimate the World War II experience for the French people, telling the Parisians that the city had been won back by them,[56] nevertheless clearly recognized this factor: "For all the satisfaction of its [World War II's] dénouement, it had left—and forever!—a secret grief in the depths of the national conscience."[57] World War II, then, is *the* burden of history for the French—less daunting than what successive generations of Germans have had and will have to carry, but a burden, nevertheless.

It is curious that Germany, which was not defeated by France in World War II, has at least until now been able to accommodate to a position of French ascendancy in Europe. In the view of Christoph Bertram, director of the Berlin think tank Stiftung Wissenschaft und Politik, this is because Germany was "destroyed" by World War II, whereas France was "humiliated." This difference has made it more difficult for the French than for the Germans to come to terms with these traumatic events. "The French constantly need to find reassurance as to who they are."[58]

But it was Germany's destruction that opened the way for French ascendancy in Europe in the last half of the twentieth century, for once France had recovered from the war, materially and psychologically, it alone was in a position to fill the power vacuum in continental Western Europe. It remained, however, for France to reform its fractious political institutions and present a coherent and strong international image. This de Gaulle eventually was to accomplish.

In the aftermath of World War II, France acknowledged its diminished place in the world and recognized that it needed to build stable relationships with the other great powers of Europe. The chief innovation in French foreign policy after World War II was not the restoration of the Entente Cordiale with Britain, which continued on much as before. Nor was it the short-lived attempt to revive France's "reverse alliance"[59] with the USSR, an alliance that had begun in 1893 when France looked to tsarist Russia as a counterweight to Wilhelmine Germany; de Gaulle's efforts to rekindle this alliance had to be put aside with the onset of the Cold War in 1947–48. Rather, it was the gradual construction of a relationship with Germany, based on mutual interest and slowly developing trust and built within the context of a European ensemble.

FRANCE SINCE WORLD WAR II: INDEPENDENCE AND MULTILATERALISM

The story of France since World War II is that of a dialectic between independence and multilateralism, played out against a background of a lack of means to back up an increasingly ambitious foreign policy. Independence was something to be constantly watched over for a country with a proud past that had just emerged, for the first time, from total occupation by a foreign power. At the same time, its reduced status as a world power made it very difficult for France to make its influence felt internationally. Hence the attraction of multilateralism: France could leverage its power by working through multilateral organizations, particularly the European Union and the United Nations.

In real and symbolic terms, this dialectic is represented by two of the great figures of postwar France, Jean Monnet and Charles de Gaulle. Monnet, a French cognac salesman who left home at the age of sixteen, had before the war established important contacts in Britain and the United States. Later he became a trusted intermediary between the Roosevelt administration and its favored candidate to bring France back into the war, General Henri Giraud. However, as the war wore on and de Gaulle maneuvered Giraud out of the way, Monnet moved his attentions toward de Gaulle. The two men could not have been more different, in physical stature and in personality. Monnet was a consensual figure who worked behind the scenes and whose slogan was "to unite men, to solve the problems that divide them, and to persuade them to see their common interest."[60] General de Gaulle was bellicose, emotional, and most of the time uncompromising; he was also an erudite product of the French school system, whose father had been a history teacher in a *lycée*. As Aron once remarked, "De Gaulle only had words at his disposal; that is why he used them with such force."[61]

Monnet, who was the author of the stillborn plan for a British-

French union amid the turmoil of June 1940, had turned his attention away from Britain and toward Germany after the war. Monnet sought a way of locking the French and German economies together so that the two countries could never go to war again. He fastened on the idea of pooling the two countries' key war-making resources, coal and steel. He found common cause with mainly Christian Democratic leaders in France, West Germany, and Italy. The result was the European Coal and Steel Community (ECSC). Ratified in 1952, the ECSC bound French and Germans together in a "community" that also included the Benelux countries and Italy. A supranational Europe, transcending the nation-state framework, was born.

The ECSC, like the other initiatives that were to culminate in the establishment of the European Union, was built on the premise that pooled economic arrangements among the Western European states (what was to become known as communitarianism) would be easier to set up than political and military ones, which would come later on. But Monnet violated this basic premise with his hastily conceived European Defense Community (EDC), intended to be the pendant of the ECSC. Much-needed German troops would be brought into the defense of Europe in a communitarian army that would also include France and the other ECSC countries. This was too much for the French sense of independence, and the Treaty of Paris of 1952 that instituted the EDC went down to defeat in the French National Assembly in August 1954.

Soon thereafter West Germany entered Western defense arrangements by the front door, becoming a member of NATO. France received compensation by obtaining a long-term British commitment to keep troops on the Continent and by securing a prohibition against German development of nuclear, biological, or chemical weapons on its soil as part of the agreement that ended the Allied occupation. As a way of codifying these arrangements, the Brussels Pact of 1948—signed by France, the United Kingdom, and the Benelux countries—was expanded to include Germany and Italy. The pact's organization, the Western European Union (WEU), turned out to be unnecessary, as it could never emerge by itself as a viable and independent military entity parallel to NATO; even its enabling statute enjoined it to seek military advice from NATO. Despite French attempts to revive the

WEU in the 1980s, it was largely absorbed into the European Union by the end of the century.

THE RETURN OF DE GAULLE

Charles de Gaulle resigned suddenly from office in January 1946, expecting to be called back by popular acclaim before long. Such did not happen until twelve years later. When he did return, in 1958, France's standing in Europe and the world had not improved much, in relative terms, although its economic recovery was well under way, thanks in part to massive aid delivered by the Marshall Plan in the late 1940s and early 1950s.

France was now a member of NATO, and part of its armed forces were under NATO's integrated command. At first France had welcomed General Dwight Eisenhower's return to Europe as Supreme Allied Commander (SACEUR). NATO not only provided protection in the face of the Soviet threat, but also supplanted European defense arrangements growing out of the Brussels Pact of 1948 that implied a British military ascendancy over France. But when Eisenhower proceeded to distribute the NATO regional commands, the French received none of the top positions and rapidly became dissatisfied. Later, when the French in 1954 rejected a European communitarian army that would not have included Great Britain, the SACEUR's military hold over NATO members' contingents was tightened through what was known as NATO's integrated command.

By the time the Germans were brought into NATO (and the WEU), even the French recognized that the major security threat to Europe was the Soviet Union and no longer Germany, though the French intellectual class as a whole, dominated by Jean-Paul Sartre, had become pervasively anti-American while remaining sympathetic to the Russian people and the Red Army for having played the chief role in the defeat of Germany. Not until the 1970s and the revelation of the existence of the Soviet gulags would French intellectual opinion turn away from the USSR.

When de Gaulle returned to power in 1958, France had been at war almost continually since 1945, indeed from V-E Day itself, when bloody riots broke out in Algeria, provoking a merciless French repression. In general, France, unlike Britain, gave up its colonial possessions with great reluctance, partly because these were considered a gauge of France's international standing.

Although the troubles in Algeria subsided, France was immediately taken up with recovering its position in Indochina, which had been lost to the Japanese in March 1945. France's remnant European population in Indochina, numbering some thirty thousand, proved unwilling to cede anything but the trappings of power to the Vietnamese, and by the end of 1946 all hopes for a peaceful solution between the French and Ho Chi Minh had disappeared. A full-scale war began that was to last until 1954, when a peace agreement was signed in Geneva, following the French defeat at Dien Bien Phu. Just three months later, on November 1, 1954, a full-scale revolt broke out in Algeria. The French army simply moved its operations from Indochina to Algeria. That war lasted until 1962, when, at de Gaulle's prodding, France withdrew from North Africa.

Throughout the 1950s, France unhappily made the transition from a diehard colonialist power to a postcolonial one. The major exception to Britain's graceful acceptance of the postcolonial age was Anthony Eden's petulant reaction to Gamal Abdel Nasser's nationalization of the Suez Canal Company in 1956. France, in the mistaken hope that the Algerian revolt could be cut off at its supposed head, in Cairo, launched with Britain (and Israel) a military operation to seize the canal. Under U.S. and Soviet pressure, the operation had to be aborted, and the Suez misadventure marked the demise of Britain and France as great powers. The outcome of this affair, during which Marshal Nikolay Bulganin implicitly threatened to drop atomic bombs on London and Paris, and the United States failed to respond strongly to the USSR, prompted France to turn toward nuclear deterrence.

De Gaulle, when returning to power, sought to change the NATO system by creating a French-U.S.-British triumvirate to run the alliance. When Washington offered no meaningful response, he proceeded over the next eight years to dismantle the French presence in NATO's integrated command and to move NATO's facilities and troops out of France, all the while preserving France's status as a member of the Atlantic Alliance. De Gaulle, with impeccable Cartesian logic, had always maintained that the alliance and NATO were two separate movements, as in a piece of music. The one was the North Atlantic Treaty of April 4, 1949, and the other was the organization that stemmed from it and that was set up in early 1951.

THE *FORCE DE FRAPPE*

As de Gaulle saw it, there were two ways in which he needed to restore France to full independence. The first was to get French forces out from under the control of the SACEUR, always an American. Though de Gaulle's withdrawal from the integrated military command in 1966 restored, at least in theory, France's freedom of movement, accords were drawn up between France and NATO from as early as 1967. These governed the employment of French forces should a hot war break out with the Soviet Union. But NATO engaged in no military actions in the forty-odd years of the Cold War. Thus the French, though constrained by the post-1966 France-NATO agreements, never had to exercise them, and so in practice they retained their strategic independence throughout the remainder of the Cold War.

The second way for de Gaulle to restore France to "full independence" was to create a nuclear weapons capability, the so-called *force de frappe*. The French nuclear arsenal, which became operational in 1969, was built not only without U.S. help but over the objections of Washington. (By an act of Congress in 1958, the British had been given access to U.S. atomic weapons information, while the French were purposely excluded.) This weapon was to become identified with French independence itself, as explicitly stated in the Defense White Paper of 1972: "if the nuclear strategic force is the instrument of nuclear deterrence, it is the will to national independence that is the foundation of it."[62]

The *force de frappe* was—and remains—above all a political instrument, aimed at making sure that other countries, including and especially the United States, respected France. It also meant theoretically that in the last resort France could act alone and against the tide of the Allied powers. However problematic the *force de frappe* may seem in today's post–Cold War world, it bolsters French confidence that the country can, if necessary, "go it alone," without the kind of desperate search for allies it conducted in the 1920s and 1930s. It allows France to more comfortably exercise its "culture of opposition to the dominant norms."

Beyond the United States and the Soviet Union, the *force de frappe* spoke most pointedly to Germany: with this instrument, France reversed its position of military inferiority to Germany that dated from the Franco-Prussian War. For the French subconscious, the *force de frappe* is the "anti-1940" or, in a broader sense, the expiation for everything that has been inflicted on France militarily since the Prussians came across the border in 1870. For France to do away with nuclear weapons, de Gaulle asserted to his Council of Ministers in 1968, would be "to restore German military power."[63]

Further, the *force de frappe* means that France, against the odds, has won out in its protracted struggle against Germany: the shock of 1870 cannot happen again; the French destiny of Alsace-Lorraine has been settled. And in part, the stridently assertive behavior of the French in European councils is a way, consciously or not, of driving home the point that France came out best in the contest with Germany. (Such assurance, however, barely conceals a growing French nervousness about the power that reunified Germany may wield in the future.)

On occasion, French negotiators even make explicit reference to the power that the *force de frappe* confers. During the EU summit at Nice in December 2000, *Le Monde* reported:

> A number of French diplomats thought it wise, in order to defend the [continued] parity of votes between Germany and France, to spread the idea that if France had 20 million fewer people than Germany, it nevertheless possessed a nuclear arsenal. Such arguments feed the traditional criticisms, notably in Germany, on the arrogance of "la grande nation."[64]

There is, however, an anomaly at the heart of French military strategy. As Alfred Grosser points out, whereas the French nuclear arm is too powerful to be used against the weak countries, the French conventional arm is not powerful enough to make itself felt throughout the world.[65] These anomalies became more accentuated with the end of the Cold War and the disappearance of the Soviet nuclear threat.

The large slices that the nuclear and space programs take out of the French military budget have meant that the quality of the French conventional forces has deteriorated. No less than 20 percent of the French military budget is absorbed by nuclear weaponry.[66] Nuclear arms also take the same share of the British budget, but as of 2002 the British were spending 10 to 15 percent more than the French on new weaponry in general. Thus the postulate that France, with its large conscript army, was the preeminent military power in Western Europe at the end of the Cold War is no longer true, and this is only partly due to the fact that the French have transitioned from a conscript army to a professional one.[67]

Despite these serious emerging deficiencies, France's military has become an effective instrument from its continual involvement in colonial wars until 1962 and its considerable experience in international peacekeeping operations in the later decades of the twentieth century. Since World War II, France and Britain have become the most interventionist powers in Western Europe.

Furthermore, a serious effort is currently being made to improve France's military posture. The military budget for 2003 was 7.5 percent higher than that for 2002. The equipment and armaments side of the budget increased by 11.2 percent in 2003. According to Jacques Isnard of Le Monde, "the objective [is] to close the gap with Great Britain."[68]

THE TRANSFORMATION OF SUPRANATIONAL EUROPE

In June 1957 the Treaty of Rome transformed the ECSC into the European Economic Community (EEC), or Common Market. De Gaulle, an avowed opponent of supranational arrangements, endorsed the Treaty of Rome on his return to power in 1958. Perhaps this is less surprising than it appeared at the time, as France was bound to be the dominant force in a grouping that included six Western European powers but not Britain.

During the 1960s de Gaulle twice vetoed the entry of Great Britain into the Common Market as a way of preserving France's ascendancy in continental Western Europe and demonstrating to the world the end of an ephemeral disequilibrium that had existed between Great Britain and France from 1940 to 1960. In the 1960s de Gaulle also sought to extend the benefits of the EEC to agriculture. He was

ultimately successful in doing so but not without causing severe dis-
ruption in the EEC. During what came to be known as the "empty
chair" crisis of June 1965 through January 1966, France refused to
attend meetings of the European Council until the council acceded to
French demands that it implement financial arrangements for the
EEC's Common Agricultural Policy (CAP). The crisis ended with the
Luxembourg Compromise, a nonstatutory agreement whereby a member country could invoke overriding national interest and veto a decision, even a decision on communitarian issues (such as the CAP),
which was otherwise subject to a qualified majority vote.[69] Four months
later the financial arrangements for the CAP were put in place.

THE ENDURING INFLUENCE OF DE GAULLE

De Gaulle's determination to "place France at the center of the world
(au milieu du monde),"[70] has left an indelible stamp on French diplomats, according to a French ambassador posted to Brussels.[71] Many of
them have sought to carry on the Gaullist tradition not only in political orientation but also in terms of manner and style.

De Gaulle's idea was that weakness had to be, and could be,
overcome by intransigence. In the depths of French powerlessness
during World War II, de Gaulle made this a matter of doctrine, with
such public statements as, "We have, in the common interest, the right
and duty to show ourselves intransigent."[72] To the Free French delegation in London he announced, "We shall have need of this intransigence up to the Rhine, inclusive."[73]

What appeals most to later French negotiators about the Gaullist
approach is that it seemed to work. In the 1960s, although France was
not at the center of the world, de Gaulle captured more than a fair
share of the world's attention. His pronouncements were at one and
the same time mysterious, unpredictable, and portentous. De Gaulle's
thinking, argues Hoffmann, contained "an element of mysticism that
Americans did not appreciate."[74] It was not always clear in Washington
what de Gaulle was getting at. At one point, Assistant Secretary of
State George Ball proposed at a White House meeting "a public and
serious approach to de Gaulle—an approach which would put to him
the question: 'what do you want?' We should seriously make the point
to him (in such a fashion that it was understood publicly): 'We are not

against you, but we don't know what troubles you, and we don't have proposals from you.'"[75]

And yet de Gaulle considered that his intentions had long been clear: he wanted to re-create the Big Three of World War I. France, on a par with Britain, would decide, along with the United States, on a world strategy, including nuclear strategy. The problem with de Gaulle's proposals, and with a number of French proposals since his time, is that they struck the United States as utterly unrealistic: France simply did not have the national power to merit its inclusion in a revamped Big Three.

Though de Gaulle provoked a high degree of interest and consternation, he was unable to fulfill some of his objectives, partly because France as a middle power did not have the clout to achieve them. The Germans dodged his effort to distance them from the United States when the Bundestag watered down the Élysée Treaty of Friendship and Cooperation, which he and Konrad Adenauer had signed in January 1963; his attempt to establish an intergovernmental political structure—the Fouchet Plan—over the EEC and thus assert France's hegemony more directly, was rejected by the other members, in particular the Dutch and the Italians; and the Soviets ended his opening toward them ("détente, entente, and cooperation")[76] by crushing the Prague Spring in Czechoslovakia in 1968. But de Gaulle was sure in his long-term vision: communism would end because the nation-state concept was too strong and would triumph over it.

Since the 1960s French foreign policy positions have hewn to the diplomatic orientations set down by de Gaulle: independence based on military strength (the *force de frappe*); a Europe of nations, not a federated or supranational Europe; and a world role for France as a champion of freedom and of the underdog. In addition to maintaining long-standing areas of French interest—Africa and the Middle East—France has extended political, economic, and cultural support to Asia, Latin America, and Québec.

The reservation about an integrated or "federal" Europe is a reflection of the French (and de Gaulle's) fixation on sovereignty and independence. The French prefer that critical aspects of policy remain the purview of national governments, decided on by unanimity in an "intergovernmental" rather than a "communitarian" framework. A "federal" Europe to the French means a limitation of their freedom of maneuver in critical areas such as foreign and defense policy. As one French diplomat puts it, "One does not impose on our country that which does not please us."[77] And the other members of the European Union realize that France is too important to be ignored. Whether this will hold as true with the membership of the union expanding from fifteen to twenty-five remains to be seen.

France has the European Commission, the representation of Europe's supranationality, constantly under its eye. The French mantra is that decisions cannot be imposed on France, which will remain master of its own choices. It will not let itself be dragged into situations not of its own making. It will not give a blank check; it first wants to know what action its partners are planning.

THE EUROPEAN ROLE OF FRANÇOIS MITTERRAND

Starting in the mid-1970s, the closeness of the personal ties between French and German leaders had a significant effect not only on bilateral relations but also in the international arena and in the construction of Europe. Both Helmut Schmidt and Helmut Kohl were generally comfortable in deferring to their French counterparts (respectively, Valéry Giscard d'Estaing and François Mitterrand) for the political leadership of Europe. The European Monetary System, the forerunner to the European Monetary Union and the euro, was started in the 1970s under the impulsion of Giscard d'Estaing and Helmut Schmidt. Political support was also provided, notably when Mitterrand supported Kohl's decision to install medium-range nuclear missiles in West Germany despite widespread domestic opposition and the hostility of the Soviets.

In the 1980s and early 1990s, led by Mitterrand and Kohl, the European Community began to take major steps toward more communitarianism. With the passage of the Single European Act of December 4, 1985, a single market was instituted, providing for the free circulation of goods, persons, services, and capital throughout the community by 1993.[78] In December 1991 it was agreed at a summit in Maastricht, the Netherlands (where the European Community became the European Union), to introduce a common currency—what became known as the euro—on January 1, 1999; the euro would become the sole medium of exchange by 2002. The Treaty of Maastricht also sketched out the idea for a European defense identity, which would emerge gradually and be linked to a common security and defense policy.[79]

Mitterrand, together with Jacques Delors, the French president of the European Commission, led the campaign for the euro, which Mitterrand saw as a means of anchoring Germany firmly to Western Europe and of lessening France's dependence on the monetary policies of the Bundesbank. Mitterrand was less interested in promoting the political integration of Europe, an idea that had greater appeal for Kohl, who, like most Germans, was ready to sacrifice some sovereignty to achieve a united Europe. This difference reflects long-standing differences between French and German attitudes toward the *nation*. As Rudolph von Thadden writes:

> [I]n France, nation and national thought have always been synonymous with the values of the [Enlightenment] and the modern world, whereas in Germany, even today, the tradition of romanticism, which expresses itself in the anti-rationalist character of its ethnic thinking, shines through [in] the terminology used. West of the Rhine the formation of the nation served to surmount the *ancien régime* and a society of orders, whereas to the east it was above all the symbol of an anti-democratic and reactionary [line of] thought not committed to universal values.[80]

The French preference is for a union of states and thus for a stronger European Council, which exercises the intergovernmental competencies of the European Union. The German preference is for a union of peoples, and thus for a stronger European Parliament and European Commission, which deliberate and decide on matters of a communitarian nature.

THE END OF THE COLD WAR AND THE QUEST FOR A EUROPEAN DEFENSE IDENTITY

With the fall of the Berlin Wall in November 1989 and the reunification of Germany in September 1990, the postwar relationship between France and Germany was altered irrevocably. France's ascendancy over Germany and within the European Union was coming to an end, or at least was about to be profoundly modified. Despite his later disclaimers,[81] François Mitterrand clearly sought to slow down or otherwise control the process of German reunification; but he was soon forced to accept that, as Hoffmann comments, "German unity was a fait accompli for all practical purposes; the problem for France was accommodation, not prevention."[82]

With the end of the Cold War, NATO seemed suddenly irrelevant to some observers, while the creation of a stronger European defense entity seemed a logical next step. In the event, however, the United States showed that it had no intention of closing down NATO, which would mean losing its military position on the European continent. Furthermore, rather than prompting the end of NATO, the settlement of the German question brought about the first *expansion* of NATO since the accession of Spain in 1982. East Germany's *Anschluss* with West Germany meant that East Germany would become part of NATO (albeit without any non-German troops on its soil). With this new acquisition, NATO began its own peaceful march into Eastern Europe, and its momentum has carried on ever since, as has Eastern Europe's fervent devotion to NATO. In the words of one French ambassador, "To its members, NATO is like a religion. We [the French] are agnostics."[83]

French intentions in the area of European defense have always been clear, at least to the French. Frédéric Bozo, writing in 1991, laid out France's long-term strategic view:

> The affirmation of a European strategic identity has in effect represented for forty years the constant ambition of the diplomatic and strategic action of France, which legitimately believes that the European upheavals of 1989 have increased both its necessity and its possibility.[84]

Thus, despite NATO's refusal to disappear in the immediate aftermath of the Cold War, France continued to press for an independent European defense identity. While NATO sought to keep such an identity within the confines of the Atlantic Alliance—recognizing "the development of a European identity in the domain of security,"[85] but not openly in the area of "defense"[86]—France and Germany secretly went ahead in late 1991 and created a separate Franco-German Corps (later mutating into the Euro-Corps, with Spain, Belgium, and Luxembourg also joining). This move, mainly pushed by the French, may have been spurred partly by French resentment over being shut out of the arrangements in the aftermath of the Persian Gulf War. Mitterrand's bitterness on this score was amply evident in retrospect, as noted earlier. French resentment over the end-of-war arrangements also played a role in the gradual distancing of France from Anglo-American policies toward Iraq over the course of the 1990s and into the twenty-first century, a process that culminated in France leading the opposition within the UN Security Council to U.S. and British moves to win UN backing for an invasion of Iraq in 2003 (see chapter 5).

In 1995 the staunchly anti-NATO Mitterrand was replaced by Jacques Chirac, who despite being a member of the Gaullist party was perceived to be free of the traditional French reservations about U.S. culture.[87] "Chirac came in on a wave of goodwill toward the U.S.," notes John Kornblum, a key negotiator with the French on the U.S. side.[88] The new president swiftly signaled his intention to effect a rapprochement between France and the military structure of NATO. The senior military figure at the Élysée under Mitterrand, General Christian Quesnot, saw Chirac's move as a clear deviation from the traditional Gaullist consensus on defense: "I remained chief of the [Élysée] military staff under Jacques Chirac for several months. There was a real break with the Gaullist-Mitterrandian heritage with regard to NATO. I am not making a judgment on it; it was a political act."[89]

But this rapprochement, which began in late 1995, was stopped in its tracks by a sudden demand by the French in the following year that they be given charge of NATO's Southern Command at Naples. As described in the first case study in chapter 5, the standoff between France and the United States led France to turn again toward an autonomous European defense identity.

This time France made common cause with Britain, which, according to Jean-David Levitte, was looking to "weaken the French-German couple,"[90] and which, like France, had become disenchanted with the tergiversations of U.S. policy in the Balkans in the early 1990s. The chances of British-French cooperation in European defense within NATO were severely limited after the French-U.S. dispute over the Southern Command, which left little prospect that the French would return to the military structure of NATO in the near future.

According to a senior British defense official, Tony Blair and his team on coming into office in 1997 were taken aback when they discovered the lack of military self-sufficiency among Europe's major powers. As the Kosovo crisis developed in 1998, the continued reluctance of the Clinton administration to contemplate the use of U.S. ground troops there prior to a settlement stood in contrast to the British and French willingness to entertain a ground intervention.[91] Another element in the background to the British change of heart, perhaps even a crucial one, was that Tony Blair, blocked by his own public opinion from joining the European Monetary Union, could demonstrate his European credentials by moving closer to the French position on European defense.

Following a number of entreaties from the French about the necessity for a European defense force, the British responded positively. After a good deal of preparatory work,[92] an agreement was reached; it was made public at the Anglo-French summit at St. Malo on December 3 and 4, 1998. Heralding an end to Britain's long-standing proscription against a defense role for the European Union, Blair and Chirac issued a joint declaration averring that "the [European] Union must have the capacity for autonomous action, backed up by credible military forces [and] the means to decide to use them . . . in order to respond to international crises."[93] "Autonomous action" was to take the form of an autonomous European defense force, called the Rapid Reaction Force (RRF)[94]—the equivalent of an army corps (fifteen brigades), totaling fifty thousand to sixty thousand troops, with an air and naval component, capable of being deployed within the space of two months, and self-sufficient to the extent that it could remain deployed for one year.[95] Over this force is an EU political-military superstructure headed by a Political and Security Committee (COPS).

The Anglo-French rapprochement on defense was, at least implicitly, a sort of insurance policy for France against the perception that its relations with reunited Germany were becoming less close. But, as with France's treaty of friendship with Germany in the EU context, there are limits to France's closeness to Britain in defense matters—exemplified by the fact that Britain is the United States' closest military ally, buoyantly affirmed by Tony Blair in Afghanistan, Iraq, and elsewhere. Thus the "spirit of St. Malo" was dampened by the falling-out between Britain and France over the issue of going to war with Iraq in early 2003. Forward movement on European defense cannot be accomplished in any meaningful way without Anglo-French cooperation, as these are the only two significant interventionist powers in Europe.

This differentiation between France and the "Anglo-Saxons" is perceivable across the diplomatic landscape. In the aftermath of the events of September 11, 2001, and following an initial outburst of support by President Chirac, the French seemed curiously absent, certainly in relation to the activism of Tony Blair. There was a *historical* reason for this, in that the French do not like to be drawn into compromising situations by the United States; but there was also a *cultural* one. The French want to know first what the plan is: "We are ready," said Chirac, "to send special forces [to Afghanistan] on condition that we know what is the nature of the mission and to be associated with the planning."[96]

But beyond this, there was from the U.S. side, post–September 11, a reflex of not stepping outside the "Anglo-Saxon" community for the planning and execution of operations: the first call goes out to the British and the second to the Australians. This was in part due to unpleasant memories over Kosovo, a NATO action that had to be conducted on the basis of unanimity.

At the outset of the war in Afghanistan, the Americans declined an offer of troop support from certain NATO allies, including the French and the Italians. Thus, even though the Atlantic Alliance's Article 5, the collective defense article in the Washington Treaty, was immediately invoked after September 11, only British ground troops joined U.S. regular combat forces in the initial fighting in Afghanistan that drove the Taliban from power.[97] However, special forces from other countries were involved, including those of France, Germany, Norway, Australia, New Zealand, and Canada. The predominantly Anglo-American force posture reflected the U.S. desire to have a free hand in conducting the campaign and to avoid the "Belgrade Bridge" syndrome whereby participating countries in the Kosovo war (read France) vetoed some of the targets selected.

As it turned out, the French did not begin to send regular troops until after the fall of Kabul, although two French ships were in the

Indian Ocean from the outset. Later, the French contributed modest forces to the international peacekeeping force in Kabul, sponsored by the United Nations and under the lead of the British, and they also dispatched a small number of Mirage aircraft to Kyrgyzstan, which took part along with U.S. aircraft in bombing suspected al Qaeda hideouts in eastern Afghanistan in March 2002—though the French exercised their discretion in determining the appropriateness of some of the targets. Subsequently, French and U.S. troops each began training a battalion of what is to be a future Afghan army.[98]

Overall, though only after the Taliban had been overthrown, the French made a considerable contribution to Operation Enduring Freedom in Afghanistan: "By the end, nearly 5,000 French soldiers, sailors and airmen deployed for the operation in Afghanistan, including about a quarter of the French Navy and the only non-U.S. combat aircraft."[99]

The U.S. decision to decline the military support of NATO in the aftermath of September 11—yet another illustration of the increasing U.S. tendency to "go it alone" militarily—precipitated another crisis in NATO, according to German general Klaus Naumann, the former chairman of NATO's Military Committee. The French, according to Naumann, are looking with amusement on what appears to be the ongoing erosion of NATO. Another, and more serious, crisis broke out in early 2003, when France, along with Germany and Belgium, refused to sanction NATO military support for Turkey in the hypothetical event of hostilities between Turkey and Iraq. Eventually, the Defense Planning Committee, an organ of NATO that does not include France, endorsed such support.

According to some NATO members, by declining the military support of NATO in Afghanistan, by going ahead with NATO enlargement, and by bringing Russia closer into Atlantic Alliance deliberations, has in effect marginalized NATO.[100] Many observers see NATO becoming more like the Organization for Security and Cooperation in Europe—a debating organization—which suggests to the French that NATO does not matter anymore.

Whether the French would like to see a complete end to the U.S. military presence in Europe is not clear. Some Americans who negotiated with the French during the arms control talks and the negotiations over

German reunification in the late 1980s and the early 1990s believe that
the French want the United States to stay in Europe, but under French
terms. The French want less of an overpowering U.S. presence concerning European issues, but at the same time they do not want the
United States to leave the Continent, as the United States serves as a
counterbalance to the emerging power of a reunited Germany.[101] This
opinion, however, seems contradicted by statements such as the following by Hubert Védrine, who questions the existence of an Atlantic security community of common interests:

> I believe the feeling of differences between the French and the
> Americans is stronger than ever; you hear things like, "They're not
> like us," "Our societies are not at all the same." The idea of a "Euro-
> Atlantic world," which NATO is so crazy about, has no resonance in
> France. And the aversion to—if not outright resistance to—hegemony
> is very strong; it's getting stronger with globalization.[102]

A former chief of staff of the French armed forces confided bluntly to
senior NATO military officers that many French leaders wanted NATO
only as an "ace in the hole." He added that "the ojective is to have the
Americans out of day-to-day defense matters in Europe."[103]

A PREFERENCE FOR POLITICAL OVER MILITARY SOLUTIONS

French negotiators, long accustomed to dealing from a weak hand,
especially during the Cold War when the country was squeezed
between the two superpowers, tend characteristically to favor political
solutions over military ones. This attitude has a European-wide resonance: the European Union emphasizes a panoply of actions that it
can bring to bear, including economic aid, police forces, peace moni-
tors, and so on. In this context, some Europeans see the European
Union as having a larger vocation in the security realm than NATO
itself. In an interview in *Le Monde*, General Jean-Pierre Kelche, chief
of staff of the French armed forces, stated:

> In the future, we would like it that, when a crisis develops, Europe
> would be able to analyze the elements and seek solutions in all pos-
> sible areas of action, including military, and then engage the means.

The solutions will not necessarily be only military ones. *The field of responsibility of the European Union is more vast than that of NATO* [emphasis added].[104]

The U.S. focus is largely on military options. The United States has been capable of the exercise of supreme military power since 1945. With the onset of the Cold War in 1947–48, the politics of force, or the threat of force, became the United States' prime instrument in its foreign policy arsenal. The U.S. sense was that it had the strength, which the Europeans did not have, to impose, or to threaten to impose, solutions to conflicts. While the Europeans acknowledge the power and the protection that the United States provided during the Cold War, they believe that the United States is overinclined toward the use of force. Europe, they feel, is a more peace-seeking culture, in part because of the tradition of European "humanism,"[105] and in part because the devastation wrought on their continent in the twentieth century has given them a firsthand appreciation of the evils of war.

For the French negotiator, seeking a political solution means holding out the possibility of peaceful options until the very end, and preferably in a multilateral framework such as the United Nations, in hopes that a military confrontation can be avoided. This temporizing approach leads at times to U.S. accusations that the French tend to play a double game. An example of this was the French initiative through the United Nations Security Council hours before the deadline for Iraqi compliance was to end on January 15, 1991, and six days after a meeting in Geneva between James Baker and Foreign Minister Tariq Aziz had ended in a total standoff. The French proposal was a resolution to the effect that if Iraq committed itself to a withdrawal and began initiating it immediately, hostilities could be avoided. Both the British and the Americans were hostile to such a resolution—suspecting that France was really seeking to preserve some credit with the regime of Saddam Hussein—and France withdrew it.

The foregoing does not mean that France renounces the use of military force as a policy. France and Britain remain the two powers most willing to use military force to protect the security of Europe. But in the Third World, and given its own colonial background, France has become very chary about military interventions without international, and particularly UN, sanction. This is especially true as regards the

Arab world, which has been the object of special French attention since the Six Day War of June 1967, when de Gaulle ended France's arms relationship with Israel because of the latter's preemptive military attack, which began the war.

The overall European view, as expressed by Javier Solana, secretary-general of the European Council and high representative of the European Union's Common Foreign and Security Policy (CFSP), is that "[w]e try . . . to develop a veritable culture of prevention of conflicts."[106] This has led U.S. commentators such as Robert Kagan to draw a sharp distinction between the two sides of the Atlantic:

> Europe, because of its unique historical experience of the past half-century—culminating in the past decade with the creation of the European Union—has developed a set of ideals and principles regarding the utility and morality of power different from the ideals and principles of Americans, who have not shared that experience. . . . Within the confines of Europe, the age-old laws of international relations have been repealed. Europeans have stepped out of the Hobbesian world of anarchy into the Kantian world of perpetual peace. . . . Consider again the qualities that make up the European strategic culture—the emphasis on negotiation, diplomacy and commercial ties, on international law over the use of force, on seduction over coercion, on multilateralism over unilateralism.[107]

From the French, and by extension the European, point of view (as these are increasingly converging), an excessive militarism risks creating endless provocations in the Third World, thereby preventing the extension of the zone of peace that has grown within the European Union, especially with the expansion to twenty-five members.

The French find the United States not only too ready to use military force but also too fond of seeing the world in simplistic, Manichaean terms of good versus evil. The French like to take account of multiple forces at play over long periods of time, an approach that U.S. leaders tend to find airy or fuzzy. For example, in late 1963 and early 1964 de Gaulle sought to bring an end to the Vietnam War through a "neutralization" of the conflict, which meant, without it being made explicit, the neutralization of South Vietnam only. This was to be accomplished by means of an international conference on Southeast Asia involving not only the United States but also interested powers such as France, India, and China. In part to set the stage for this, de Gaulle recognized the government of the People's Republic of China in early 1964. The Americans could not lead this initiative alone, de Gaulle told a U.S. emissary, George Ball, because if they did it would not succeed. A large conference had been attempted in 1954 in Geneva, the French president recalled, and though the talks had taken a very long time, this in itself was not a bad thing. If a world conference of this type could be put into being, it would change the state of mind of the Vietnamese people and produce a détente.[108] In the margins of Ball's telegram to Washington reporting his conversation, two remarks were scribbled: "Nonsense" and "How fuzzy can one be?"[109]

In a like manner, the Americans tended to dismiss French arguments against going to war against Saddam in early 2003. France argued in the Security Council that no casus belli existed. However, France had no alternative to war to propose except to note that the new inspectors on the scene in Iraq had in effect put Saddam in a box, from which he could not launch an attack. With 160,000 of their troops deployed in the desert, the U.S. and British governments clearly wanted a more definitive resolution of the problem posed by Saddam.

FRANCO-GERMAN RELATIONS AND THE FUTURE OF EUROPE

The French-German relationship has become deeply embedded institutionally in the forty years since de Gaulle and Adenauer signed the Élysée Treaty in 1963. Despite German reunification and the coming to power of Chancellor Gerhard Schröder, who had very little experience of working with the French, German officials still tend to accept—though with less readiness than before—France's preeminent position in continental Western Europe. There are a number of reasons for this. Germany as a state came late into being and is still today less unified politically than is France. The German colossus that loomed over Europe from the middle of the nineteenth century to the middle of the twentieth no longer exists as such. Germany is wary of military involvement and strongly tinged with pacifism. According to John Kornblum, "There will be no rebirth of the Germany that the world knew. In World

War II much of the German social fabric was destroyed, as happened once before in the Thirty Years War, which was followed by two hundred years of German passivity. The Germans still have a sense of trauma and shock. They will continue to give the impression of hitting below their weight. The Germans are out of the danger business."[110] Kornblum sees the future of French-German relations as a "complex shadow dance," with relations both friendly and unproductive, but certainly peaceful. Unlike the British, who saw their World War II experience as a reaffirmation of their culture, because they did not lose, the Germans and the French "have a bond of common mutual destruction and a determination not to let it happen again." This "unbreakable lock that binds them together" stems from their hereditary enmity that goes back to the seventeenth century and is exemplified by the "red phone" that is in constant use between the two countries.[111]

Rudolph von Thadden, Chancellor Schröder's coordinator of French-German affairs, looks to the distant past to help explain today's Franco-German relationship:

> France and Germany are like two brothers, whose father is Charlemagne. Italy is like a sister, patient, indulgent, and not intended to be a rival, as are the two brothers. France wants to be considered as the elder of the two brothers. France was the leader in fighting for human rights and in promoting universal values; and in medieval times France led in fighting for Christianity and was known as the elder daughter of the Church.
>
> But France has two disadvantages. The first is that the second brother, Germany, got the imperial crown—the Holy Roman Emperor of the Germanic Peoples. The second disadvantage is that the second brother is a little bit stronger than the first one, France. It is a drama that has been going on for twelve centuries.

In the contemporary world, von Thadden observes, things tend to go sour between the two countries when Germans forget, or ignore, the fact that the French want to be the "elder brother."[112]

The Germans, however, have been increasingly inclined to ignore this fact. Among the German political class, there is a growing sense that the glow is off the relationship with France, that, in the words of Jochen Thies, "the days of the French-German special relationship are over." Exchange assignments between the two countries' civil and diplomatic services are diminishing in number. Germany is increasingly conscious of its strength and less prepared to take a back-seat to France in European councils. As a senior German diplomat puts it, "Germany will no longer be the stirrup-holder for France."[113]

This development has not gone unrecognized among the French, who remain obsessed with Germany's latent power. As Thies remarks, "They fear us. I feel their fear. It comes from the times they were de-feated by us—they only won in coalitions—and from our size, our phys-ical strength. Germany, with eighty-one million people, is still too big for Europe."[114] In the view of *Le Monde* correspondent Daniel Vernet:

> Europe will no longer be a *"jardin à la française,"* as defined by a former adviser to Chancellor Helmut Kohl, [by way of] emphasizing that the Common Market and then the European Community had been conceived in Paris and constructed according to the principles of the French administration. . . . The intellectual hegemony that France exercised over European integration, from Jean Monnet to Jacques Delors, belongs definitely to the past.[115]

The French acknowledge that adjustments in the French-German relationship are thus in order. As Arnaud Leparmentier observes:

> A problem in the French-German relationship is that for a long time it was dominated by France. Today, a reunified Germany is asking for a re-equilibrium—reform of the Common Agricultural Policy, lowering of its contribution to the [EU] budget at Brussels, taking into account its demographic weight in qualified majority voting in the European Council, and the use of the German language [in the European Union]—[all of] which are not illegitimate, but they call into question French pre-eminence.[116]

French enthusiasm for the European Union has diminished. This is partly because France no longer has the dominant role: the European Union is no longer a *jardin à la française*. The *Anschluss* of East Germany and the jump in the population of a united Germany—together with the inclusion of other non-Latin countries (Finland, Sweden, Austria) in 1995 and the further admission of more countries from the Slavic fringes of Eastern Europe, which

increases the number of EU members from fifteen to twenty-five—
means that France's influence will inevitably be reduced.

The strains in the Franco-German relationship were evident in
the unseemly wrangle at the Nice summit of the European Union in
December 2000 over the issue of whether Germany, with twenty million more people than France, should have greater weight in the
European Council's qualified majority voting system. France, though
holding the EU presidency and therefore constrained by custom to
forgo national goals, scandalized its partners by pursuing a chauvinist
agenda, notably insisting on the same voting weight as Germany. The
other Europeans came to Chancellor Schröder during the meeting
and offered to support the position that Germany should have somewhat greater weight than France. But Schröder gave way, confiding to
an adviser that had he done otherwise, "I would have ruined my relations with France."[117]

Two years after Nice, the two countries' leaders staged a spectacu-
lar turnaround that mended relations on the political level if not on the
cultural level. In a testimony to France's ability to seize the moment
and negotiate accordingly, Jacques Chirac and Gerhard Schröder
announced in October 2002 after a secret negotiation that the Common
Agricultural Policy would be extended until 2013, a decision that was
highly favorable to the French.[118] Schröder's position on the United
States, which had been highly critical of his opposition to a war with
Iraq—a repudiation, in Washington's view, of a previous commitment[119]—was strengthened by this newfound rapprochement with the
French. It was further strengthened in early 2003 when France and
Germany acted in unison in the UN Security Council in opposing the
United States going to war with Iraq. Notwithstanding the growing cultural divide between France and Germany, their two leaders appeared
to realize that they must work more closely together for the future of
Europe, and that the French-German "locomotive," which long provided the impulsion for the construction of Europe, had to be put back
in running order.

Meanwhile, France, like other EU members, continues to wres-
tle with the question of the *finalité* of the European Union. In English,
"finality" essentially means "end"; in French, *finalité* means not only
"end" but also "purpose." The *finalité* of the European Union has

been a matter of debate for years. For the smaller countries, and for Germany, as well as Italy, some degree of national sovereignty should be sacrificed to allow the European Union to become more integrated, or "federal"—the latter being a distinctly negative buzzword for the French. To them—and even more so to the British—the idea of giving up more sovereignty is anathema, and there is little support for anything more far-reaching than what is sometimes described as a "federation of nation-states"—whatever that vague rhetorical phrase might exactly mean.

But even on this sensitive issue the renewed "marriage of reason" between Germany and France was able to find a compromise. This was contained in a joint proposal of the two governments, submitted on January 22, 2003, to the Convention on the Future of Europe, which was charged with producing a draft constitution for Europe. The compromise proposed by France and Germany, which was met with considerable opposition from the smaller EU members, provided for a dual presidency: a president of the European Commission elected by the European Parliament, and a president of the European Council, elected by council members for a term of up to five years. This dual presidency, it is argued, reflects the fact that the European Union is both a union of states (reflected in the council) and a union of peoples (reflected in the commission and the parliament).

The French-German proposals of January 2003 were largely adopted in the convention's draft constitution, approved by the European Council at Thessalonika on June 20, 2003, for submission to a subsequent Intergovernmental Conference.

The work of the convention, chaired by former French president Valéry Giscard d'Estaing, proved once again that the European "project," as it is referred to, moves ahead when the Germans and the French work together. A major concession made by the French, as reflected in the draft constitution, is a redefinition of the system of qualified majority voting, which in the future will require a majority of the member-states representing at least 60 percent of the population of the European Union as a whole. This was a concession to Germany and undoes the arrangements of the Nice summit, but it will not go into effect until 2009. Another concession made by the French, and reflected in the draft constitution, is to accept, as least in principle, that the European Parliament should have a say in determining the CAP budget. The French, however, did resist German pressure to change the voting system for decisions on the Common Foreign and Security Policy from qualified majority voting to a simple majority.

WHERE DOES FRANCE STAND TODAY?

Belgian jokes are prevalent in France, and they are of the deprecating variety. However, a French diplomat, writing in *Le Monde* on May 2, 2003, quoted another kind of Belgian "story": "France and Belgium resemble each other because they are both middle powers. The difference is that only one of them knows it."[120]

France still lives with the nostalgia of *la Grande Nation*, but the reality of its international stature is less grandiose. The twentieth-century notion of the Big Three never adequately functioned, chiefly because of the mismatch between the rising power of the United States and the declining power of Britain and, especially, France. Recognizing this, the United States never treated France on an equal plane with Britain, most notably in terms of intelligence sharing, military planning, and strategic consultation. Resentful of this unequal treatment, de Gaulle dropped out of the NATO integrated command in 1966. Nevertheless, the myth of the Big Three persisted, being reaffirmed as recently as the Gulf War of 1990–91, until finally it was shattered by the war against Iraq in March–April 2003.

Where, then, does France stand in today's world? It has had considerable success in becoming the leading influence in the European Union, though this is beginning to fade with German reunification and the expansion of the European Union from fifteen to twenty-five members. Nevertheless, despite this new trend, harmonization of relations within the European Union, and of the European Union's relationship with the United States, cannot effectively be accomplished without the French being a part of such a process.

An upbeat, though relatively balanced, position of where France stands in the world—but which in no way renounces France's ambition to make itself felt worldwide—was offered by Hubert Védrine at a meeting of French ambassadors at the Quai d'Orsay on August 28, 1997:

[France] is neither an actor among others nor a "middle" power, which is an improper term. She is not "the" hegemonic power. And she is not a superpower in the classic sense of the term. What is she? She is one of the seven or eight powers with worldwide influence. That is to say, one of the great powers of the world that have the means of a truly global policy.[121]

4

The Process

The Process and Stages of Negotiation

> Although he was flattered when John Stuart Mill hailed him as the
> creator of a new political science, [Alexis de] Tocqueville was not the
> precursor of the number-crunchers and algebraicists of today. . . .
> Tocqueville's model was Montesquieu. Like Montesquieu, Tocque-
> ville emphasized the centrality of *moeurs*, the congeries of beliefs
> and values and the "habits of the heart" that provide the cultural
> soil in which political institutions can grow.[1]

In what can be thought of as analogous to the viewpoint of Tocqueville, the French have a very different outlook on the *process* of negotiations than do, for example, the Americans. There is no French
equivalent of the word "process" in the sense of its meaning in
English of "a particular method of doing something, generally involving a number of steps or operations,"[2] which may help to explain why
French diplomats have tended to regard the notion of a negotiating
process with disdain or at least little interest. As Alain Lempereur puts
it, if "what we negotiate" refers to *content* or *substance*, if "who we
negotiate with" refers to *relationship*, and if "how we negotiate" refers

to *process*, then the French are much less process oriented than the Americans.[3]

The idea that negotiation consists of a series of elements and stages, each of which can be carefully dismantled and weighed to determine the mechanism by which a diplomatic encounter operates, is both unappealing and unpersuasive to most French negotiators and until recently has inspired very few French scholars to examine the subject. "The French," comments a German diplomat, "think that [negotiation] comes naturally; that they know by their education what French interests are. They rely on the sharpness of their minds. They don't pay attention to procedural matters."[4] Indeed, typical French *énarques* are likely to consider that, having mastered at Sciences Po and ENA the codes that have gained them entry into France's elite class, they will be able to handle any situation.

The French are less process oriented not only than the Americans, who pioneered the study of the negotiating process, but also than their fellow major powers in Europe, Germany and Britain. Christoph Bertram remarks that "French policy expresses France. It is a way of claiming one's identity. It is not to shape or change things. The Germans are interested in process. The French defend status. They are suspicious of process. The 'toolbox' approach to negotiations is foreign to them."[5] A senior British civil servant has the following view on how the French approach the negotiating process:

> The French do not focus on process or on the interests of the country with which they are negotiating. They focus on the interests of the French instead. It is not so much a scientific process as an artistic performance. The British put themselves in the position of the person they are negotiating with: what is the best tactic; how to proceed, etc. This reflects an appreciation of how the other thinks. The French are not interested in getting inside the thought of others.[6]

This indifference to the negotiation process, it should be noted, is beginning to change under the influence of globalization. For example, the subject of negotiations has been taught at ENA since the late 1990s and is now also studied at the French business school ESSEC.[7] Even so, as this chapter shows, the French tradition of conducting negotiations primarily to assert French status and only secondarily to reach agreement by working within or manipulating the negotiating process continues to this day.

Furthermore, while the French may have little interest in dissecting the negotiating process, their own negotiating style is nonetheless amenable to such dissection. As this chapter demonstrates, there are distinct traits in the French approach to negotiations, some of which are evident throughout a negotiation, others of which are more pronounced at different stages of the negotiating process.

Americans tend to conceive of a negotiation as a linear progression through a series of stages that lead from opening moves through a middle game to an endgame. In contrast, according to Lempereur, the French see a negotiation as a spiral of activity. This outlook, coupled with the fact that the French are not particularly respectful of deadlines or point-by-point agendas, can lead Americans to conclude that discussions with their French counterparts are leading nowhere; the French impression, however, may well be that the discussions are progressing, but in a circular fashion.[8]

Even so, most French diplomatic negotiations involve at least four stages. The first is the preparatory stage, during which a negotiating position is proposed by the Quai d'Orsay or arbitrated by the Secrétariat Général du Comité Interministériel (depending, respectively on whether it is a classic foreign negotiation or a matter that is treated in the EU context). The position lays out the goals that France wishes to achieve but gives the negotiator some flexibility in how to present and argue for those goals.

The second is the opening, or presentation, stage, which usually begins in the following manner, according to Jacques Andréani:

> The French classic negotiator begins with an exposé in the style of Sciences Po—intellectual and logical—and seeks to convince the interlocutor of the soundness of his reasoning. But this leaves others unimpressed. Interlocutors like, for example, the Dutch, are interested in give-and-take.[9]

The third stage, the middle phase, is by far the longest, even though it is typically marked not by a gradual convergence of the two sides through a process of give-and-take but by a persistent French refusal to compromise and an increasingly prickly atmosphere as the French exhibit a mixture of superiority and defensiveness that may mask inferiority. Having presented what he or she conceives to be a logical, correct solution at the outset of a negotiation, the French negotiator has little inclination to veer away from it. Maurice Couve de Murville, generally known to French diplomats as "the Master," who served as foreign minister, ambassador to Washington, and briefly prime minister toward the end of de Gaulle's presidency, imparted this cardinal rule to the Quai d'Orsay:

> The important thing in a negotiation is to defend one's point of view. An agreement can come as an extra. The objective is not to arrive at a negotiated solution; it is to defend one's point of view.[10]

If, however, France discovers a reason or perceives a need to reach agreement, negotiations enter a fourth stage, during which the French side, finally tempering Cartesian logic with a certain "peasant" realism, reluctantly comes to a compromise. Once the French side accepts the idea of a compromise, agreement can often be hammered out swiftly. To quote again from Couve de Murville, when he was asked about a marathon discussion on agriculture in the European Union:

> For the first quarter of an hour, I presented the position of France. From then until the twentieth hour, I presented the position of France. At the twentieth hour, I negotiated the position of France.[11]

This chapter broadly parallels these four stages in its exploration of the various facets of French negotiating behavior. The chapter begins by describing the pyramidal decision-making structures that establish the negotiating positions France will adopt in bilateral and multilateral forums. This section also indicates the level of team discipline and individual flexibility on the French side of the negotiating table. The second section focuses on the presentation stage, during which French negotiators, armed with a clear idea of their final position, lay out at length the logic of the French position. The third section of the chapter—which, like the third stage of a negotiation, is the longest—explores a variety of key characteristics of French negotiating behavior, traits that are evident throughout the negotiating process but that are very visible during what

might be called the intransigent stage. In addition to examining the
importance that French negotiators attach to relationship, their simultaneous sense of superiority and inferiority, and their resistance to compromise, this section looks at the use made of language, time, back
channels, entertainment, and the media. The fourth section examines
French tactics during the endgame and French attitudes toward implementation of agreements. A fifth and final section offers a brief sketch
of the distinguishing characteristics of French negotiators other than
diplomats and bureaucrats, notably, businesspeople and members of the
military.

STAGE 1: DETERMINING NEGOTIATING POSITIONS

The Decision-Making Apparatus

The decision-making structure that determines the stance taken by
French diplomatic negotiators reflects not the egalitarian ideals of the
country's revolutionary tradition but rather the enduring reverence for
the authority of the state and the hierarchical nature of the political
system. "There is a contrast between French ideals and French realities that in no other country is so huge," comments Rudolph von
Thadden. "The ideal is equality but in fact no other nation has as
much hierarchy as France. The French president is a republican king.
There is no equality at all. He is the queen bee."[12] A former French
academic who is now a senior government official emphasizes the
heavy administrative structure of the state:

> France is first and foremost an administration. It is a republic, not a
> democracy. The republic is a pyramidal decision structure; it is hier-
> archical. The president of the republic decides. In France, the presi-
> dent does not have to consult and deal with the legislature, as is the
> case with the president of the U.S.
>
> The U.S. can have several irons in the fire in foreign policy. It
> is a democracy, based on "multiple elements." France speaks with
> one voice. The U.S. perspective of a network *[la toile]* [of decision
> makers] is unfamiliar to the hierarchical French.
>
> In France there is the rule, and how it is applied. France is a

normative country. This stems from two main elements: the long history of the administration; and the [rationalist] method of thinking.[13]

The idea that "France speaks with one voice" is supported by a study by the Commissariat Général du Plan, the French planning commission that was created by General de Gaulle in the aftermath of World War II and initially headed by Jean Monnet. The commission is under the authority of the prime minister, who in November 2000 directed that it make a study of French policies in the European Union and international contexts. Published in December 2002, the study found that

> [t]he great advantage of the French system, notably with respect to American and German structures, lies in its ability to arbitrate issues. The entire organization of the cabinet of the prime minister is oriented in this perspective. It is therefore exceptional in France that on European and international subjects one hears French representatives presenting conflicting analyses. Only the British system seems more efficient from this point of view, due to an exceptional quality of circulation of information.[14]

Whereas in the United States a network of academics, business leaders, and officials go in and out of the government, in France little such communication and exchange occurs between different sectors. French officials are reluctant to share information with nonofficials, whom they tend to regard as unqualified to understand it.[15] The study by the Commissariat Général du Plan notes the paucity of privately sponsored think tanks in France, an under-attendance of French officials and academics at international conferences, and an overemphasis in France on diplomatic history at the expense of public policy studies.[16] The consequences are significant:

> In several areas the strategy of influence of France is seriously dysfunctional. It is as though she has not understood that her influence is not spread primarily through chanceries, and she has not organized the diffusion of her positions through nonofficial channels which are often more efficient, and also she has not understood the importance of the academic world for spreading her concepts.[17]

Foreign policy in France is the affair of the executive branch, and in particular of the president, following the evolved custom (as imposed by de Gaulle) of a "reserved domain" for the chief of state in foreign affairs and defense. To be sure, other actors are also involved in shaping policy, typically the prime minister, the foreign minister, and top-level officials from the Ministries of Foreign Affairs, Defense, and Finance, as well as from technical ministries (such as Transportation and Industry) that have an interest in a particular policy matter. The preparatory work for foreign negotiations begins at the Quai d'Orsay and moves to the Hôtel Matignon (the prime minister's office), where efforts are made to reconcile the positions of the various players. If this cannot be done—and during periods of cohabitation, when the president and prime minister are from competing parties, differences of opinion are common—the matter is passed to a higher level. The role of Matignon vis-à-vis the Élysée (the presidency) and the Quai d'Orsay varies, of course, depending on the personalities involved. In the case of the failed return to NATO (see chapter 5), Prime Minister Alain Juppé, who had previously been the foreign minister, played a key role in pushing the rapprochement with NATO. In the Iraq crisis of early 2003 (see chapter 5), Prime Minister Jean-Pierre Raffarin played a minimal role in a negotiation that was run tightly by President Jacques Chirac and Foreign Minister Dominique de Villepin.[18]

Interagency coordination in France, in preparation for a negotiation, has points in common with the same process in other countries. But there are also some particularities. There is the fear in France that conflicts will see the light of day, and this fear becomes intensified with the phenomenon of cohabitation or split government. There is a hesitancy about setting out these conflicts on the table, and there is an awareness that there comes a moment when one must stop. This is in part due to French history and the very strong sense of identity that the French have about their history; that is to say, the French are in a permanent state of being afraid of themselves and of their unpredictability.[19] As Jean-Marie Guéhenno puts it, there is always the question of whether the French, in arguing among themselves, are just going through a "psychodrama," or whether it is something more serious. The French concern about not breaking too much crockery has the effect of increasing the difficulty of coming to an agreed position, and at the same time, when a position is arrived at, it is at a certain level of generality.[20]

It follows, then, that great efforts are made to ensure that con-
flicting opinions within the ranks of the government do not come to
public attention. When consensus is achieved, it is put in writing in a
memorandum known as *un bleu* (a blue).[21] An agreed-on position is
often pitched at a level of generality that facilitates reaching interagency consensus but at the same time leaves some flexibility for the
official doing the negotiation. And yet French officials are constrained
not to fail, although their brief is not as detailed as, for example, that
of their British counterparts, and although they have a certain leeway
as individual performers in negotiations. They feel the weight, and the
power, of the state structure behind them. The solidity and the collective discipline of the state apparatus is an advantage, contends
Jean-David Levitte:

> I read with great interest the books of Henry Kissinger. His mem-
> oirs are a description of the functioning of the American power
> structure. What he describes is what only the leading country in the
> world can allow itself; that is to say, when the president arbitrates a
> decision, those who were defeated in the arbitration immediately
> begin the next stage, which is to arrange leaks to the press and to
> lobby the Congress, in order to demolish the arguments of those
> who won. The combat never stops. Thus you have the president,
> around whom there are different circles of power who fight among
> one another, in order to be triumphant in their ideas, in their per-
> sonal interests, or in their weight as personalities. In our system,
> when, for example, there is a restricted meeting following the
> Council of Ministers, where you have the president, the prime min-
> ister, the minister of foreign affairs, the minister of defense, and the
> chief of staff of the armed forces, a decision is taken, and the state
> acts as one man. And you don't have this combat [which is] typically
> American.[22]

According to Levitte, even during the most recent period of
cohabitation (which ended in June 2002), the collective discipline of
the French state apparatus was more apparent than in the case of
France's major European allies, Germany and, to a lesser extent,
Britain. The contrast was all the more striking because the French
government was made up of opposed parties, whereas the British government was in the sole hands of Tony Blair's Labour Party and the

German government in the control of more or less like-minded coalition partners under the chancellorship of Gerhard Schröder.

Another advantage enjoyed by French negotiators over many of their counterparts is the limited role that the national legislature plays in foreign policy. Although there are new challenges to executive authority in France, in that parliamentarians and others have sought to point the finger at corrupt practices of high officials, France's overpowering and hierarchical state structure leaves little room for real accountability. Public officials are not brought to account in the same way that the more independent U.S. judicial system does its work. Similarly, there is not enough power in the National Assembly to challenge effectively the state apparatus. Finally, as Stanley Hoffmann observes, the French press has less influence on foreign policy than is usually the case in other countries.[23] All these factors have a bearing, not surprisingly, on the behavior of the French at the negotiating table, as a senior British diplomatic official describes:

> The French do not have a parliament or public that would question what they do. They do not have a brake on their theatricals. Hence they can walk out of meetings. Hence the French individualistic and prima donna approach. They have a large degree of discretion. They can pull tantrums. A British minister would be called down to Parliament for such behavior. The French can put all their stakes behind an issue as they did in the Uruguay Round.[24]

Negotiations within the European Union

Much of France's negotiation takes place not in a strictly bilateral, nation-to-nation framework but increasingly within the European Union. The trend has been not only welcomed but also engineered by France, which values the European Union as a means both of sustaining its status and strength within Europe and of leveraging its power against the United States. (The same is true with regard to the United Nations and other multilateral organizations in which France is able to enhance its influence, especially with regard to the United States.) The importance France attaches to the European Union is reflected in the quality of the diplomats it sends to EU forums and the efforts it makes to ensure that it marshals its forces effectively.

A senior U.S. State Department official provides an outspoken view from the outside as to how the French operate within the European Union:

> European solidarity means agreeing with the French position. If France is isolated, then the others should agree with it. If France is in the majority, then the others should toe the line.
>
> France makes use of its compatriots in the European Commission. France sends its finest *énarques* to Brussels, and Paris keeps in close touch with them. The ambassadors France sends to the EU are well prepared, subtle, and effective.
>
> The French assemble coalitions, such as the "Club Med" [Mediterranean] countries. They see themselves as the intellectual leaders in such coalitions. They are brutal in enforcing discipline. The others in the coalitions say, "If we break with them, they'll take it out on us."
>
> The Germans are hopelessly disorganized, with a chaotic interministerial process in preparing for negotiations. They only put their foot down when they have to pay. . . . The British . . . operate in a similar way [to the French], but less brutally. . . . The French have the most cohesive and homogeneous foreign policy elite in the business.[25]

The latter assertion is not gainsaid by the Commissariat Général du Plan: "If we put ourselves in a comparative perspective, we cannot but recognize the overall quality of the French diplomatic apparatus."[26]

France practices what one German diplomat describes as "personnel diplomacy": it sends its best people to the European Union and to other international institutions. It does not, as Germany does, use the European Union as a dumping ground for individuals burned out in domestic politics. The French officials sent to the European Union are younger, perhaps by as much as eight years, than their German counterparts. They are trained earlier and they arrive in very important posts at a relatively young age. The sense of their being members of an elite brings a self-assuredness that belies their age.[27]

These officials operate within a complex system. If the matter at hand is a "Pillar One" subject (and as far as negotiations are concerned, this means trade in goods and services, including agriculture), then France must deal with the supranational or communitarian

European Commission, which is authorized to conduct external trade relations on behalf of all EU member countries. However, the commission is subject to some oversight by the intergovernmental European Council,[28] the supreme organ of the European Union and its prime legislative entity.[29]

The European Council is the designation for regular meetings of heads of state or government for strategic overview of policy and for launching new initiatives.[30] Foreign policy and defense fall into the purview of the European Council. Legally, there is only one council, but it operates in no fewer than seventeen different modes or formations. If the meeting is of other than heads of state or government, the council is known not as the European Council but as the Council of Ministers. Furthermore, a particular Council of Ministers meeting may have a specific designation. For example, the General Affairs Council is composed of the foreign ministers of the member countries.[31] The Council of Ministers may also take the form of a meeting among ministers with other specialties (e.g., finance) or a meeting among the ambassadors from the member countries assigned to Brussels as the permanent representatives to the council. These ambassadors form themselves into a Committee of Permanent Representatives, which goes under the acronym COREPER, in the French version.

The COREPER is the engine of the council, taking preparatory material from the various working or expert groups that form part of the General Secretariat, which supports the council, and transforming it into material for submission to the council. The COREPER is split into two groups: COREPER #2, on which the ambassadors are represented, deals with subjects that are more vital to the national interest, such as foreign affairs, defense, justice, and finance. COREPER #1, on which the deputies to the ambassadors are represented, deals with agriculture, industry, and the European Union's internal market.

The French ambassador to the European Union serves both as France's permanent representative in Brussels, in which position he must promote French interests, and as a member of the Council of Ministers, a task that involves working with his fellow permanent representatives in trying to find a compromise acceptable to all.[32] Historically, the French approach has been intransigent and confrontational, as in the "empty chair" crisis (see chapter 3) that led to the Luxembourg

Compromise in 1966. Gradually, however, French diplomats have accustomed themselves to EU negotiating ways and have developed a degree of flexibility.[33]

While the Quai d'Orsay determines the French position for EU negotiations on foreign policy, other ministries also play a role in shaping the negotiating stance on other topics.[34] The different policies promoted by the various ministries are arbitrated by the Secrétariat Général du Comité Interministériel pour les Questions Européennes (SGCI, General Secretariat of the Interministerial Committee for European Questions), which fashions a coordinated position. The SGCI was first created to handle the French approach toward Marshall Plan aid. It was subsequently brought into play in connection with the creation of the European Coal and Steel Community and the abortive European Defense Community. Since the creation of the Common Market in 1957, the SGCI has coordinated negotiations conducted in the EU framework.

Representatives of multiple government entities are present in the SGCI, making it difficult to reach an arbitrated position. The SGCI includes not only officials from the main substantive ministries—the Ministry of Finance, the Ministry of Foreign Trade, and the Ministry of Agriculture—whose interests are almost invariably at stake in EU decisions, but also representatives from technical ministries such as Telecommunications and from the Quai d'Orsay, the Élysée, and Matignon. Matignon has overall responsibility for the work of the SGCI.

The French mission in Brussels, which has a staff of 150 and which is in constant contact with the SGCI, usually divides dossiers into "low-option" and "high-option" ones, the latter being those in which it is necessary to defend the French position to the hilt. If negotiations with the other members of the Council of Ministers reach an impasse, the mission will contact Paris to see whether the government will lower its demands. If the case is extremely important to the government, the president and his staff will take the matter up at the next meeting of the European Council.

According to Gérard Araud:

> The system functions rather well in Paris for the elaboration of positions [in the EU], and it is rare to perceive divergences or national contradictions such as one sees with the Germans or the Italians.

This is evident in the existence of the SGCI, which centralizes the preparation of instructions for negotiations in the European Union, among all the technical ministries concerned.[35]

Still, preparations in the SGCI venue are not as elaborate as in the British Cabinet Office, according to a senior British diplomatic official:

> In Britain there is an inter-Whitehall consensus leading to a single position. There is small room for maneuver. There is no position set until the secondary points are worked out.
>
> The French system is more individualistic. There is a broad set of instructions coming out of the SGCI for the beginning of negotiations—a set of points they want to achieve. After these guidelines are set down by the ministers, a small group of French officials come together on an issue. Generally, there is less structure, less collective activity.
>
> A French negotiator is a solo performer who sets off to negotiate an issue. The French representatives report back less.[36]

This view is echoed by Sir Michael Jay, permanent undersecretary of the Foreign Office:

> In EU matters the British coordinate carefully in advance, with a clear brief that cannot be exceeded without referring to London. You know that you are not going to get much further with the British for this reason. The French do have a sort of process, a coordinating mechanism in Paris beforehand, to work out an approach and the objectives. But French preparations are not to the same level of thoroughness. The French negotiator will have more authority and will feel more confident in the position he takes without referral. At times he will act without being covered back home; hence he may not be able to deliver. French individualism can lead to greater flexibility during negotiations but can be disruptive if it winds up in a disavowal.[37]

Thus, although the French do stake out a prepared position beforehand, it is likely to be less staffed out and developed in detail than that of their British counterparts. According to Nicolas Tenzer, the French do not spend a great deal of time in the specifics of preparation for a negotiation, although they do set down the general guidelines. Nor do they do much interpersonal work in advance, in terms of establishing contacts with their foreign interlocutors.[38]

Although the British seem to be the leaders in terms of advance preparations and thoroughness, a senior German Foreign Office official in turn concedes the superiority of the French over his own compatriots in preparations: "The French are well prepared, better than the Germans on the average. They are well up on facts and figures, due to their education in the *grandes écoles*."[39]

The U.S. tendency to pose options in preparatory papers is not in the French mind-set. According to a French diplomat:

> Americans examine all the possible options, even the remote ones, in an exhaustive analysis, then they eliminate them, one by one. [When they get into substance] the French go right to the heart of the subject. They never pose options. They are synthetic and less detailed. The Americans are analytic and detailed. The French have fewer people involved in a negotiation than the Americans and therefore are less bureaucratic.[40]

STAGE 2: OPENING MOVES

A Positional Mind-Set

The French mind-set is "positional"; that is, French negotiators come to the table with a clear idea of what is to be their final position. By the time negotiations begin, French officials have adopted a unified view of French goals and they abide by it throughout the following discussions. (Such unity is less marked among the members of U.S. negotiating teams, who, though having spent much time and effort settling interagency differences beforehand, still come to the table each representing different constituencies or points of view—political, military, economic, and so forth.)[41] Moreover, the position adopted is typically calculated to serve long-range objectives rather than to secure short-term advantages. Many observers have remarked on the French ability to set long-term objectives and to hold to them. For instance, Col. (ret.) Bruce Bach, a U.S. NATO official and a veteran of discussions with the French, contends that "the French are like the Asians. They focus on the long-term objective and are very patient. They are willing to give up tactical advantage here and there. Strategically they never lose sight of the goal."[42]

The positional approach may be gradually shifting toward a more flexible outlook, a consequence, argues Lempereur, of "more and more young administrators and diplomats [being] educated beyond the doors of French *grandes écoles* and receiv[ing] some international exposure that is not purely that of the French embassies abroad."[43] For the present, however, the positional mind-set remains dominant.

The degree of clarity and consistency about French diplomats' final position is attributable in no small part to their faith in the Cartesian method. According to Gilles Andréani, head of the Analysis and Forecasting Center at the Quai d'Orsay, when it comes to negotiating, the French emphasis is on determining at the outset what is the best solution. The important thing is to be right, and to achieve this one employs deductive reasoning. Bargaining and compromise are secondary; after all, why change what has been worked out by an exercise of reason? This characteristic is one of the chief features that distinguish French diplomats from negotiators from other countries.[44]

Dissertation *and* Effet d'annonce

Well educated in the art of disquisition, a French negotiator characteristically starts out seeking to seize the initiative with a long peroration. As a French diplomat asserts, "The one who wins is he who speaks first."[45] It is important for the French to seize the floor *(occuper le terrain)*.[46] Indeed, even in a one-on-one meeting or in a small group, a French interlocutor will often begin by making a speech.

There is an overall term for the French style of presentation: *dissertation*, the dictionary definition of which is "a written exercise that pupils in the upper classes of the *lycées* and those in the faculties of letters have to write on literary, philosophical, and historical subjects."[47] In the last year of the *lycée*, students have to take between seven and eight hours of philosophy each week, giving them ample opportunity to polish their craft of dissertation and ensuring that it becomes a prominent part of the intellectual baggage they will take with them should they enter the ranks of the French diplomatic elite.[48]

Some, like Levitte, regard *dissertation* as a dubious blessing:

> I call it cursed dissertation *[maudite dissertation]*, because we have learned in primary school, then in secondary school, then at Sciences Po, to make brilliant presentations; but with the same brio we can demonstrate the contrary of the previous demonstration, and

with the same implacable reasoning. It is a method of thinking which is good for being brilliant in the salons but which is not efficacious in bilateral or, especially, multilateral negotiations. There, listening to the other, and getting an understanding of the interests and the objectives of the other, is the point of departure—after which one can make brilliant demonstrations. And especially, one must not be too artificial in speeches related to national objectives, as everyone else present knows that these are at the core of the matter.[49]

When French officials are in this mode of *dissertation*, they are generally less inclined to listen to what others have to say and more inclined to display panache and create an impact—what the French call an *effet d'annonce*. This can be counterproductive, as many French themselves readily concede. In the words of Araud, "The French are victims of their combined love of concept and brio, which, in a negotiation, leads them into long and brilliant digressions to explain the luminous logic of their position rather than to concrete propositions of amendments or of texts which are without glory but much more effective."[50] The shortcomings of the French penchant for *effet d'annonce* are also evident to France's negotiating partners. "The French are very good at setting out bold, eye-catching ideas," notes one senior British diplomatic official,

> not in transforming them into detail. They benefit from having a French flag on an idea. They like forcing the agenda and being bold. They are less good at the staff work to flesh out a position, the underpinning, the depth of analysis. The important thing is the initial idea and to make sure they are driving the agenda. They get impatient over how to put it into practice. They leave it to others . . . to fill in the details. They lose points that way.[51]

Furthermore, and again according to Araud, the Cartesianism of the French is such that they

> see in each position an ensemble of possible consequences in their obsession with [plotting a chain of causality] . . . : A implies B which implies C and on to Z and sometimes beyond. Not for an instant do they imagine—contrary to the British—treating each problem in isolation or even contradicting themselves, if necessary. Logical they are and logical they must remain, because "coherence" is a sacred imperative. Therefore, every decision becomes dangerous.[52]

The dangers of too strict an adherence to Cartesianism are also noted by former White House official Anthony Blinken: "If something doesn't fit into a logical scheme intellectually, the French have difficulty with it. The French are strong, but not in a creative process. They can be thrown off."[53]

French theoretical rigidity and British pragmatism stand out in bold relief, notes a senior British diplomat:

> The French are most comfortable when they can define a set of principles. When the French start talking about pragmatism, we start worrying. When we start talking about principles, they start to worry. The British shy away from principles. The French like structure, a set of principles, a framework, and they are rigid in sticking to it. Issues of face, prestige, and pride figure in. The idea is to go back to Paris having delivered an outcome in conformity with French principles. Personal standing gets mixed up in the success of a negotiating enterprise.[54]

The French often save what is most important in a presentation until last. This is in line with the French adherence to deductive reasoning. One starts with the principles, and then one gets to the facts. An exposition must have a beginning, the development of the argument, and an end, or "summing up." The U.S. style is quite different. The facts are stated up front and, often to the French observer, in a very direct and blunt fashion. This is not unrelated to the celebrated legal formula of Oliver Wendell Holmes, Jr.: "It is the merit of the [Anglo-Saxon] common law that it decides the case first and determines the principles afterwards."[55]

Americans often have had the experience of listening to a French interlocutor drone on, leaving those on the other side of the table wondering what is the point. Suddenly, at the end of an extended presentation, the French negotiator presents his conclusions. "You have to pay the closest attention to what the French negotiator says at the end," remarks Ambassador George Ward Jr., a U.S. diplomat who has worked extensively on European security questions.[56]

L'Honnête homme

The *énarque* is aware of the French tradition of *l'honnête homme* (the honest man), which dates from the seventeenth century and which holds that one is expected to express oneself on any subject with clarity.[57] (The qualifier "honest" refers not to honesty in the modern sense of the word but to honor and connotes the idea that a man is respectable and courteous, in addition to being cultivated.)[58] As Gilles Andréani observes, "The French are brought up to have an idea on everything, even when they do not have a direct influence on the matter at hand. This is evident in ministerial meetings in France. The object is to demonstrate that one's thinking is well founded, and not necessarily to arrive at a solution."[59]

This custom has disadvantages as well as advantages, as evidenced in the report of the Commissariat Général du Plan:

> By tradition, France, in contrast to a number of its partners, including certain great powers, believes that it is necessary to have a position on each subject that comes up in different councils and committees. She defends it with seriousness and rigor, and with a single voice, and after internal arbitrations conducted with efficiency. However, this tendency can cause perverse effects in terms of the "visibility" of French priorities, of the capability to conclude a compromise on what is essential, and of the ability to make a greater investment on subjects that are for France the most important for the national interest.[60]

STAGE 3: THE MIDDLE GAME

The Importance of Relationship

Lempereur posits a sliding scale between "relationship" at one end and "content" at the other, the issue being how much "relationship" there must be before getting into "content." At one extreme are the Chinese, for whom there should be no "content"[61] until a "relationship" is established. At the other extreme are the Americans, who go quickly into "content." The French are somewhere in between, and Lempereur refers back to Cardinal Richelieu to prove his point—in particular, Richelieu's dictum that "negotiations" should continue regardless of whether there are issues to be discussed. Wrote Richelieu in his *Political Testament:*

> States receive so much benefit from uninterrupted foreign negotiations, if they are conducted with prudence . . . it is absolutely nec-

essary to the well-being of the state to negotiate ceaselessly, either openly or secretly, and in all places, even in those from which no present fruits are reaped, and still more in those for which no future prospects seem likely.[62]

The French view, according to Lempereur, is that one will not get anything done, even if one is the boss, unless a relationship is established. The U.S. attitude is indifferent to such a consideration; it can be characterized as "first come, first served" and is reflected in an urge to get right down to the business at hand.[63] A German observer reflects this distinction, as related to his own countrymen: "[T]he French need a comfortable atmosphere for negotiations. The Germans can start quickly."[64]

In the view of Gérard Errera, former number-three official in the Quai d'Orsay and subsequently French ambassador to London, negotiation is not possible when there is not a minimum of confidence among the negotiators. Errera draws an example from his own experience: the negotiations on nuclear waste at the International Agency for Atomic Energy in Vienna in 1986–87. Errera was told by his French colleagues that he was "crazy" if he thought he could achieve an agreement. The spokesperson for the nonaligned countries was the Nigerian delegate, who began by haranguing Errera. Errera asked him if he was out to make propaganda on an issue that was of interest to all of them. Before long, a minimum of confidence was created, and an agreement was achieved. The lesson here, according to Errera, is:

> Establish a minimum of confidence and frankness. Respect the person opposite you; make yourself respected by the person opposite you. The goal of a negotiation is not to arrive at a solution but to defend a position, recognizing that the position of the other is as respectable as yours. The result depends on the importance of the stakes.[65]

France as a High-Context Culture

Another way of looking at the question of "relationship" versus "content" is the distinction between *high-context* and *low-context* cultures, as developed by Edward T. Hall[66] and others. This distinction, as Kevin Avruch points out, relates most centrally to language:

> The core of this distinction is a linguistic or paralinguistic one. A high-context communicational style . . . is one in which most of

the information is "in the person" or the physical context in which the communication takes place; relatively little; in the explicit . . . message itself. By contrast, a low-context style or message is one wherein most of the information or meaning is to be found explicitly in the . . . message. In high-context communication, language use is expressive; in low-context communication it is instrumental.[67]

Raymond Cohen also emphasizes the central factor of language as it is manifested in high-context and low-context cultures:

> A high-context culture communicates allusively rather than directly. As important as the explicit content of the message are the context in which it occurs, surrounding nonverbal cues, and hinted-at nuances of meaning. . . . The low-context culture, exemplified by the United States, reserves a quite different role for language. Very little meaning is implicit in the context of articulation. On the contrary, what has to be said is stated explicitly. Indirection is much disliked. "Straight-from-the-shoulder" talk is admired.[68]

A "straight-from-the-shoulder" bluntness is not in keeping with the French style; hence, when Gerhard Schröder, in one of his first meetings with Jacques Chirac, plunged right in at the beginning of lunch and asked Chirac what he thought about the situation in Afghanistan, the French leader was startled.[69] The French prefer to wait for the appropriate moment, after a certain amount of scene setting. The French expression *entre la poire et le fromage* (between the pear and the cheese) is an allusion to the habit of discussing important business at the *end* of a meal.[70] The French philosopher Michel de Montaigne used the expression that one needs to speak *à l'heure* (at the right moment).[71]

Another example of low-context or instrumental communication is reflected in a French-U.S. meeting of May 11, 1992, in the aftermath of the Persian Gulf War, during which Secretary of State James A. Baker demanded of French foreign minister Roland Dumas, "Are you for us or against us?"[72] The French typically would call such an approach naive or Manichaean. But the Americans, on the other hand, would call it blunt.

As U.S. secretary of state, James Baker was generally considered a tough and effective negotiator, as when, in the aftermath of the Gulf

War, he helped relaunch the Arab-Israeli peace process at the Madrid summit in October 1991. Negotiations experts Michael Watkins and Susan Rosegrant describe Baker's work at Madrid as that of "judicious diplomacy."[73] The view in Paris was somewhat different. During a visit to Paris in November 1990 in the midst of the looming crisis with Iraq, Baker drew this observation by Admiral Jacques Lanxade head of President Mitterrand's military cabinet at the time:

> Jim Baker, although a lawyer by profession, seemed to me in the course of an interview . . . a rather rigid individual, not very gifted for mediation, and with little regard for the French. This profile would not be the most apt for the final diplomatic attempt at a conciliation with Iraq shortly thereafter.[74]

Fons Trompenaars draws the distinction between high-context and low-context cultures in terms of its operational implications for negotiations:

> Context has to do with how much you have to know before effective communication can occur; how much shared knowledge is taken for granted by those in conversation with each other; how much reference is there to tacit common ground. Cultures with high context like Japan and France believe that strangers must be "filled in" before business can be properly discussed. Cultures with low context like America and the Netherlands believe that each stranger should share in rule-making, and the fewer initial structures there are the better. Low-context cultures tend to be adaptable and flexible. High-context cultures are rich and subtle . . . and may never really be comfortable for foreigners who are not fully assimilated. . . . Westerners working for Japanese companies are never wholly "inside." It is similarly hard to feel fully accepted within the richness of French culture with its thousands of diffuse connections.[75]

Form and Content

Related to the distinction between high-context and low-context cultures is that between *form* and *content*, which follows the divide between Latin and Catholic, on the one hand, and and Protestant Germanic/Anglo-Saxon, on the other. The perception that the French emphasize form at the expense of content is so undisputed that it has become almost a cliché. For von Thadden, it is basically a question of a Latin way of looking at things.[76] For example, a German invited to dinner will bring flowers for the hostess but will take the flowers out of the wrapping and present them straightaway to her. The Frenchman, on the other hand, will also bring flowers but will take care over the presentation of the flowers, what surrounds them, that is, the *emballage*. This will leave the hostess to exclaim first and foremost on the beauty of the *emballage* and only later on the flowers themselves.

This contrast between Latin and Germanic outlooks extends to many domains, according to von Thadden. For the former, the *appearance* is important, as in women's clothing, perfumes, and so on. The German wants to know the content. The same idea is found in the writings of Tacitus, who stated, "The Germans never see the outside." Adds von Thadden, "Nothing has changed since the Romans." In the domain of nature, the Germans prefer to see things in their original state. The French style is typified by the trimmed gardens and trees of Versailles. "Nature has to be cultivated," Brigitte Sauzay, Chancellor Schröder's adviser on France, remarked to von Thadden.[77]

The question of form over content has a direct bearing on the conduct of negotiations. It is the view of Robert Hunter, former U.S. ambassador to NATO, that since the French place a higher value on form in relation to substance, if they get satisfaction on form they may yield somewhat on substance. It is Hunter's opinion that this emphasis on form in part has to do with the perceived overall standing of the country: "what de Gaulle called *la gloire*"[78]—meaning, essentially, the image of France.

What is more, as noted earlier, the French are in the habit of presenting an argument in an elegant fashion. The result is that a well-presented argument tends to be accepted by them even though it may not be the best course of action. This habit of presenting an argument in marshaled and orderly fashion to justify a position has a double effect: first, it leads to a certain rigidity, but second, it can result in an acceptance of the other's position provided the latter is well (and elegantly) argued.

A Simultaneous Sense of Superiority and Inferiority

French statements about the importance of establishing a relationship and winning respect may sound unconvincing to many foreign diplomats who have sat through the lengthy middle phase of negotiations while French negotiators have switched back and forth between assertions of the rightness of French positions and accusations of the hegemonic designs of other nations. This simultaneous projection of a sense of superiority and inferiority stems, as noted in previous chapters, from a dialectic between the tradition of *la Grande Nation* and the culture of the underdog, and from the mismatch between French ambitions and French power.

This ambivalence of attitude, stated a French ambassador posted to Brussels, "can lead to two problems":

> a weakness in diplomatic technique which consists in fighting over issues of formulations or symbols while others bother only with those things that directly affect their concrete interests; and a defect in terms of a general attitude that people often characterize as "arrogant" or "aggressive." It seems to me that this is the reverse side of an inferiority complex, of a lack of confidence in oneself, [and] of a sense of discomfort in an international environment. It is said that there is a French pretension in favor of the defense of universal values which results from a false notion of the importance of ideas in the world and a true perception of the relative weakness of France in seeking to defend them.[79]

Not surprisingly, foreign interlocutors often find it difficult to deal with the French, whose attitude can change so dramatically both within and between negotiations. For instance, the cordial and cooperative relations between the British and French following the St. Malo agreement on European defense in December 1998 stand in contrast to the harsh exchange of words between Tony Blair and Jacques Chirac in October 2002, when Blair was stunned to learn of the secret French-German agreement on agriculture, from which the British had been excluded. In their meeting, the sharpness of Blair's reproach led Chirac to exclaim, "I've never been talked to like that before." Although Blair later made up with Chirac through an overly flattering message to the French president on his birthday, the two governments in 2003 again disagreed sharply over the issue of war with Iraq, with Foreign Minister Jack Straw criticizing Chirac for having said he would veto a second Security Council resolution "whatever the circumstances." Chirac made this statement in a television interview on March 10, before the resolution was due to come up for a vote. Nevertheless, British and French contacts continued, in contrast to French-U.S. relations, which entered a deep-freeze starting in early February 2003, albeit with some ongoing diplomatic exchanges.

Similarly, the Franco-German wrangling over voting weights at the Nice EU summit in December 2000, like Chirac's blunt rejection of Schröder's proposal in March 1999 to modify the Common Agricultural Policy,[80] stands in stark contrast to the mutual self-esteem displayed during the elaborate celebrations of the fortieth anniversary of the Élysée Treaty in January 2003, when the parliaments of the two nations gathered together at Versailles.

As for French-U.S. encounters, these are more often than not a wary experience for both sides—except for military-to-military relations, which are typically good. A senior British Foreign Office official, speaking in 2002, observed:

> The French and the Americans are very opposite. On the French side, there is defensiveness, anxiety, and jealousy about American power. There were bad vibes over Kosovo. The French have a chip on their shoulder *plus* a fascination with American power. The French shoot from the hip in public, and this grandstanding grates in Washington.
>
> The French have a constant misunderstanding with the Americans; they clash all the time. The British have a ringside seat in all this. The French view of the Americans is that they never listen, they're unilateral, and they couldn't care less about Europe.
>
> However, with a real threat, all three will usually be there—Americans, British, and French. The British make their influence felt through the inside. The French have at the Americans in public but sort things out in private.[81]

In this regard, Americans show little appreciation for the fact that the outwardly aggressive style of French public communications belies a perception in Paris that most of the time things are going to be worked out in private.

Speaking in May 2002, a senior French diplomatic official referred to "the neurotic nature of French-American relations: never better than in a crisis, never quiet in peacetime."[82] May 2002, of course, preceded the Iraq war crisis of early 2003, when the British, the French, and the Americans did not remain together. Jacques Chirac and Dominique de Villepin made the portentous decision, sometime around mid-January 2003, to break the Big Three alliance of the twentieth century and oppose the Anglo-American war in Iraq.[83] The reaction of the Bush administration was more severe than anticipated, prompting this comment by Philippe Roger, author of *L'Ennemi américain*, in the aftermath:

> The word "consequences," used by Colin Powell to indicate there would be actions taken against them, struck the French particularly, because prior to that time the French had practiced anti-Americanism with the thought that there would be no consequences.[84]

A senior State Department official with long experience in France also characterizes the relationship between the two countries as "neurotic":

> We find the French hard to deal with. There is no convergence on what is acceptable behavior. The French think it is acceptable to out-maneuver us. They can support us strongly on one issue and isolate us on the next. Between the British and us, there is as little daylight as possible on issues. The French look at things differently. That's why we get mad at them. It is hard to deal with this change of temperature.
>
> All EU countries find the French exasperating. They can be arrogant, haggling over little points. They can be egotistical. They will not be budged. They have the self-confidence of a large European power, as do the British. The Germans get nervous if they're isolated. The French attitude is, "I feel confident when I'm isolated because I am assured that this is the correct position." They are not interested in building a consensus but on imposing their position. There are irremediable differences between the French and the American viewpoints.
>
> Relations with the French military are excellent. The "headquarters" of the antifeeling is in the Quai d'Orsay and the European Bureau of the State Department, where there is gratuitous mutual bashing.[85]

Ambassador George Ward also points to the singularity of the Quai: "The quality of the air in the Quai is different: it is ideology, self-love, grandeur."[86]

Although there is a widespread cultural and intellectual arrogance toward the United States within France as a whole as well as among French diplomats, French actions toward the United States generally have a defensiveness about them, reflecting the marked imbalance in the respective power positions. In this regard, it is striking to recall the many instances in which the French have displayed an exaggerated, even misplaced, sensitivity—as when a French official expressed dismay that, after simultaneous terrorist attacks in May 2002 in Chechnya and Pakistan, the latter against French technicians, the U.S. press emphasized the Chechnya event at the expense of the one in Pakistan, despite the fact, the official noted, that France is an ally of the United States.

Over the course of the 1990s, as Anthony Blinken comments, France developed a broad strategy aimed at moving diplomatic action to international forums, especially the United Nations but also the Organization for Security and Cooperation in Europe (OSCE), the Organization for Economic Cooperation and Development (OECD), and NATO. By tying the United States to these institutions and forming alliances with other member-states, France has sought to leverage its power vis-à-vis the United States. France can also use the rules of these organizations—for example, the NATO requirement that decisions be made unanimously—to place itself in the role of a holdout.[87] Similarly, on issues—especially trade issues—involving Europe and the United States, France has found that it can work effectively through the European Union, lining up allies with whom better to confront the more powerful U.S. partner. As a French diplomat puts it, "We like the multilateral."[88]

French officials are acutely conscious of the fact that they are not treated as equals by the Americans; they are particularly resentful that they are not accorded the same respect shown to the British. They are hypersensitive to any sign of condescension on the part of their U.S. interlocutors, and they tend to exaggerate the import of remarks that the latter may consider to be no more than routine statements of fact. The French see expressions of U.S. bumptiousness about its role in the world—for example, former secretary of state Madeleine Albright's infelicitous phrase, "We are Americans, we stand tall, and therefore we see farther"—as intolerable arrogance.

A highly developed sense of national pride produces a distinct French aversion to losing. Of the three French "fears" that von Thadden enumerates, one is the fear of losing. The other two are the fear of being bored *(ennui)* and the fear of appearing ridiculous. This starts in the school system and its fierce competitiveness, leading to the notion that "a Frenchman can't lose." In an Olympic competition, if a French contestant wins a silver medal, he or she will point not to that but rather to the fact that the gold medal was lost.[89] If a French team loses in an important contest, such as the 1-0 defeat at the hands of Senegal in France's opening match in the 2002 World Cup, a relative blackout descends on the event, as if it is just too painful to contemplate. Winning, however, brings out the triumphalist rooster cry *(cocorico!)* of *le coq gaulois.*[90]

This French aversion to losing is pronounced in diplomatic negotiations, in part because of the memory of having had to play so often with a losing hand, especially from the 1920s to the 1960s. "In entering negotiations," observes Ulrike Guérot of the German Council on Foreign Relations, "the French always have to win; if they can't, they need to have an 'exception,' as in the 'cultural exception' [in the audiovisual negotiations during the Uruguay Round of the GATT in the 1990s]. The French approach is rather rough, and there is no culture of compromise."[91]

The French, more often than not, find themselves outnumbered, including and particularly linguistically. In the 1980s they fought a rearguard action against the introduction of other than economic subjects in the G-7 meetings because they were outnumbered by "Anglo-Saxons"—even the Japanese being considered, in this forum, as "Anglo-Saxons." The French, it should be noted, are not only accustomed to being alone but also reconciled to it, for it allows them to practice the "burden of being right,"[92] that is, finding the right solution and sticking to it, even if one is without means or even allies to back it up. Napoleon, who virtually always carried on his campaigns without allies and against alliances, once famously remarked to an Austrian diplomat: "How many allies do you have?

Five? Ten? Twenty? The more you have, the better it is for me."[93] The sentiment endures. For instance, during a meeting in the 1980s of the High-Level Task Force on Conventional Arms Control, U.S. delegate Stephen Ledogar observed to his French counterpart, Benoit Daboville, "You're isolated." Daboville replied, "Wonderful! That's just the way we like it."[94]

There is one exception, however, to the French serenity in being isolated, and this concerns the Germans. Sir Michael Jay puts it this way: "In NATO the French interest seems to be in being apart. In the EU, however, they do not want to be isolated. They are not happy when they are apart from the Germans."[95] This tendency was very evident when Gerhard Schröder replaced Helmut Kohl in late 1998. Kohl had long been close to the French, and to François Mitterrand in particular. One of Kohl's sayings was "I always greet the tricolor [the French flag] several times. Show reverence. Do it first; then you get along."[96] It was Kohl who had held hands with Mitterrand in a ceremony at the war memorial at Verdun in 1984. This was not in the style of Schröder, the first post–Cold War chancellor: "I could never do that," he remarked to an adviser. "We must look ahead. Thanks to those before me, we don't have to say to each other every day: 'we will not go to war.'" Later, Schröder came to realize the importance of symbols in the French-German relationship and took steps to restore them.[97]

When he was installed as chancellor, Schröder even considered, for a moment, making his first foreign trip not to Paris but to London. He was persuaded, however, to go to Paris first. Nevertheless, Schröder's initial intention became known to the French, who immediately became nervous about their relationship with Germany. Thies recounts:

> The Germans gave too much to the French for many years. The
> French started to believe they could get whatever they wanted. This
> came to an end with Schröder, who was not in command of French
> history and culture and not listening to people who know France.
> The situation changed to a too-normal relationship that was uncomfortable to the French. The shift of the capital to Berlin was also difficult for the French, who had liked staying in Bonn. For them,
> Berlin was too far away, too in the east.[98]

A Reluctance to Compromise

In most diplomatic negotiations involving Western powers, the middle phase is marked by a process of give-and-take, with negotiators looking to reach agreement by trading concessions, reframing intractable issues, or otherwise creating the conditions that can enable a deal to be struck. In negotiations involving France, however, the middle phase is typically marked by a persistent French refusal to compromise.

This intransigence has at least two historical sources, one centuries old, the other much more recent. First, an enduring sense of France as *la Grande Nation* inspires a reluctance to dishonor that stature by engaging in horse trading and encourages a taste for imposing a settlement rather than negotiating an agreement. As Araud comments:

> French society is a society of authority and not of consensus. Contrary to the northern Europeans, the French negotiator seeks a "victory" over others rather than an accord with others, which leads him to neglect the "little countries" and favor the big ones, which are the keys to success. Furthermore, he is not afraid of being isolated.[99]

Second, there is the legacy of de Gaulle. As one French ambassador observed, there is a pervasive "de Gaulle effect" in the way French negotiators are conditioned to negotiate.[100] This is reflected in a continuing attachment not only to some of the foreign policy strategies championed by the former president (see chapter 3) but also to the Gaullist comportment itself.

Behind de Gaulle's aloof facade was the fact that he had fashioned himself from an early age as a military leader. As an officer, he sought not to curry favor with his subordinates but rather to instill in them a measure of fear. In dealing from a position of weakness with allies in wartime and subsequently, he practiced brinkmanship with relish, yet when facing extreme pressure he generally would beat a discreet retreat. De Gaulle was always testing the mettle of others and found that few could match his. He was confident of the validity of his tactic of using strong-arm measures. He confided to one of his wartime commanders, Paul Legentilhomme, "With the British you have to bang on the table. Then they fold."[101] He mocked Harold Macmillan's ineffectual attempt to gain British entry into the Common Market over France's objections. Said de Gaulle to his Council of Ministers on December 19, 1963, a few days after an inconclusive and not very satisfactory meeting with Macmillan at Rambouillet:

> These very practical questions cannot be decided on the basis of sentiment. He [Macmillan] was melancholic and so was I. We prefer the Great Britain of Macmillan to that of the Labour Party, and we'd like to help him remain in power. But what can I do? Other than sing him the song of Edith Piaf: *ne pleurez pas*, Milord! (don't cry, my Lord).[102]

In a press conference shortly thereafter, on January 14, 1963, de Gaulle shocked the Western alliance by turning down Britain's membership in the Common Market and by refusing French participation in the U.S.-sponsored Multilateral Force (MLF) for NATO.

De Gaulle's was the practice of machismo politics on a grand scale but always presented as an unsentimental pursuit of the national interest; and for French diplomats, the memory is focused on the fact that, for de Gaulle at least, it could be carried off. As the general himself put it, "Our greatness and our strength consist solely in intransigence concerning the rights of France."[103]

French negotiators still widely employ de Gaulle's tactics: making extreme, even outrageous, demands (or simply, as Robert Hunter puts it, "throwing up window dressing" as a device to distract the opponent and/or to get their own way); threatening to boycott negotiations or to walk out of negotiations that are in progress; and refusing to agree until the last minute. A German diplomat has this unsparing, if half-admiring, observation:

> They have a nastiness of political interventions that we cannot tolerate. We want to be loved. We go for harmony. The French want to be respected. They do not need other partners. We hunger for harmony.
>
> If you criticize the French, this makes them stronger. They do not bend on issues. Criticism tells them they are right. They grow with criticism.[104]

Gilles Andréani, who shares in part the German diplomat's view, finds it is interesting to contrast the French and the Germans in the way they negotiate and, in a larger sense, in the way they have sought to reestablish themselves after World War II. The Germans insert themselves into the group in negotiating with others. The French do exactly the reverse: they seek to be less consensual and to distinguish themselves from others.[105]

Andréani elaborates on what could be called the French "culture of noncompromise":

> During a negotiation, the important thing for the French is to be right, and to demonstrate this by disquisition rather than by compromise and bargaining. Unlike many others, they do not feel a compulsion to compromise. They consider that it is to the overall benefit in a negotiation to have a party present who is disinterested, who has a different point of view, and who therefore can be of service. Though they acknowledge that this outlook can be irritating, they emphasize that overall it is useful.[106]

Almost invariably in the European Union, France plays the role of the holdout. This is treated as a commonplace in the French press, as though there were no use in not admitting it. For example, during the EU summit in Laeken, Belgium, in December 2001, *Le Monde* commented on the French position regarding possible locations for the headquarters for newly created EU agencies:

> Showing little willingness to share, France attracted some bitterness in showing itself incapable of making a concession, although it had obtained that morning approval for [its candidate] Valéry Giscard d'Estaing to be president of the Convention on the Future of Europe.

The German view of this French culture of noncompromise appears to be generally disapproving, if resigned, as in this observation by a senior official in the German Foreign Office:

> The French pretend to be calm and cool, but if their sacred cows are called into question they get emotional. The French take much more time to come to a compromise. They "loop" around. Perhaps this is a Latin thing. They are tough, but they know they have to come down to a compromise. The Germans and the Anglo-Saxons, when they know they have to come to a compromise, they do it in a more gentlemanly way.
>
> The French hold the line, even if it is untenable. They have a way of ignoring things if they want to keep a line. They just keep repeating. This is more effective in multilateral settings. One cannot have this kind of confrontation in a bilateral exchange.[108]

Often in multilateral negotiations, especially on defense, U.S. and French negotiators wind up at loggerheads. The other allies become frustrated at a French-U.S. impasse, and some will dress down the French for allowing such a situation to happen; others will come to the Americans and ask them, "Why don't you do something to settle with the French?" U.S. negotiators suspect often the French try to make things as painful as possible for them before finally agreeing.[109]

Some French officials are critical of this culture of noncompromise, of a focus on victory rather than on agreement. Levitte, for example, reflects:

> It is very curious, because at the beginning I did not quite perceive this, but when you are in a negotiation, you must always listen to the other. If you wish to bring him over to your ground, you must show him that you have understood his world, his position. And then one moves toward a compromise. It is never a victory of one who gains one hundred, and the other who gets zero. Rather, it is always fifty-fifty or seventy-thirty or eighty-twenty. Listening to the other, and presenting things in a way that is attractive, that is, attractive in the eyes of the other, is the ABC of multilateral diplomacy.
>
> But we French have learned in our schools to give demonstrations *(faire des demonstrations)*, what is called a *dissertation*, that is to say, a plan in two parts, two subparts, an introduction, a conclusion; and here are the stages we must all necessarily follow. And thus you lock up the others in an implacable logic but which is, naturally, your own and which ends in meeting your objectives. And the others are irritated to see that you paint a picture as if France was the only one to think of the general interest; whereas this general interest, which is unfolded with impeccable reasoning and which the others are urged to follow, actually serves the particular interest of France.[110]

Another problem caused by the general distaste for compromise is that it disinclines the French side to prepare a possible fallback position. As the first case study in chapter 5 describes, the French thought it eminently reasonable to ask that a Frenchman be given charge of NATO's Southern Command at Naples as a quid pro quo for France's decision to rejoin the NATO command, and they prepared no alternative strategy should the United States refuse the French request. As it turned out, and as most French officials now agree, French expectations were unrealistically high and set the stage for a diplomatic failure. And behind these high expectations lies an endemic French problem, which we saw again in the Iraq crisis of 2003: the inadequacy of French means in relation to French ends—both in terms of material power and therefore of real influence.

The Use of Language

French negotiators pride themselves on their eloquence and their ability to present a logical, carefully ordered argument. The worst insult that can be laid at the foot of a French negotiator, according to several French interlocutors, is that of "incoherence."[111] More generally, to imply that one's interlocutor is unintelligent appears to be the surest way to upset a French negotiator, who, behind a crystalline Cartesian facade, is typically highly emotional.

The emphasis on precision and beauty of expression is virtually a national fixation. As Pierre Nora has observed, "What nation would make aesthetics of expression the ultimate foundation and the supreme legitimacy of the word of authority? What state would take the pains to confer on an academic company the exclusive mission of putting together a dictionary of the language?"[112] "For the French, like the ancient Greeks," remarks Lempereur, "there is a unity of the good and the beautiful: what is right can only be elegant and vice versa. This moral aestheticism or aesthetic morality may look odd to many Americans, but it is very much in coherence with the general sense of harmony that one finds in ancient thought and eastern philosophy."[113] This "unity" devolves into the political realm as well. As the writers Jean-Marie Goulemot and Éric Walter note: "[L]iterature serves to unify the national conscience at the same time that it legitimates the republican nation-state. Is it [not] sufficient to point out the strange complicity which, in France, associates literature and politics, the writer and the statesman?"[114]

There is something, in no small part wrapped up in the language, that sets the French apart—far apart—from the Anglo-Americans. As the great French historian Fernand Braudel is quoted as saying, "France *is* language [emphasis added]" *("La France c'est la langue")*.[115] If Britain and the United States are "separated by a common language," as the saying goes, the French and English languages are uncommonly different. French is a language of precision ("Everything which is not clear is not French");[116] English is a language of flexibility.

Between the two languages there are frequent stumbling blocks to translation and many "false friends" *(faux amis)*—words and phrases that look the same but are not. For example, in order to verify a point, a U.S. diplomat asked a Maghrebian interlocutor if he was "serious," not realizing that he was calling into question the Maghrebian's character and reliability.

According to Guéhenno, the crispness of the French language is like a corset that is more constraining than a fluid language like English. The strong grammatical structure of French underlies, and even dictates, the order of how an argument is presented. Ideas are laid out in a sequential fashion, in which counterarguments and paradoxes, so dear to the French heart, are set forth in order, generally in the framework of dialectical reasoning, making use of the thesis-antithesis-synthesis chain of argument. This sense of order is carried along and even exaggerated by the formalism of French syntax. A presentation must have a beginning, the development of the argument, and an end.[117] All this is in keeping with the ascendancy of rational form over content, part of the key elements of what François Azouvi refers to as the "Cartesian spirit": "[T]he inaugural gesture of rupture with the past and the greco-latin culture, the subordination of content to rational form, and naturally, the choice of the French language."[118]

The French have an undoubted difficulty with the looseness and flexibility of the English language, and this is a major reason, other than attitudinal conflicts, for the chronic difficulty encountered with the French in the drafting of joint communiqués. As many observers, including Robert Hunter, have noted, words are very important to the French, and this is evident in the way they pore over the language in joint communiqués.[119] This tradition goes back centuries. In the words of Cardinal Richelieu: "It is absolutely necessary . . . to utilize as negotiators those people who know the weight of words and how best to employ them in written documents."[120]

A case in point is the definite article, over which there have been many linguistic struggles, most famously and most controversially over

UN Security Council Resolution 242 concerning the Israeli evacuation of territories occupied in the Six Day War of June 1967. In the French version of this resolution, which exists as the official version side by side with the English one, the reference is to Israeli withdrawal *"des territoires,"* which means "from the territories." The English version does not contain the definite article but merely states withdrawal "from territories" occupied in the conflict. This bit of finesse has given the Israelis (and the Americans behind them) the justification for not withdrawing from *all* the territories they occupied in 1967. But according to Robert Hunter, "This sentence was deliberately negotiated in this way, so that each side could cite its own version and both were 'equally authoritative.' This was the 'magic' of 242."[121]

The formalism of French and the enveloped style of presentation can become an excuse for the absence of substance or a face-saving way to cover the lack of preparation or of real interest in the subject. "To speak without saying anything is easier in French than in English, as one can make use of all the redundancies of the language," observes Guéhenno. "The clarity of language can camouflage the clarity of ideas."[122] This idea is akin to that expressed by an eighteenth-century writer, Béat-Louis de Muralt: in most countries "expressions are born of thought," while in France "it is the reverse; often it is expressions that give birth to thoughts."[123] But as Tony Judt points out, de Muralt's observation

> is more than a witty aphorism: the importance of rhetoric and style in France are incontestable, shaping thoughts and ideas under an unquestioned discursive authority, in contrast to England, for example, where the vernacular and the literary had merged into a rich, but open, almost anarchic language. With rhetorical primacy, there came abstraction, a power attaching to language and concept independently of the thing they thought to express or describe.[124]

Paradoxically then, besides being a paragon of precision, the French language is also a paragon of abstraction, or, as Judt characterizes it, "This [French] genius for abstracting. reifying, and generalizing."[125] Particularly in literary French, the presentation can be so abstract and enveloped that it is at times difficult to discern the real meaning as intended by the author.

French tends to remain at a level of generality that can leave much unresolved. This characteristic, states Guéhenno,[126] gives the French the opportunity to camouflage the meaning more easily. As Jean-Philippe Mathy comments, the "French rhetorical style, which can make the most abstract speculations seem convincingly real, [has been] diagnosed as a specific trait of French culture."[127]

The abstract character of the French language is such that misunderstandings can arise over the meaning of a communiqué, particularly in relation to the more direct and confrontational U.S. style. In other words, the reading of a text in English may not be the same as the reading of a counterpart text in French. Although a communiqué is supposed to be a codification of what has been achieved, a French text, based on the notion of "good faith" (or "common ground"),[128] may have the wording "the understanding was such-and-such." This often turns out to mean that the French will continue the negotiations after the agreement is reached. The net effect is that both sides may be left with the impression that the other is acting in bad faith.[129]

The French try to see to it that the original drafts of documents, which often carry the day, are first written in French. This is frequently the case in the European Union, where the working languages are French and English. (Above the working level, a representative to the European Union will speak in his own language, if an interpreter is available.)[130] In the two main cities where the European Union is located, Brussels and Strasbourg, the majority of people have French as their first language. Even in Luxembourg, where the European Court of Justice sits, French is understood by everyone. If delegates from member countries cannot conduct themselves with ease in French, they are at an immediate disadvantage.

The view of one German diplomat, echoed by many European counterparts, is that the French characteristically use language as power.[131] At the Paris Peace Conference of 1919, which led to the Treaty of Versailles, the French argued that their language alone should be the official language for documents, as it was more precise and at the same time capable of greater nuance; besides, French had been the language of international communication and diplomacy for centuries. In the end Prime Minister Georges Clemenceau had to back down, and both English and French became the official language for documents.[132]

Sometimes, however, the French use English for effect, as was the case at the pivotal St. Malo meeting in December 1998, when the British agreed to a defense role for the European Union. The French put forward their text, but in an English translation, a practice that is not "abnormal," according to Errera, who was the leading French negotiator at St. Malo.[133] This text turned out to be the basis of the St. Malo declaration, although in discussing the final touches to it, Jacques Chirac agreed, by way of a concession to the British, to "put a little bit of NATO in it."[134] Another example was Dominique de Villepin's impassioned speech before the UN Security Council on February 15, 2003. De Villepin's oration against war in Iraq, in English, was received with sustained applause, which was unprecedented in such a forum.

The Use of Back Channels

It is not uncommon for some politically sensitive negotiations to be conducted through back channels instead of the usual diplomatic channels. One type of back channel is direct contact between one president or prime minister and another. Another type involves the intelligence services establishing secret contacts to convey particularly sensitive information. In the 1960s, 1970s, and 1980s, the latter variant was employed on a few occasions to transmit information between Washington and Paris. In the 1960s, for instance, the CIA chief in Paris, Al Ulmer, was used to convey a warning to de Gaulle about the existence of unnamed Soviet spies at high levels in the French government and in de Gaulle's own entourage. Such was the suspicion in Washington of Soviet penetrations in France that the United States took the unorthodox action of going directly to de Gaulle on the basis of unproven assertions by a Russian defector, Anatoly Golitsyn. Ulmer was used because the U.S. ambassador, Amory Houghton, did not want to become involved (perhaps in part because the information was unspecific and unproved). In the event, de Gaulle appears to have shrugged the matter off, having a low opinion of intelligence matters in general, which he considered as *subalterns* (inferior).

An example in reverse was François Mitterrand's use of his security service, the Direction de la Surveillance du Territoire (DST), to convey information to the United States and to request U.S. technical support in the case of a high-level Soviet agent recruited by the DST, code-named "Farewell." The agent's revelations about Soviet industrial espionage resulted in the expulsion of forty-seven Soviets from the embassy in Paris in 1983. Ironically, several years later, a Soviet scientist came to Paris to brief Mitterrand on "Farewell" (who had since been apprehended and executed by the Soviets) and led Mitterrand to believe that the Americans had manipulated him, specifically into taking action against the Soviet embassy.

De Gaulle's attitude (and Mitterrand's) toward the intelligence and security services is widely shared in France, which helps explain why covert channels have rarely been used. In the recent period, they have fallen even further out of fashion, especially following the unprecedented expulsion in 1995 by the French of four diplomats from the U.S. embassy and one other individual accused of being CIA personnel. Usually such incidents are handled quietly behind the scenes, but in this case the interior minister, Charles Pasqua, decided to exploit the incident publicly.

In contrast, France's diplomatic corps has a very long and distinguished reputation, and French leaders typically trust the professionalism of their diplomats to defend national interests and transmit sensitive information. Even so, when a matter concerns the presidency directly, or when negotiations between foreign ministries have reached an impasse, a French leader will open a back channel between himself and the leader of another country. In the Élysée, such back channels are usually managed by the sherpa, whose foremost function is to prepare the president for the annual G-8 economic summits. In the first five years of Jacques Chirac's first presidency, the position was held by Jean-David Levitte. Occasionally, as during wartime, the back channel may be managed by another highly trusted and well-connected official, such as the military adviser to the president. During the first Gulf War, for instance, the channel was in the hands of the military adviser, Admiral Jacques Lanxade.

In the French-U.S. context, the back channel is known as the "blue line" and is a direct electronic connection to the White House, in the person of the national security adviser. In the Mitterrand presidency, at least three different individuals handled the blue line contact at different times: military adviser Lanxade, sherpa Jacques Attali, and the secretary-general of the Élysée, Hubert Védrine. The first case study in chapter 5 describes how the French-U.S. negotiations over a French return to NATO during the Chirac presidency were taken out of the normal negotiating channel and put in the charge of the sherpa (Levitte) and the national security adviser (Sandy Berger). This connection sometimes involved personal meetings. For instance, Levitte went to Washington in early 1997 in an abortive effort to find a compromise over the issue of the French return to NATO. Earlier, during the Gulf War, Lanxade made a number of visits to Washington to coordinate strategy with the national security adviser, General (Ret.) Brent Scowcroft. During the crisis in 2003 over the war in Iraq, the French ambassador to the United States, Jean-David Levitte, sought to reconnect the personal relationship between Jacques Chirac and George Bush by going to White House adviser Karl Rove. The result was a phone call between the two presidents on April 15, 2003, the first since February 7.

Although not used often, this back channel between the Élysée and the White House almost invariably works better than the normal liaison between the State Department, which is accustomed to finding the French difficult, and the Quai d'Orsay, which is the traditional bastion of Gaullist orthodoxy.

Lanxade has this view of the back channel contact between the Élysée and the White House during the 1990s:

> Bush appreciated Mitterrand. There was a personal relationship. It was a period of a high point in U.S.-French relations. There were regular summits. The Clinton-Chirac relationship was superficial, although apparently amicable. For French-American relations to work well, there must be a good relationship between the presidents, and below them, someone who handles the dossier, either the military chief of staff in the Élysée or the diplomatic adviser. Without preparatory work at the lower level, it does not work well.[135]

When the U.S. government seeks to relay sensitive intelligence information to Paris, it usually does so by sending a special emissary to the Élysée or to Matignon. In 1962, for example, Dean Acheson, who had been called back by President Kennedy as a special adviser, met with General de Gaulle along with Sherman Kent of the CIA, to show proof of the existence of Soviet medium-range ballistic missiles in Cuba. In 1986 General (Ret.) Vernon Walters pleaded unsuccessfully with François Mitterrand and Jacques Chirac for permission for U.S. warplanes to overfly France en route to attacking Libya.

The Use of Entertainment

For the French, as Alain Plantey remarks, "negotiation has a cultural base,"[136] meaning that all aspects of French culture are brought into play, from language, to art and architecture, to entertainment. France, since the days of Charles de Gaulle and his intellectual foil, André Malraux, has had a minister of culture.

Ambassador Plantey's opinion is echoed by Ambassador George F. Ward Jr.: "French culture is the dynamic in *all* negotiations. It is the background music."[137] A more pointed comment, but reflective of the same pervasive emphasis, is that of John Kornblum: "The Russians and the French have great psychological similarities: a grand past that got lost."[138]

For the French, food is an important part of the culture. "This country does not have an ordinary relationship to food," writes Pascal Ory:

> In the seventeenth century, French culture became hegemonic in Europe for at least two reasons: firstly because the political system that supported it was triumphant and influential; next because the longtime relationship which the political power in this country maintained with symbolic production (in modern terms, with artists, savants, and ideologues) functioned, thanks to absolutism, to the maximum. If French cuisine tended to become a reference, it was in the same way, although obviously with less prestige, as the language codified by Richelieu . . . or painting codified by Colbert.[139]

A British historian has limned the difference in the culinary traditions of France and England in the following manner:

> In France, the culinary model was that of the Versailles monarchy: curial, ostentatious, sophisticated. Its ideal host was the Sun-King [Louis XIV], reigning over a dysfunctional and even domesticated

nobility. The English model on the other hand was that of a liberal aristocracy, exercising the essence and the reality of economic and political power: rural, puritan, and practical; its ideal host was the gentleman, an integral part of a relatively open elite, the gentry. Nothing further was necessary for the two culinary languages not to understand each other.[140]

The following comparison with German cuisine (by a French author) is distinctly unflattering:

> If the "meatballs of the Black Forest" are heavy, thick, [and massive], like German thought, literature and art, there is in quiche lorraine, in the liver of Périgord, or in the bouillabaisse of Marseilles . . . all the refined richness of France. . . . The taste for gastronomy is innate in the race.[141]

At the Congress of Vienna, the ever-present Foreign Minister Talleyrand said to his new master, Louis XVIII, "Sire, I have more need of casseroles than instructions," prompting this commentary by Pascal Ory: "This pleasant formula, assuredly a pragmatic philosophy of the defeated, nevertheless marked the entry into an era of a sort of politics of gastronomy. 'Meals,' asserted Brillat, 'have become a means of government.'"[142]

Excellent cuisine, or what the French call *la bonne chère*, has long been used to impress and please visitors, not least diplomats. In the matter of hospitality, the French are on high ground, supremely confident that French cuisine and wines are unsurpassed, and practiced in the art of elegant presentation. Even a simple meal in a French home is marked by a certain order and elegance. At the same time, the presentation tends to be understated; it is not forced, except in commercial negotiations, when it becomes more ostentatious. In political negotiations, the atmosphere is more austere. At official receptions and meetings held in the splendor of buildings such as the Quai d'Orsay, the Élysée Palace, and Matignon, the atmosphere is institutional and formal; one observes a strict dress code and does not deal in first names.[143] The effect can be mesmerizing. As one German diplomat remarks, when one comes to Paris for diplomatic negotiations, one is likely to be "lulled" by the atmosphere: "the Empire furniture, the receptions—you forget who you are."[144]

The French are usually eager to host international conferences, at which they can display their cultivated taste in the decor and amenities of the conference site. A number of key conferences and ceremonies have been held in Paris over the past century, starting with the Paris Peace Conference, which lasted for six months in 1919. During the Cold War the French hosted secret talks between Amercans and Vietnamese, and also between Americans and Chinese, and it was the Paris Agreement of January 1973 that ended the war between the United States and North Vietnam. The French government assiduously vies for Paris to be the site for the signing of international agreements, as was the case in 1995 with the signing of the agreement brokered in Dayton, Ohio, to end the Bosnian war. In the fall of 1989 the French built a conference hall featuring a huge table within the Kleber Conference Center for the purpose of hosting a CSCE conference. By sponsoring such gatherings, the French seek to enhance their prestige, particularly in a European context, and to gain some negotiating advantage by both awing and delighting their foreign interlocutors. Given the beauty and charms of Paris ("the city of light," as it is known), many foreigners are happy to oblige their hosts.

"French negotiators," comments a senior U.S. diplomat, "are conscious of their advantages as representatives of France. They are in the business of winning hearts and minds with a good meal and good wine. Call it *traiteur* diplomacy: using these tools to gain a little extra sway. The French can go either way: *mano a mano*, or using all the finery of French culture and cuisine to wow you."[145]

Use of the Media

Paris, like Washington, is active in manipulating the media to gain an advantage in a dispute or in a negotiation. For instance, France used the press to try to win a favorable outcome in the Uruguay Round of GATT negotiations (see chapter 5). Yet Paris and Washington tend to have different views about the process by which the other shapes media coverage. The French impression, as Levitte articulates, is that the U.S. system, with its checks and balances, inspires infighting within and among U.S. government departments and agencies to shape foreign policy and negotiating positions; this conflict then spills over into the press as the various players leak stories intended to bolster their causes. In France, in contrast, the government "acts as one man" and there is not the same phenomenon of interagency wars waged in the press.[146]

The U.S. impression is that the central government in France has the power to directly influence the tenor and substance of media reports and thus can use the media as an instrument to advance its policies. This U.S. perspective, however, tends to ignore the fact that the French media have grown more independent than was the case a generation ago. We are a long way from the de Gaulle period, when French television (ORTF) was a government corporation and when investigative reporting was still in its infancy. In 1985, for example, when French intelligence agents blew up the Greenpeace ship *Rainbow Warrior*, which was in New Zealand to protest French nuclear testing, *Le Monde*'s investigative reporting team went to work, eventually producing conclusive proof that the operation had been carried out by a previously unidentified group of French agents. Still, investigative reporters in France are not yet as aggressive or as unrestrained as their U.S. counterparts. Moreover, certain subjects, particularly money and sex, are considered more or less private and are handled delicately. The French, for example, would not produce an implicitly prurient report like that written by Kenneth Starr about the sex scandal involving President Clinton.

STAGE 4: ENDGAME AND IMPLEMENTATION

The Use of Time

French diplomats tend to be a good deal less concerned with time than many other Western negotiators, especially Americans. This readiness to engage in protracted discussions has several sources. First is the fact that the French, à la Couve de Murville, regard negotiation above all as an exercise in defending France's position rather than in reaching agreement; if agreement seems unattainable, they are content to restate the French position repeatedly while the negotiations splutter and stall. In the words of a senior German Foreign Office official cited earlier: "The French hold the line, even if it is untenable. They have a way of ignoring things if they want to keep a line. They just keep repeating."

Second is the French reluctance to compromise on a position that strikes them as perfectly logical; à la de Gaulle, French diplomats have no qualms about saying *"Non!"* even if it means that a negotiation will ultimately lead nowhere. If they consider their position to be the right one, that is, based on reason and logic, they will generally not oblige the other side by making statements designed to foster better transitory relations. On more than one occasion, U.S. negotiators have believed that they were making incremental progress on an issue with the French, only to hear the French restate their overall principles—a move that the Americans considered backtracking at best and duplicitous at worst. An example of this occurred when the *New York Times*, citing senior French officials, stated on August 29, 2002, that "the new center-right French Government has decided to stop criticizing American war planning against Saddam Hussein and instead maximize its leverage with the United States by stressing areas of agreement."[147] Indeed, this new departure of stressing the positive aspects of the bilateral relationship was the avowed policy of the incoming French government, as made plain from the outset by Foreign Minister Dominique de Villepin in conversations with State Department officials.[148] However, on the very next day, August 30, this departure from the past seemed to be contradicted by a new statement from Jacques Chirac to the effect that any resort to force against Iraq would have to be sanctioned by the United Nations. "One sees the appearance of the temptation to legitimize the unilateral and preventive use of force. This is a worrying development," he said.[149] To the French, this was not so much a criticism of the U.S. position as a reaffirmation of French principles, particularly in the face of a statement by Vice President Dick Cheney on August 26 that inspections in Iraq would accomplish nothing.

Third, with a historic distaste for entering into agreements that it cannot control, and with the consciousness of playing from a weak hand, France is loath to be pushed into an agreement, especially by the United States. Often, when the United States enunciates a position, it expects that its allies, being lesser powers with lesser responsibilities, will follow along without much debate. In the nineteenth century Alexis de Tocqueville detected what he saw as the U.S. passion for unanimity.[150] France, however, is in a special position: being outside the military structure of NATO, it has the unspoken status of being a less than complete ally and therefore possessed of a greater margin of maneuver.

There is a strong French reflex against the "tailism" of the 1930s that led to France's greatest disaster, in 1940—or more generally against what the French call *suivisme* (following along). Hence there is an overpowering urge to maintain an independence of position. If the United States wants unanimity in the Western position badly enough, the French calculate that they have only to play for time until Washington makes the necessary concessions to the French position. As we will see in the Iraqi case study in chapter 5, this calculation is not always accurate.

Fourth, on a more philosophical plane, the French seem to calculate that because theirs is a reasoned position and consistent with historical realities, others will overcome the impulse of the moment and gradually come to acknowledge the validity of the French arguments. Thus, there is a strong temptation to play for time. The debate over Resolution 1441, which paved the way for the inspectors to return to Iraq, was stretched out over a period of seven weeks in the fall of 2002, largely because the French were playing for time and insistently pressing their point of view.

Negotiators seeking to overcome this dilatory approach on the part of the French counterparts have at least two options, but neither is very compatible with the French style. One option is to set deadlines. If, however, there is no sense of compulsion on the French side to reach an agreement, the deadline will simply be ignored. (As we will see in chapter 5, the French in early 2003 resisted the idea of coming to closure on the inspections regime in Iraq in order to meet the U.S. meteorological requirement for a possible military operation before the hot weather set in.) The second option is the so-called one-text procedure—entering a negotiation with a text and asking the other party to comment on it. (In the case of Resolution 1441, the French countered this procedure with a pressure tactic of their own: by letting it be known they had a text of their own that they nevertheless would not table.) In general, U.S. negotiators want to proceed quickly to a text. French negotiators, however, are reluctant to do so. The French, who tend to use language precisely, generally will not be satisfied with an informal translation from an English into a French text; they will wait for an official translation and they will expect it to be a very good one. Moreover, when confronted with a text, the French may prefer not to comment on it but to discuss the general principles of the negotiation at hand.

A Swift Endgame

As this chapter has emphasized, French diplomats usually enter a negotiation with a clear conception of what is to be their final position, and they defend it in a tough and intransigent manner. Throughout the middle game, the French seem immovable. But sometimes, as the negotiation appears destined to conclude in failure, there is a sudden shift in the French position and a compromise is found. Negotiators from most other countries seek to build confidence with their opposite numbers from the outset and work together to find a solution, but not the French, who will let frustration, even ill feeling, build throughout the lengthy middle game but then reach agreement in a cooperative, even cordial, fashion.

Here we evoke once again the strain of "peasant realism" of the French, or what is described as the "French solidity," based in part on the peasant past of most of the French population. As a French ambassador posted to Brussels put it, "the peasant good sense is never very far off" and has saved France from many "disasters."[151] This "peasant realism" is based in part on a sober appraisal of the country's power position in relation to others. In the EU context, the French position has often been intransigent, behind which is an appreciation that France is too important for the European Union to do without, and that France's political influence within the union has been pervasive from the outset. With the United States, on the other hand, France has been in a position of weakness from 1919 onward. Even as truculent a personality as de Gaulle generally had to give way before U.S. power in a real military crunch during World War II. With the European Union, on the other hand, de Gaulle saw fit to boycott it for ten months in 1965–66 until he got—more or less—his way.

There does seem to a certain rhythm in the way the French stick to a position and then suddenly come to closure in negotiations, as indicated in the remarks of Couve de Murville and others cited earlier in this study. Valéry Giscard d'Estaing, president of the European Convention, posed on the dais, at the opening of each session, two statuettes, one a tortoise and the other a dragon. Asked the meaning of this, Giscard replied, "The tortoise is for tenacity, the dragon is for the final acceleration."[152]

The power to produce a shift in the French negotiating position generally comes from Paris and, more particularly—though it depends on the gravity of the situation—from the Élysée, home of what von Thadden has described as a "Republican King." In France's pyramidal, top-down decision-making structure, it is the president who has the ability to end a negotiating impasse by modifying the original negotiating position—a position, it should be remembered, that was carefully arbitrated among different components of the French government before negotiations began. Furthermore, in the hierarchical French system, the top leader is usually happy to flex his muscles in this way and demonstrate that the final decision is his, not that of his subordinates. In the protracted negotiations that led to the passage of UN Security Council Resolution 1441 on Iraq in November 2002, the French position came together with the U.S. position at the eleventh hour, thanks to a decision that clearly was made by President Chirac himself. The actual negotiation was conducted primarily between Secretary of State Colin Powell and Foreign Minister de Villepin, with the latter acting in the closest coordination with Chirac. The diplomats at the Quai d'Orsay and the French military, who had participated in the Gulf War of 1991, were essentially kept out of the decision-making picture.

In similar fashion, as the case study in chapter 5 will show, the French concluded that they could not achieve more than they already had in the course of the long Uruguay Round negotiation and came suddenly to an agreement. Here it was a case of an intervention by President François Mitterrand, who had been advised by his fellow socialist, European Commission president Jacques Delors, that it would be wise for the French to conclude the agreement.

On a level, or a matter, that is less Olympian, the French negotiator paradoxically exhibits a certain leeway in terms of improvisation. Partly this derives from the cultural style of the French, as a senior British diplomatic official describes:

> The French are instinctive negotiators. They have an individualistic style, are well prepared, and tough. They are fast on their feet and not constrained by their mandate. They have a strong personal investment

in the outcome. They do not have elaborate instructions for negotiations. A quick call often settles an issue. It is an informal, personality-
based process. Leeway is allowed. It is ad hoc, intuitive. The British
have a more elaborate process, with a close examination of text.[153]

The French emphasis on finding the right solution, based on logic
and reason, and presenting it at the outset inherently tends to limit the
possibilities of a fallback position, and this can put a premium on a
French negotiator's ability to improvise. Conversely, as Robert Hunter
notes, the French attraction for logic and reason is such that if the position of a negotiating partner is eminently logical and well argued, the
French negotiator will often risk supporting it, even though it may lack
something in substance and even if it differs from the position given to
him or her before the start of the negotiation.[154]

The fact that French negotiating teams tend to be relatively small
encourages this readiness to improvise. According to a French diplo-
mat, a U.S. delegation can include as many as sixty persons, while the
French team numbers only five. But this has certain advantages. The
French team is tightly organized and can come to a quick decision.
Also, the chain leading back to a major decision in Paris is short.[155]

The French willingness to improvise contrasts with the German
practice, which is highly disciplined, and also with the British
approach.[156] The latter is, as Jay points out, thoroughly staffed out
beforehand, with the effect that not many changes in the British position can be anticipated in the course of negotiations.[157] The U.S.
approach can reflect a degree of improvisation, based on characteristic
U.S. pragmatism and also the presence of competing constituencies in
a negotiation. But on the other hand, the U.S. approach can also be
tough-minded and unbending, based on the reflex of a superpower
accustomed to expecting to get its own way.

Implementation

There are mixed opinions on how the French conduct the implementation phase of an agreement. These differences have to do partly with
the contrasting individual experiences of negotiators who have dealt
with the French. On the one hand, according to Hunter,

> [s]ince the French have a clear idea of what they want, they can
> relate their immediate negotiation to long-term strategic goals that

may even be years into the future. In negotiations, they are disciplined and work as a team. But if they finally come to an agreement in a negotiation, they generally adhere to it.[158]

Hunter contends that if he and his French counterpart, Gérard Errera, had been allowed to continue their negotiations over a full French return to NATO, they could have arrived at an agreement. Instead, the negotiation was taken out of their hands and conducted by representatives of the White House and the Élysée (see chapter 5).

On the other hand, a number of other observers would take issue with Hunter's assertion that the French abide by the agreements they have signed and would instead argue that for the French, implementation is really a process of constant renegotiation. In the opinion of a German specialist on France, a penchant for "renegotiation" goes deep into the French psychology itself:

> For the French, a decision can be modified. For Germans, a decision taken should not be modified. For the French, decision has another meaning: it can mean negotiations afterward; it can mean modification. It is an intellectual game: there should be enough ambiguity to allow for a change. The French are flexible, and they do not take themselves so seriously.[159]

The question of "seriousness" as between the French and the Germans recalls Guéhenno's and Vimont's earlier observations that the French predilection for moving from one concept to another ("an intellectual game," the latter called it) is made possible by a habit of ambiguity that can be aided by the generality of the French language, which is dialectically both abstract and precise.[160]

It is obviously the case, and not just for the French, that the ambiguity of an agreement ipso facto lends itself to a renegotiation. As we will see in chapter 5, UN Security Council Resolution 1441, painfully concluded after seven weeks of negotiations, had, in the words of one observer, "no timetable, no road map, and no cutoff date" (for determining Iraqi compliance).[161] It was bound to become the subject of renegotiation among the council members.

Other elements of the French mind-set and intellectual tradition likewise encourage a readiness to renegotiate. For instance, the French preference for deductive over inductive reasoning disinclines them to regard an agreement as setting an inviolable precedent and encourages them to believe one can always reexamine an agreement in light of basic principles. The French approach, contends Lempereur, is that one can start over again from the beginning with—to use a French figure of speech—*cire vierge* (virgin wax).[162]

OTHER ACTORS

The portrait of French negotiating behavior presented in this chapter is based on the approach taken by government officials—chiefly, diplomats—not by other groups within French society. Even within this relatively narrow professional group differences exist in negotiating behavior. For instance, Ambassador Jacques Andréani draws distinctions between French politicians ("who are often anxious to come to an agreement, and therefore they tend to be too easy to please") and French civil servants ("generally tenacious about defending the national interest . . . they often come across as self-important and arrogant"). Among the latter, Andréani singles out for praise officials from the Finance and Foreign Commerce Ministries who conduct negotiations in the European Union and who "know their métier and are overall very effective."[163]

While the aim here is not to capture every nuance and facet of every French negotiator—such a task would obviously be impossible—but to provide a composite picture of the approach French diplomats take, some mention should also be made of two other groups whom foreign diplomats may encounter during negotiations: businesspeople and members of the military.

Business Negotiators

Generally, French businesspeople tend to be more open to the outside world and more open to foreign innovations than French diplomats. In recent decades, French business has become increasingly internationalized, and a vibrant French entrepreneurial class has sprung up. As noted in chapter 1, foreign ownership of French firms increased from 10 percent in the mid-1980s to more than 40 percent at the beginning of the twenty-first century, and French companies have made a number of global acquisitions.[164] Many French businesspeople are thus well accustomed to international travel and are more or less at ease in English.

Over past decades, French civil servants have played a significant role in business-to-business negotiations, partly because of the large role of the state in the economy, and partly because it has been the practice for a significant number of elite civil servants to move over late in their careers into more lucrative positions in the private sector. This phenomenon, known as *pantouflage*—defined by *Le grand dictionnaire Larousse* as "leaving a civil service post to work in the private sector"[165]—is becoming less common as privatization continues at an increasing rate in France.[166]

Many of today's business executives did not come up through the ENA route but through business schools such as HEC and ESSEC. In addition, an increasing number of French business managers have worked and studied in the United States (usually for an MBA or in an advanced management program). The Harvard Business School Club of France, for example, has more than twelve hundred members.[167]

The business negotiator who does not come from the elite *énarque* class is inclined to be more pragmatic than his civil servant counterpart and more sympathetic to the Anglo-American mind-set than a product of the Quai d'Orsay is. Even if he or she is an *énarque*, the French business negotiator will likely have a more flexible and cooperative approach than a French diplomat, according to a senior British diplomatic official: "Business negotiators are often ex-*énarques* who are parachuted in. Still, the French businessman has developed an Anglo-Saxon coloration that is pretty successful. The *énarque* mold appears less now in the French business community. Before there was a single type. Now it is less so."[168]

The Military

Particularly since the discussions that began in 1995 over a new relationship between France and NATO, U.S. officials have gradually come to realize that French military officers do not enjoy the same status as their U.S. counterparts. In the United States, the military has become the guardian of the country's role as the sole superpower, as well as its principal protector against terrorism. In France, however, the military does not have the prestige of the senior civil servant caste.

The French military characteristically take a backseat to civilian officials. The French army is known as *La Grande Muette* (the Great Silent One) because military officers are not supposed to express political opinions in public. Civil dominance over the military is ingrained in France's republican tradition. With this tradition has gone a preference for an army of citizen-soldiers and a distrust of a professional military corps that might produce an antirepublican strongman. This distrust has diminished in recent years—as evidenced by the ending of conscription in 2002 and the move toward a smaller, more professional force—but it has by no means disappeared.

The British, who have had extensive military exchanges with France, have long recognized this special status of the French military. "In France, there is less respect for the military than is the case here [in London]," notes a senior British diplomatic official. "When there is a clash, the Quai always wins out over the military, who are much less an equal player. Here there is a genuine equality. Military advice is given a serious hearing."[169]

According to Bruce Bach, who was then serving in the U.S. military at SHAPE Headquarters, negotiations in the 1990s revealed a general lack of understanding within the U.S. defense community, both civil and military, as to how the French are organized. The French minister of defense, the Americans discovered, has nothing like the power of his U.S. counterpart ("He's a beans and bullets person"). In France the Quai rules supreme:

> Many Americans were so used to our system that they expected the same thing from the French. They saw things mostly through the eyes of Admiral Lanxade, the chief of staff of the armed forces [CEMA]. He appeared to be on a par with General Shalikashvili, his counterpart, and with General Colin Powell [Shalikashvili's predecessor]. He seemed to be an important figure and not just inside the military, and he was thought to have influence over President Mitterrand. We thought that Lanxade could deliver. But the Quai never intended a French return to NATO, at least not until their long-term goals on the EU side could be satisfied. The fledgling objective of achieving an EU security and defense policy after Maastricht needed to be given a

chance: a NATO military structure strengthened with the French in it would clearly present a major obstacle to their longer-term aim of an eventual EU military capacity.[170]

Nevertheless, some enhancement of the military role in strategic decision making in France was instituted in 1993, when President François Mitterrand and Prime Minister Edouard Balladur began France's second cohabitation. The first cohabitation, in 1986–88, with an activist defense minister, André Giraud, had been marked by dissensions; in the early 1990s France was involved in the Bosnian conflict and a harmonious position at the top levels of the government was deemed imperative.[171] Thus, a new procedure was introduced, that of a Restricted Council of Ministers to handle the management of crises. The council functions along the lines of the National Security Council in the United States. It meets once a week, on Wednesdays, following the weekly Council of Ministers meeting, is chaired by the president, and includes the prime minister, the foreign minister, the defense minister, the chief of staff of the armed forces (the CEMA), and often the head of the president's military staff, the general secretary of the Élysée, and the general secretary of national defense. The main result of this innovation is that the chief military officer in France, the CEMA, is now, at least institutionally, involved in political-military decisions at the highest level.[172] The CEMA is also present, along with his German counterpart, at the French-German summit meetings, which were held twice annually until the French-German quarrel at the Nice EU summit in December 2000 and every six weeks thereafter.[173]

French officers now typically emerge from St. Cyr rather than the École Polytechnique, or St. Cyr's naval counterpart, the École Navale. Though both St. Cyr and the École Navale are classed as *grandes écoles*,[174] these institutions offer two-year programs and are not considered to provide the equivalent of a university education. As officers advance in their careers, they are also likely to attend one of the military schools, such as the Collège Interarmé de Défense.

According to a senior French defense official, the French military are something of a caste apart—"a little bit like Jesuits." There is a tradition that the army can do no wrong, and this emerged with force in the Dreyfus affair, which was not only a trial of a Jewish captain from

Alsace, but also an issue of whether the army could have erred in accusing Captain Dreyfus. Although the military in the French administration, as in the Defense Ministry, are exceedingly polite to their civilian superiors, they keep to their own traditions. It is significant in this regard that the military cabinet of the Defense Ministry does not change when a new government and a new defense minister come in; the civilian cabinet of the minister does change. Still, a certain politicization has taken place in recent years with the establishment within the ministry of a Department of Strategic Affairs (Direction des Affaires Stratégiques [DAS]), controlled by civilians, the top echelon of whom are appointed by the administration in power.[175]

5

Case Studies
NATO, Iraq, and
the Uruguay Round

T
HE THREE CASE STUDIES IN THIS CHAPTER were chosen as illus-
trations of *current* French negotiating behavior and as such
they reflect the changes that have taken place in French society and attitudes over the past generation. To be sure, many of the
characteristics exhibited in recent negotiations can also be found in
earlier crises involving France and the major Western powers—for
instance, the Suez crisis in 1956 and the furor created by the French
withdrawal from the NATO military command in 1966. However, to
underline the currency of the portrait of French negotiating behavior
presented in this volume, the cases examined here are all drawn from
the post–Cold War period.

The first case concerns the dispute in 1996–97 over whether
a European (and more particularly a Frenchman), rather than an
American, should head NATO's Southern Command in Naples. On
the outcome of the dispute hung the French decision on whether to

rejoin the military structure of NATO and become again a full member of the military alliance. In the end, the French decided against a return to the structure, and this issue became the most serious dispute between France and NATO (meaning essentially the United States) in the decade following the end of the Cold War.

The second case, involving the creation of a new weapons inspection regime for Iraq in 1999, which led eventually to the decision to go to war in 2003, produced what was arguably the most serious long-term crisis in the history of French-American relations. It brought into relief the deep fissures that have existed between the two countries for more than two centuries and that belie what Philippe Roger has characterized as a "shared mythology of eternal friendship" that has produced a "pasteurized past."[1]

The third case, the conclusion of the Uruguay Round of the GATT in 1992–93, illustrates how commercial and cultural issues are handled within the European Union and how France interacts within this system. The European Union as a unit negotiated for EU member-states in the Uruguay Round, with the EU external trade commissioner and the agriculture commissioner acting under the supervision of the European Council and the Council of Ministers. The French role, though behind the scenes and indirect, was important and in some respects even decisive.

All three cases reflect France's position as a "stand-alone" power both in the sense of serving as a pole of attraction for other parties to rally around, as has often been the case in the European Union, and as a country eager to stand up for its principles, notably that of national independence, and of independence from U.S. dominance in particular.

The cases also illustrate many other of the characteristics of French negotiating behavior described in the previous chapters: the sense of representing the authority of the French state and the grandeur of its traditions; the feeling of being on the defensive in the face of an Anglo-Saxon world that has been in the ascendancy for more than a century; the confidence in the power of reason and the French capacity to exercise it, even to the point of obstinacy and self-isolation; and the ability often to come to a compromise based on an innate sense of realism—as has been evident in the way France has been able to adapt to the changing dynamics in the European Union and other multilateral organizations.

Case 1: The Dispute over NATO's Southern Command

Overview

In 1996 the French proposed a change in NATO's Southern Command at Naples, which had always been headed by a U.S. admiral. This command is one of two regional commands under the Supreme Allied Commander Europe (SACEUR), who is based in Mons, Belgium, and has always been a U.S. general officer. The dispute that followed was the first public flare-up in the France-NATO relationship since 1966, when France quit the integrated command and ordered NATO troops to withdraw from its territory.

As even most knowledgeable French officials now admit, the French overreached themselves in this dispute. As one French diplomat sums it up, "Whoever put it in Jacques Chirac's head to ask for the Southern Command? This was setting the bar rather high."[2] At the same time, however, the disagreement was spurred by the Americans, who mounted their high horse about accumulating French demands, saying in effect, "Enough is enough! *Nyet!*"[3] Although the French were humiliated by the blunt and public U.S. refusal to meet French demands, the more lasting regret appears to be on the U.S. side. As a number of U.S. officials at the NATO organizational headquarters in Brussels and at its military headquarters in Mons[4] now acknowledge, U.S. inflexibility doomed the negotiations to failure, a failure that encouraged France to press for the development of a European defense force apart from NATO. As Gérard Errera, the French ambassador to London and former ambassador to NATO, notes, "If these negotiations had succeeded, St. Malo [where the British and the French came together on the idea of an autonomous European defense force] might never have taken place."[5] And as a consequence of the decision made at St. Malo, there are now two more or less independent military organizations existing on the same terrain, in Europe: NATO and the autonomous defense force of the European Union.[6]

What the French seemed to have wanted in exchange for a commitment to make a full return to NATO was the establishment of a relatively free-functioning European defense identity *within* the Atlantic Alliance. The French hoped to accomplish this by creating a strictly European chain of command internally within NATO: it would run from the deputy SACEUR (who would be a European) down through the chief of the Southern Command at Naples, who would be a Frenchman. The Mediterranean is of paramount interest to France; there is a French naval presence in the Mediterranean Sea itself, a large North African population in metropolitan France, and considerable political turmoil and poverty in the countries of the Maghreb, just across the Mediterranean from France (in this context, it is often said that the Maghreb is to France what Central America is to the United States). For these reasons, the French attached great importance to their request that the Southern Command be given to a European—by which the French really meant a Frenchman.

The core U.S. position was the obverse of the French position: the Americans perceived the need to preserve, especially in the nuclear context, a solely U.S. chain of command. It would run from Washington, to the SACEUR, to the Southern Command, and to the Sixth Fleet in the Mediterranean with its complement of nuclear submarines. As we shall see later in this chapter, the reality is that NATO has never had any operational authority over this exclusively U.S. chain of command from Washington down to the Sixth Fleet. Though Jacques Chirac recognized that special arrangements would have to be made for the Sixth Fleet should France take over the Southern Command, the French leadership in general did not grasp the significance that the Americans attached to the command at Naples, especially in terms of the command and employment of the nuclear submarines in the Sixth Fleet. (Even some connected with the French military endorse this judgment, among them Admiral (ret.) Jacques Lanxade, former chief of President Mitterrand's Military Staff who later became chief of staff of the French armed forces.)[7]

The fundamental incompatibilities between the French and U.S. positions virtually ruled out any hopes of reaching a mutually acceptable agreement. Moreover, other factors prevented the two sides from putting together even some limited compromise or a face-saving solution. One of these factors was the inability to transcend the long legacy of distrust and suspicion between France and the United States. Another was the personalities of the leading players, and in particular the personality of French president Jacques Chirac. On the one hand, Chirac appeared to break the mold of French reserve about the United States, setting in motion preparations for a full French return to NATO through a planning study conducted under the auspices of the chief of staff of the French armed forces. On the other hand, Chirac had a hussar's temperament and was known for acts of political impulsiveness. Not only did he aim too high in this case (though his aim was based on logic), but he engaged himself personally on the issue with President Clinton.

This case illustrates not only the impact on negotiations of incompatible policies and impulsive personalities, but also a number of significant and enduring differences between the French and the U.S. negotiating styles. While the French approached the negotiations with a long-term goal, the Americans approached them pragmatically and on a step-by-step basis. The French adopted a dialectical approach, shifting back and forth in an attempt to rationalize and synthesize two seeming opposites: reconciliation with NATO and greater independence from NATO. The U.S. approach was to make progress pragmatically, on an incremental basis, without any backtracking. And whereas the French side was tightly disciplined and unified, the U.S. side was clearly made up of several constituencies that were not always working toward the same end.

French Moves toward Rapprochement with NATO

According to John Kornblum, who became the chief civilian negotiator on the U.S. side as assistant secretary of state for Europe, the origins of the Southern Command dispute go back to the fall of 1995.[8] At that time, the members of the alliance were engaging in wide discussions on the restructuring of NATO and the redefinition of the alliance's role in the post–Cold War world. This debate included the French, who were reconsidering their own position on NATO, now that the Cold War was over.

At this point, according to Kornblum, NATO members conceived a major innovation, which was the designation of a deputy

SACEUR, who would be a European, under the American SACEUR. In this new setup, the European deputy SACEUR would be able to use NATO military assets (communications, airlift capabilities, and so forth) for European operations in which the Americans would not want to or need to become involved. In the context of this new arrangement, the French informally gave their U.S. counterparts to understand that they would consider a return to the integrated command structure of NATO.[9]

Negotiations on the French-NATO relationship began in fall 1995 and were conducted in three different contexts: the NATO context, the bilateral French-U.S. context, and the context of the Quad (the United States, the United Kingdom, France, and Germany).[10] The Quad had originated as a discussion forum within NATO of the four countries focusing on Berlin and had evolved into a group that reviewed the international situation as a whole.

While the relationship of France to NATO was being discussed in the post–Cold War context, so was the relationship between the European Union and NATO. Often the two subjects overlapped. The European Union's Treaty of Maastricht, signed in 1992 and ratified in 1993, mentioned for the first time a Common Foreign and Security Policy (CFSP) that could lead eventually to a common defense for EU members. The NATO summit at Brussels in 1994 recognized the European Union's European Security and Defense Identity (ESDI), which was an outgrowth and an operationalization, at least in concept, of the CFSP.

According to Philippe Guelluy, who was diplomatic adviser to Defense Minister Charles Millon at the time, the experience in the former Yugoslavia was key in the French reevaluation of its strategic position. As the Bosnian war was being brought to a close, with the intervention of NATO, the French were participants in the operation but not members of the NATO command structure. French rethinking took the following shape:

> Europe could have a pro-NATO policy without developing a European Security and Defense Identity, but the reverse could not be true; that is, there could not be a European Security and Defense Identity that ignored NATO.
>
> Until that point, the European Security and Defense Identity had been conceived of as being *outside* NATO. During a second pe-

riod there was an attempt to do that *within* NATO. [But finally] a change had to be brought about so that this identity could be created [along] with NATO.[11]

The accession of Jacques Chirac as president in June 1995, just as the Bosnian war was heating up, provided a further impulsion to the French move back toward NATO. Chirac immediately became an advocate of a tough policy against the Bosnian Serbs, unlike his predecessor, François Mitterrand. The NATO intervention soon followed, and the war was swiftly brought to a close. In December 1995, a month after the Bosnian peace accords were achieved, France announced that it was returning to the Military Committee of NATO. This was a step toward a full return of France to NATO: the Military Committee was a policy body over the NATO military command structure but was not strictly speaking a part of the command. (Actually, France had remained on the Military Committee since its break with NATO in 1966 but not as a voting member.) As the negotiations proceeded, there were encouraging signs that France before long would rejoin the NATO integrated command. Kornblum, however, had the feeling that "things were going too well. We shouldn't assume this is easy," he told his French interlocutors.[12]

The French Team

From the French side, the initiative for a full return to NATO originated with a team of technocrats who sold the idea to the incoming president, Jacques Chirac, as well as to his prime minister, Alain Juppé, who had been foreign minister in the previous government.[13] Ultimately, however, according to a senior French defense official, the decision to consider a return to NATO was made at the highest level, by Chirac himself, who, unlike Mitterrand, was not known to be hostile toward NATO.[14] Chirac had long signaled his intention to revise the standoffish French position toward NATO. For instance, at a reception in honor of reserve officers in Paris on February 8, 1993, he had remarked that if France wanted

> to play a determining role in the creation of a European defense identity, it must take into account [the] state of mind of its partners, and reconsider to a large degree the form of its relations with NATO. It is clear, in effect, that the necessary rebalancing of relations within the

Atlantic Alliance, relying on existing European institutions such as the
WEU [Western European Union] can only take place from the inside,
not against the United States but in agreement with it.[15]

But while Chirac was favorably disposed to the idea of readjusting
France's relations with NATO, the majority of the French political class
did not support such a radical departure in French defense policy. On the
contrary, powerful elements within the political class were staunchly
opposed to France returning to NATO, notably the communists, the
"historic Gaullists" (sometimes referred to pejoratively as the "paleo-
Gaullists"), and the socialists, who had just lost the presidency to Chirac.
From the beginning, this lack of a political constituency in favor of a
return to NATO was a principal weakness of the French initiative.

At the working level, this initiative was in the hands of a group of
some twelve technocrats, all of whom knew one another well and
worked together in harmony. They included advisers from four elements of the government: the Élysée, Matignon, the Defense Ministry,
and the Quai d'Orsay. The French team hoped that it could convince the
French establishment that both a reform of NATO and a French return
to NATO could be accomplished. The team had two starting assumptions: first, France had to adjust itself to the reality of what was happen-
ing in Bosnia, where it was cooperating in a NATO intervention without
being a full member of NATO; second, France had to draw closer to
NATO if it was to persuade its major European partners, chiefly
Germany and Britain, to go along with its initiatives to create a
European defense entity. Approaching NATO would not only remove
the suspicions of France's European partners that it was trying to distance Europe from the United States but at the same time help France's
efforts to create a genuine European defense.

Overall, the French team sought to reform NATO by giving the
Europeans greater freedom of maneuver within the alliance, for example, in conducting by themselves operations with the support of NATO
in cases where the United States would not get involved. This ambition
reflected the French tendency to think in dialectical terms by taking two
opposites—a European defense identity and a U.S.-controlled NATO—
and generating from them a synthesis, which would involve greater freedom of action for the Europeans and greater freedom from U.S. domination—all of this within the context and the confines of a military

alliance. To most U.S. officials, however, the inherent paradox only served to strengthen the notion that the French were not being straight-forward, that they were trying only to undercut NATO and its sacrosanct principle of unity of command. Further, the Americans could not visualize many situations in which Europeans would run NATO-supported operations in which the United States would not want to become involved. Nevertheless, it was the *principle* of freedom of action and nondomination that the French were eager to assert.

The French team piloting the new initiative wanted to announce the first step toward a rapprochement with NATO in a dramatic way. This step, the return of France to the Military Committee of NATO, would be done by Foreign Minister Hervé de Charette at a meeting of the North Atlantic Council in Brussels in December 1995. The idea was to do this with panache, to surprise and impress the audience at Brussels, and thereby create a dynamic that would move the process forward.

The reaction to de Charette's announcement was indeed favorable. The European members of NATO were surprised and pleased, especially the British, who had long wanted to reform NATO, especially by streamlining the organization of the regional commands. The Germans were more hesitant and wanted time to study the French opening. The Americans, too, were pleased with the French approach. At last, the U.S. side felt, the French are coming to their senses; their real place is in NATO. But this alone was not the French goal, which remained the creation of a European defense identity. This initial misunderstanding set the stage for subsequent disagreement and discord. Chirac set out the French position on February 1, 1996, several weeks after the Brussels meeting:

> France is ready to assume its full share in this renovation process. She demonstrated this in announcing a few weeks ago her rapprochement with the military structures of the organization. And I wish to confirm today the spirit of open-mindedness and availability with which France approaches this adaptation of NATO, including the military side, as long as the European identity can assert itself fully therein.[16]

Following the meeting in Brussels in December 1995, the French team in Paris sought to make concrete the idea of a European defense identity within NATO. The team visualized creating a dormant but permanent European structure that could be activated when required and that would operate under the strategic command of the Western European Union (WEU). This structure would be for operations conducted by Europeans, using NATO assets, but in which the Americans would choose not to participate.

The Berlin Ministerial Meeting

After the French announcement at Brussels, the U.S., British, French, and German ambassadors to NATO met in Bonn to discuss follow-on steps. According to Errera, the French representative, he and his British counterpart, on returning from Bonn to Brussels, put their thoughts down on paper concerning the principles that would be involved in putting together an ESDI within the framework of the WEU but operating within NATO.[17]

In March and April 1996, the four ambassadors resumed discussions on the basis of the British-French draft and arrived at the text of a communiqué that would be issued at a NATO ministerial meeting in Berlin on June 3. The communiqué contained no brackets—that is, there were no disputed points—although the German ambassador's reaction to the British-French draft was more cautious, perhaps because it allowed for too much freedom of action for an ESDI.

The text arrived in Washington, where, it was assumed, officials had closely followed its evolution. This turned out not to be the case, and the result was that Washington in effect overruled the U.S. ambassador to NATO, Robert Hunter, in demanding that the text be revised. As it turned out, the amendments to the text were largely cosmetic, and the basic idea of organizing a European defense pillar around the WEU that would use NATO assets for conducting European-only operations—in other words, giving wide freedom of action to the Europeans—was retained. However, though the text largely stood intact, the political effect, in Errera's words, was "disastrous." In Washington, the text was viewed as a "holdup" of NATO led by the French and the British.[18]

A U.S. delegation, led by an obviously annoyed Secretary of State Warren Christopher, arrived in Berlin and the document was signed.

According to Gilles Delafon and Thomas Sancton, Christopher initially said, "I don't want to sign this blankety-blank communiqué."[19] But at the insistence of President Clinton, who wanted a settlement of the issue, the communiqué was adopted, and with it, principles that were acceptable to the French.[20] In Errera's view, it is necessary to keep this background in mind in order to understand the severe U.S. backlash that occurred later in the summer of 1996 when the French introduced yet another new proposal: giving the Southern Command to a European.

The Berlin communiqué made mention of "militarily coherent and effective forces capable of operating under the political control and strategic direction of the WEU," as well as "European command arrangements" that would permit the "rapid constitution" of such a "military force." Also, the WEU would use NATO capabilities and assets for missions to be performed by the WEU.[21] All this seemed not too far off from the French team's goal of creating a dormant structure that the WEU could activate and command.

In addition, the Berlin communiqué charged NATO's Military Committee with coming up with "recommendations for a military command structure better suited to current and future Euro-Atlantic security." With this evocation of the issue of NATO's internal reform, it was logical to assume, at least from the European point of view, and especially from the French perspective, that, a priori, reform was considered necessary.

In his speech at the Berlin ministerial meeting in June 1996, Foreign Minister de Charette said that he agreed with the principles advanced at the meeting. The French would wait and see how these principles would be put into practice. He added that he would not exclude the possibility that the French would return to NATO.

The French appear to have thought that a real turning point had taken place with the signing of the Berlin communiqué. The communiqué did not merely reaffirm the need to develop an ESDI but also acknowledged that the WEU could take charge of purely European operations, including the planning of them, while borrowing NATO assets for these purposes, such as communications, intelligence, and airlift.

It was following this moment, a moment of French euphoria at the end of the Berlin ministerial meeting, that things seemed to go sour, both in terms of the attributes of an ESDI and in terms of the internal reform of NATO. Although all sides at Berlin had accepted the principle of reforming NATO, the Americans in the aftermath held to the principle of unity of command—that is, that command responsibility should not be split. Among the Europeans, however, even the British (or so believed the French team) viewed the unity of command principle to be unacceptable as it made the NATO structure "too heavy" and "too American."

According to one U.S. negotiator involved, the U.S. approach could be summarized in the following formula: flexible on principles, firm on details.[22] But as previous chapters have noted, the French negotiating approach is typically very different: once the principle has been agreed upon, the details can be put into place in a more or less logical manner. This difference in approach helps explain the disappointment that was to follow the Berlin meeting: for the French, the principle of European-only operations under the strategic direction of the WEU, using NATO assets, had been achieved in the Berlin communiqué. The rest—that is, the details—would naturally fall into place.

In the viewpoint of the French team, new factors intervened to change the situation that the Berlin ministerial meeting seemed to have resolved. First, and under the rubric of the need for NATO reform, the French government raised the bidding by introducing a new demand—namely, that a European be given the Southern Command. Second, the "diehards" on the U.S. side sought to "take revenge" on what had been decided at Berlin. The result was that the consensus forged at Berlin fell apart. However, Kornblum, whom the French considered one of the U.S. diehards, maintains that this view represents a pronounced misreading of the situation, in that he himself had largely conceived the proposals of the Berlin ministerial meeting.[23]

The Raising of the Southern Command Issue

In the background to the French government's apparently sudden focus on the Southern Command in 1996 lay the fact that a restructuring of NATO commands was already in the offing. The changes, which became official in 1996 and effective from 1998, were the following: the number of strategic commands would remain at two—the Atlantic Command, headed by an American (Supreme Allied Commander Atlantic [SACLANT]), and the European Command, also headed by an American (Supreme Allied Commander Europe [SACEUR])—but the number of regional commands under the SACEUR would be reduced from three to two—the Northern Command, designated Allied Forces North Europe (AFNORTH) and located at Brunssum, the Netherlands, and the Southern Command, designated Allied Forces South Europe (AFSOUTH) and located at Naples, Italy.

In the new setup, German and British officers were to rotate between the positions of chief of the new Northern Command and the deputy SACEUR (DSACEUR). The Americans held on to the Southern Command. This left, in effect, no room for the French, who wanted something for themselves that would put them on a par with the British and the Germans, should France decide on a return to NATO. Hence the French came to focus on the Southern Command at Naples, which had jurisdiction over the Mediterranean. Among other things, a French presence in Naples would enhance the maritime cooperation among France, Italy, and Spain that had been launched in the 1990s under the EurMarFor (European Maritime Force) Program.[24]

Although the French phrased their proposal in terms of the Naples post going to a European rather than an American, they were clearly seeking the position for themselves. It seemed to them logical that because the other two top European positions, the Northern Command and the deputy SACEUR, alternated between the British and the Germans, the Southern Command should go to a Frenchman if the Americans relinquished the command to a European. According to European observers, the French made a tactical mistake in melding together their espousal of a greater role for Europe in NATO with that of a greater role for France in NATO. This only served to confuse the issue. The French should have made clear at the outset that what they were seeking—the Southern Command—was for themselves.[25]

But it was not just a question of finding some room for the French should they return to the integrated command. To make such a move would constitute on the internal French scene a "heavy political gesture," in the view of Errera. It would have to be explained in credible terms to French public opinion and especially to the French political class. When Charles de Gaulle left the integrated command thirty years earlier, claiming that power within NATO was skewed too heavily in favor of the United States, he was able to elicit public support for the move without much difficulty, despite the fact that the Soviet threat remained high. Now the Soviet threat had gone, but the power imbalance, which de Gaulle had so decried, remained. The Berlin ministerial meeting had begun a process of reform within NATO, but the integrated command structure was unaffected. Therefore, there would have to be a new threat, or else a thoroughgoing reform of the structure to correct the power imbalance within NATO, in order for the French public to be convinced that a return to the NATO military structure was necessary.[26]

The Role of the U.S. Sixth Fleet

Related to the issue of the Southern Command was the question of the U.S. Sixth Fleet in the Mediterranean. The U.S. admiral in charge of the Southern Command wears two hats. He is both a NATO commander, titled commander, Allied Forces South Europe (AFSOUTH), and headquartered at Naples, and a U.S. commander who commands U.S. Naval Forces in Europe and is headquartered in London. In the latter position, he comes under the U.S. European Command (USEUCOM), which is headquartered at Stuttgart.[27]

The Sixth Fleet remains under U.S. command (that of the U.S. Naval Forces in Europe) except in wartime, when it is placed under the jurisdiction of NATO and augments NATO's Standing Force Mediterranean (STANAVFORMED), a procedure that is known within NATO as a "transfer of authority." This arrangement might seem clear cut, but the reality is more ambiguous. For example, elements of the Sixth Fleet have supported NATO forces in Bosnia (IFOR and SFOR), which are under the command of AFSOUTH. But these elements play a *supporting* role, and therefore there is no transfer of authority to NATO. Nor was there any transfer of authority of the Sixth Fleet to NATO during the Kosovo campaign.[28] In fact, there has never been a transfer of authority from the Sixth Fleet to NATO throughout the history of the Atlantic Alliance.

Kornblum considered that the Berlin ministerial meeting had largely solved the problem of the relationship between NATO and a European security identity. He had an altogether different view of the Southern Command proposal, which the French raised officially in the weeks preceding the Berlin meeting. French officials told Kornblum that because the new aircraft carrier the *Charles-de-Gaulle* would deploy in the Mediterranean, where it would work alongside the U.S. Sixth Fleet, France would find it difficult to accept an American in command at Naples. Kornblum, who considered that the French, in their thirty years of absence, had forgotten how NATO worked, replied that all units in the Mediterranean remained under *national* control. To the French, this issue was not a minor one, considering the name of the ship and its military importance. Because the keystone of de Gaulle's policy was a rejection of the integrated command of NATO, it was difficult for the French to conceive of this ship being under a U.S. admiral in charge of NATO's Southern Command.[29] The fact that all fleet elements in the Mediterranean remain under national command seemed to be secondary to the French. What counted most was the *appearance* of a ship named the *Charles-de-Gaulle* being under NATO command, especially in the eyes of French public opinion.

According to the then chairman of NATO's Military Committee, General (Ret.) Klaus Naumann, the French ideas for changes in the alliance's command structures were first broached to him informally by the chief of staff of the French armed forces (CEMA), General Jean-Philippe Douin, in Brussels in the early summer of 1996.[30] Douin suggested to Naumann that the chairman of NATO's Military Committee should be an American and should be given full command authority. Under him should be a European SACEUR. Douin did not make clear the issue of the command of SACLANT. Naumann informed Douin at that time that there was little chance that the proposal would win approval by the Military Committee.

Ironically, the idea of a European SACEUR appears to have derived, at least in part, from a conversation in Norfolk, Virginia, between Douin and the SACLANT, General John Sheehan, during a visit of the French CEMA to the United States. As Errera relates it, General Sheehan intimated to General Douin that there was a U.S. plan to have a super *(grand)* commander in chief, an American, under whom there would be a SACLANT, who would also be an American, and a SACEUR, who would be a European.[31]

Two other factors appear to have been at play here to influence the French CEMA during his visit to the United States. The first was that, according to the French team, Douin's U.S. counterpart, General John Shalikashvili, led Douin to believe that even more far-reaching (though unspecified) reforms in NATO beyond those of Berlin would be possible. The second was the publication at this time of a RAND study recommending that, in the short term, Europeans take over the NATO commands that were on their territory.[32]

According to Errera, Douin returned to Paris and argued with President Chirac the merits of a European SACEUR. Chirac readily saw that this idea was something that could be explained to the French people as a good reason for reentering the NATO military structure.[33]

Chirac instructed his defense minister, Millon, to raise the idea with William Perry, the U.S. secretary of defense, during a visit to London in July 1996. Millon did so, and Perry, ever the gentleman, responded, "Why not? We could think about this."[34]

After Millon returned from London, a few people within the French government were momentarily elated, believing that the French proposal was going to be accepted. But in Washington, a veritable machine sprang into action to defeat the French idea. Those in the Pentagon and the State Department who had looked with disfavor on the concessions made at the Berlin ministerial meeting now effectively said (in Errera's characterization), "Enough is enough! *Nyet!*"[35] In August 1996 Perry notified Millon that the United States would not support a proposal to create a super-commander over the SACLANT and the SACEUR, and to appoint a European as the latter.[36]

Douin then met again with Naumann and presented a new French position: the Military Committee would be left the way it was, there would be no super-commander, and Americans would continue to occupy the SACLANT and SACEUR positions, but Europeans would receive better representation at the next level of command, with all regional command positions, including the Southern Command, going to Europeans. The Americans were not enthusiastic about this new idea.[37]

Letters Exchanged between Clinton and Chirac

In the meantime, in a letter to President Chirac dated August 14, 1996, President Clinton stressed the critical importance of NATO enlargement in the upcoming period while stating in general terms that he favored an adaptation of the Atlantic Alliance. Responding in a letter dated August 28, Chirac said that he understood the difficulty of setting up a new Euro-American high strategic command, headed by an American, under whom would be an American SACLANT and a European SACEUR, but that he would like to hear Clinton's opinion on it nevertheless and keep it open as an option for the future. As for the NATO regional commands in Europe, north and south—which should go to Europeans—France was ready to participate in them. It would be necessary in this connection to find an appropriate mechanism to solve the problem of the Sixth Fleet. Chirac concluded by stating that if these propositions were adopted, France "would be ready to take its place in this renovated Alliance."[38]

Chirac's August 28 letter caused consternation in Washington, where it was felt that substantial concessions had already been made to the French, particularly at the Berlin ministerial meeting.[39] On September 26, Clinton replied to Chirac, mentioning at the outset that he did not think that the idea of a new supreme command above the SACEUR and the SACLANT was feasible. He continued:

> Jacques, I must be frank. . . . Although I am in agreement overall with the idea of a rotation of commands at the regional and sub-regional levels, I cannot accept that this principle be applied to the Southern Command. . . . The weight of engagement of American forces, the stabilizing role of our presence in the region, and the need to guarantee public and political support here in the United States for the continuation of our military contribution to the Alliance—all this requires keeping an American commander at the head of the Southern Command.

The president concluded by assuring his counterpart that, following the implementation of the Berlin agreement, "other adaptations will be possible in order to reinforce the transatlantic partnership that we both desire."[40]

On October 10 Chirac sent a second letter to Clinton, stating that "giving the [Southern] Command to a European is part of a political and strategic vision," and that politically the posts given to Americans and Europeans should be in balance:

> In order that the new transatlantic partnership acquire its full signifi-
> cance, it is necessary to establish an equilibrium in the responsibilities
> within the Alliance. Since the two strategic commands of NATO
> (SACLANT and SACEUR) remain, for the foreseeable future, in
> American hands, it seems legitimate to me that the two regional com-
> mands be given to Europeans.
>
> [One must take into account] the new importance that the
> Europeans must accord to the Mediterranean world, which is so
> nearby to us. In demographic, economic, political, and strategic
> terms, the Mediterranean constitutes a major stake for Europe. It is
> indispensable for Europe and for the Alliance, that the Europeans
> assume their full responsibilities there, obviously in close associa-
> tion with the United States. The Euro-American partnership would
> be reinforced.[41]

At the bottom of the letter Chirac penned in the following: "Bill, this is very important to me."[42] Clinton did not reply to this second let-ter. However, in a speech in Chicago shortly thereafter, Clinton made the turndown explicit and public, declaring, "The United States will continue to be the leader of NATO, especially in the southern region."[43]

In the view of the French team, Chirac's request had not been unreasonable. Further, the team considered that Chirac's overall strategic initiative of a return to NATO, of which the Southern Command formed a part, deserved a hearing and should not have been treated by the Americans "as if it were the end of the world."

What may have seemed reasonable to the French was quite unacceptable to the Americans, who had the impression, rightly or wrongly, that the French were overreaching. Moreover, the French had engaged in their passion for unilateral diplomacy. Chirac had sent his missive on August 28 without preconsultations with his principal allies, although he did send a copy to British prime minister John Major and German chancellor Helmut Kohl. It turned out that not all the allies were in favor of Chirac's Southern Command proposal. The

British, as usual, were loath to fall out of step with the Americans. The Germans, in the person of Defense Minister Volker Rühe, supported the French position in a NATO defense ministers meeting on September 25 at Bergen, Norway, to the displeasure of his U.S. counterpart, William Perry. The Turks wanted the Americans to remain in command at Naples because Ankara needed them as mediators in Turkey's disputes with Greece. The Italian position was ambiguous: the Italians said to the French that they supported the French idea but then telephoned Washington recommending rejection of the French proposal.[44] (The French had not told the Italians about Chirac's démarches; the Italians were subsequently informed by Washington.)[45]

Against the advice of some of his advisers, Chirac had gone straight to the top, to his counterpart, Clinton, in making the Southern Command request.[46] In so doing, Chirac bypassed not only the normal diplomatic channels but the military channels as well, even though the issues concerned first and foremost the military. This bypassing of the military had been a problem at the Berlin ministerial meeting of June 1996, whose communiqué had basically been worked out by the NATO ambassadors, and in the wake of which the U.S. chairman of the Joint Chiefs of Staff, John Shalikashvili, reportedly commented, "The ambassadors have won a battle but not the war."[47] Chirac's initiative reflected the French lack of awareness of how the position of the military in their country differed from that of the military in the United States, where the chairman of the Joint Chiefs of Staff can exercise considerable influence in Washington power struggles if he chooses to do so.

In retrospect, members of the French team consider that their plan was overoptimistic. They had not anticipated that Chirac's August 28 letter would prompt the Americans to get tough. The diehards had decided, "Let's cut them [the French] down to size." The diehards' eagerness to teach the French a lesson was accentuated by a developing crisis over Iraq, which culminated in France refusing to extend the no-fly zone in southern Iraq from the 32d to the 33d parallel (see the following case study). The hard-liners found significant support in Washington, where many feared that the French were trying to insert themselves between Washington and the Sixth Fleet.

Strong feelings developed on Capitol Hill, notably in the House and Senate Armed Services Committees, which have tended to regard the navy as the "pearl" of the U.S. armed forces.[48]

In the fall of 1996 the French witnessed what they saw as an orchestrated campaign in the U.S. press against Chirac's proposal—what several French officials have referred to as a "carpet bombing"—including reports claiming that the French wanted to take control of the U.S. Sixth Fleet.[49] Kornblum, however, dismisses notions of an orchestrated press offensive, claiming, "The U.S. isn't disciplined enough to conduct a press campaign."[50]

The U.S. rejection of the French proposal was made yet more emphatic when the new defense secretary, William Cohen, reaffirmed it before the U.S. Congress in early 1997: "It's clear. It's categoric. It is not negotiable."[51] At the same time, several members of Congress made disparaging remarks publicly about the French.

The affair turned out to be acutely embarrassing to the French government, and particularly to Chirac, who had invested his personal prestige in the matter. Members of the French military reacted sharply to the U.S. demurrer: they considered it untenable for France to return to NATO without any changes being made in NATO's structure. The French government's reaction, however, was one of immobility: it had advanced a proposal that it considered to be reasonable and had no backup plan in case that proposal was rejected. There were no tactical movements from the French team for four to six weeks.

A Search for Other Solutions

It took some time for tempers to cool in Washington and Paris in the fall of 1996. French team members, thrown off stride by the blunt and public U.S. refusal, came to the view that they had better swallow their pride. They tried coming up with other solutions, such as splitting the Southern Command in two, and they sought to win the other Europeans to their point of view. At the same time, Chirac's diplomatic adviser, Jean-David Levitte, was sent to Washington to defuse tensions.

In December 1996, however, relations were further strained by the alleged public "walkout" by Hervé de Charette during a toast in Brussels given by the NATO secretary-general, Javier Solana, in honor of Warren Christopher, who was stepping down as secretary of state. The reality was that de Charette was in the middle of a press conference, which he had already left once, and he had to return to it. However, the U.S. press interpreted de Charette's exit as a snub of Christopher.

Robert Hunter, former U.S. ambassador to NATO, considers in retrospect that a compromise could have been worked out with his French counterpart, Errera, if they had been allowed to continue their negotiations.[52] However, the matter was taken over in early 1997 by the White House and the Élysée, the former in the person of National Security Adviser Sandy Berger and the latter in that of Jean-David Levitte.

One prospect held out to the French, stated Hunter, was that the issue of the Southern Command could be revisited later, if the Europeans first demonstrated that they were pulling their weight militarily in the Mediterranean.[53] The basic U.S. position, according to Hunter, was "What do we have to offer the French and still keep the Southern Command?" One of the compromises envisioned was the creation, under French command, of a second Rapid Reaction Corps headquarters similar to the one that had been created in NATO's Northern Command (AFNORTH) area.[54] However, any compromise that did not include appointing a Frenchman as head of the Southern Command was contrary to the French vision of a future European security structure and was thus unacceptable.

Hunter's assertions are borne out by Naumann, who, following the U.S. rejection of Chirac's proposal, worked with Shalikashvili to come up with a compromise. What they subsequently presented to Shalikashvili's counterpart, Douin, and to Errera was the following: the Southern Command would remain in the charge of an American; the European mission of the deputy commander at Naples would be strengthened; and the issue of who would be in charge of the Southern Command would be reviewed in a couple of years, on the condition that the Europeans increase their military capability in the Mediterranean in the meantime. It was not easy to persuade Washington to agree to the review clause, but this was finally achieved. Douin gave the impression that this compromise would be acceptable to the French.[55]

In Naumann's account, the stage was set for finalizing the compromise during the Denver economic summit of the G-8, due to start on June 20, 1997, at which time there would be a bilateral meeting between Presidents Chirac and Clinton. Chirac would raise the issue

and Clinton would respond with the offer. According to what Shalikashvili told Naumann, Clinton had the compromise proposal in writing in his pocket. However, in their meeting, Chirac did not raise the
issue, and the matter died there.[56] According to Admiral Jacques Lanxade, who confirmed what he called this "unofficial compromise" plan,
the matter was not handled well at the level below the chiefs of state.[57]

The U.S. military seemed to place much stock in the renewed
negotiations of early 1997, considering that the compromise being
worked out could have resulted in a full return of France to NATO. A
State Department official intimately connected with the NATO process
echoes this view. According to him, Chirac's government held out the
possibility that France might rejoin the NATO military structure at the
time of the Madrid NATO summit, due to start on July 8, 1997.[58]

Whatever commitments the French government may have made
in the spring of 1997, the situation was suddenly changed when
Chirac decided to hold a legislative election in May 1997, which his
party, the Rally for the Republic (RPR), proceeded to lose. Chirac's
lack of sound political judgment in scheduling an early election while
still enjoying a parliamentary majority ushered in a third period of
cohabitation in France in the space of a dozen years, with the socialists leading a coalition government. Thus, by the time of the Denver
G-8 summit, Chirac had lost his majority in the National Assembly.
He probably decided that a compromise over NATO was now impossible and that it was useless even to raise the matter with Clinton.
(Chirac may not even have liked the plan in Clinton's pocket, for what
the United States was prepared to give—limited flexibility on
European-led operations, and a commitment for a later review of the
Southern Command issue—was distinctly short of what the French
had envisaged as the price of their return to the NATO structure.) The
new prime minister, Lionel Jospin, and foreign minister, Hubert
Védrine, had both consistently criticized Chirac's rapprochement with
NATO. For instance, in a statement to Agence France Presse on
February 4, 1996, Jospin said that he had aligned himself with
Mitterrand's position, that he was "not favorable" toward the rapprochement of France with NATO, and that he hoped that France's
"autonomy of decision" would be oriented toward the construction of
a European defense system.[59]

According to the State Department official cited earlier, "There was no way that a cohabitation government could have secured a return [to the integrated command]."[60] However, while the prospective French return to NATO remained stalemated, the French retained their *"acquis"* (benefits): membership on the Military Committee, attendance at defense ministers' meetings, and a presence on NATO's International Military Staff.[61]

In retrospect, the French team concluded that an independent European defense capability would have come anyway, as it is now slowly being created, and that Mitterrand was right in refusing to consider rejoining NATO's integrated command. The incident over the Southern Command reinforced French suspicions of U.S. dominance of NATO, suspicions that were further accentuated by the subsequent disputes between the Americans and the French over NATO's conduct of the war in Kosovo. In the French team's view, a future French president will think twice before undertaking a new French rapprochement with NATO; the team members also believe that if Clinton had shown some consideration for Chirac's proposal, instead of turning it down flat, the two sides might have found a way to overcome their difficulties.

Most U.S. officials seem to consider that the French raised the Southern Command issue for the sole purpose of enhancing their prestige and stature. Furthermore, the subsequent experience of the war in Kosovo, NATO's first war, served only to sharpen the perception among U.S. officials, particularly senior military officers, that the only way to run a war is with the United States in charge. After witnessing the constraints of the unanimity rule in NATO's supreme political body, the North Atlantic Council, the U.S. military concluded that when it came to an actual war, NATO could become as much of a political encumbrance as it was an effective military instrument. Sharp differences arose within the North Atlantic Council, particularly between the Americans and the French, about which targets in Serbia should or should not be hit. These differences were reflected in a remark after the war attributed to General Michael Short, NATO's joint air force component commander, that "a country that furnished eight percent of the overall [air] effort over the Balkans should not be in a position to restrain American pilots who were carrying 70 per cent of the load."[62] Short was clearly referring to France. On the French side, notably among the French military, there was a sense of relief that the French had remained outside the NATO military structure, in view of the perceived high-handedness of the Americans in the conduct of the war in Kosovo.

Conclusion

This case illustrates a number of characteristic features of French negotiating behavior, not least the French capacity to set a long-term goal, argue deductively, be confident of the logic of their approach, and yet also value form over content and act audaciously. In this instance, the French long-term objective was a return to NATO that would result in greater autonomy for Europe from the United States and a greater role for France within the Atlantic Alliance. The French showed themselves capable of judging clearly what U.S. actions would or would not be compatible with this goal as against what offers were basically cosmetic. In this regard, Robert Hunter's formulation of "What do we have to offer the French and still keep the Southern Command?"[63] illustrates the wide gap in the positions of the two sides.

Adopting a typically deductive approach, the French established clear principles—the need for freedom of action for an ESDI within NATO and a reform of the NATO command structures. These were stipulated or at least evoked at the Berlin ministerial meeting, and the French then expected the details to fall into place. At the same time, they convinced themselves of the irrefutable logic of their own position, namely, that if France were to return to NATO, it should of course expect something from NATO in return, and that for various reasons (among them the long-standing French interest in the Mediterranean region and the fact that other command positions were already shared by the Americans, British, and Germans) the Southern Command was the most appropriate quid pro quo. France, as one of the three major European members of NATO, could surely not be expected to return to NATO's military structure and meekly join the back of the line, so to speak, for command positions. Confident, or so it seems, that their negotiating partners would likewise see the French position as unassailably logical, the French made no contingency plans in case the other side rejected their demand for the Southern Command. Thus, when the United States publicly and unambiguously did just that, the

French government initially responded by doing nothing, as though shocked into immobility.

Characteristically, too, the French were attracted to the Southern Command no less for its symbolic than for its operational power. The command at Naples was enticing because it signified France's ambition to be the preeminent European power in the Mediterranean zone, where the new French aircraft carrier, named, of all things, the *Charles-de-Gaulle*, would be operating. With a penchant for panache and audacious action, the French seized on the Southern Command idea and escalated their demands in the middle of the negotiations on NATO reform by asking specifically for the Naples post, which had been in U.S. hands since the beginning of the alliance. The "hussar" Chirac may not have fully realized that the Naples post was sacrosanct to the Americans, who wanted to maintain total and unambiguous control all along a chain of command that ran from Washington down to the Sixth Fleet, with its component of nuclear submarines.

This case also demonstrates the French readiness, even eagerness, to act alone. Chirac appears not to have consulted his principal European allies before he decided to send a letter to Clinton asking for the Southern Command, although, as noted earlier, he did send a copy of his letter to Prime Minister John Major and Chancellor Helmut Kohl, who were the leaders most concerned in the event of a redistribution of the major NATO positions.

It should be noted that, despite the humiliating outcome of its attempt to secure the Southern Command, France's long-term goal was by no means a foolish one. Had France secured its aims, the result would have been a greater role for Europe in the alliance and the prospect of strategic harmony between Europe and the United States. It was U.S. hegemonism more than French self-delusion that stood in the way of an agreement that would have benefited all parties over the long term. The United States, through its military presence in Europe as the commanding power in NATO, had become accustomed to a position of strategic preeminence. Former national security adviser Zbigniew Brzezinski, with characteristic crispness, has even gone so far as to describe Europe as "a de facto military protectorate of the United States."[64] Thus not only was it difficult for the United States to accept a greater role for Europe within the Atlantic Alliance and specifically a greater role for France; it was also difficult for many of the other NATO partners to do so, having been so long accustomed to U.S. dominance of the alliance.

CASE 2: NEGOTIATIONS AT THE UNITED NATIONS OVER WEAPONS INSPECTIONS IN IRAQ (1999–2003)

Overview

This case traces the attempt to revive the weapons inspections regime in Iraq in the late 1990s and how this attempt eventually led to war in March 2003. The emphasis is on debates within the UN Security Council and in particular the negotiations and the impasses that occurred there between the United States and France. Three principal events took place in the Security Council: Resolution 1284 of December 1999 set up the new inspections regime (United Nations Monitoring Verification and Inspections Commission [UNMOVIC]) and replaced the old one (United Nations Special Commission on Iraq [UNSCOM]); Resolution 1441 of November 2002 paved the way for the inspectors to return to Iraq; and a follow-on resolution was presented in February 2003 that would have sanctioned military measures against Iraq but was withdrawn because there was not a majority for it in the Security Council.

The outcome was that on March 20, 2003, the Americans and the British went to war against Iraq without specific Security Council approval and over the objections of four other major powers: France, Germany, Russia, and China. It also led to the worst-ever crisis in the bilateral relationship between the two "oldest allies" in the Western world, the United States and France, as Washington accused Paris of leading the charge against a UN endorsement for going to war. In the words of Walter Russell Mead, speaking at a conference in May 2003, "unfortunately, the result in American opinion of what's happened in the last few months, is that it is now much more plausible in the United States to think of France as a cunning enemy rather than as a difficult friend."[65] This is bound to have an effect on how each side views the other's negotiators in the future.

The question to be asked is how such an impasse in French-

American relations could have developed. How could it have come about that, following the Iraq war, President Bush's national security adviser, Condoleezza Rice, stated publicly that the administration's formula for the future was to "punish France, ignore Germany and forgive Russia."[66] George Bush himself said he did not expect that Jacques Chirac would be visiting the Crawford Ranch in Texas "anytime soon." Even Colin Powell, the leading moderate in the Bush administration, said there would be "consequences" for France, prompting the following observation by Philippe Roger, author of *L'Ennemi américain:*

> There is a key phrase in the American response to the situation, which has been, "there will be consequences," and I found it extremely interesting that this phrase, which is being widely replayed by the French press, has struck the French enormously, and I think . . . for one good reason, which is that for more than a century, the French practiced anti-Americanism with the secret idea that there would be no consequences.[67]

Part of the reason for this downturn in relations was that a warm relationship between President Bush and President Chirac was lacking. Chirac's visit to Washington right after 9/11, hailed in public as a welcome demonstration of friendship, had been scheduled beforehand and did not produce useful chemistry between the two leaders. After Dominique de Villepin's "sandbagging" speech on January 20, 2003, in which he threatened for the first time to veto a resolution for going to war, catching Colin Powell unawares, the bilateral relationship went steadily downhill. Still, Bush did not have the personal animus against Chirac that he had against Gerhard Schröder, who, Bush maintained, had lied to him about supporting the war in Iraq.[68] Bush reconciled with Schröder at the United Nations in September 2003.

That what can arguably be called the worst crisis ever in French-American relations could have happened under a French president who is basically not anti-American (unlike a number of his predecessors) is only one of the paradoxes in this strange turn of events. But this French president, Jacques Chirac, is also an opportunist, in the clearly political sense that he is mindful of his public opinion—overwhelmingly against a war in Iraq, as was the rest of Europe—and also mindful of the opportunity that the situation offered up to him to advance his political interests and those of his party, reconstituted in 2002 as the Union for a Presidential Majority (UMP). Talk of yet another presidential run by Chirac in 2007 did not surface until his prestige rose with his opposition to the U.S.-led war in Iraq.

The train wreck in the bilateral relationship, however, goes far beyond personalities. In a larger sense, it is a reflection of the loosening of ties between the United States and Europe since the end of the Cold War and also of the growing hostility in European public opinion against the unilateralist policies of the Bush administration over such issues as the Kyoto Protocol and the International Criminal Court.[69]

Clearly, there were errors on both sides. "We have had our share of mistakes," admits a senior Bush administration official. "But fundamentally we have fallen victim to a different reading from many of our friends about the necessity of dealing with the problem of Iraq."[70] Here we come back to an endemic fact in French-American relations: a distrust of the other's motives and a lack of intimate knowledge of the other's intentions.

The Inspection Regime in Iraq

In 1991 the Security Council's Resolution 687 set up the United Nations Special Commission on Iraq (UNSCOM) as part of the ceasefire arrangements that emerged from the Persian Gulf War. Among the provisions of Resolution 687 was the authorization to use force against Iraq if necessary to bring peace to the region. The purpose of UNSCOM was to detect and destroy Iraq's chemical and biological weapons of mass destruction (WMD) and medium-range missile programs. The International Atomic Energy Agency (IAEA), part of the UN system of organizations, was charged with detecting and destroying Iraq's nuclear weapons. As long as this inspection process remained uncompleted, economic sanctions were imposed on Iraq.

The UNSCOM regime for the inspection of WMD functioned for more than seven years. It accomplished much in the destruction of Iraqi WMD, but it was not 100 percent successful, and it ran into more and more difficulties as it came close to locating Saddam Hussein's most vital stocks of weapons. The verdict of Patricia Lewis, director of

the United Nations Institute for Disarmament Research (UNIDIR), is
as follows:

> [UNSCOM learned] most, but not all, of what there was to know
> about Iraq's nuclear, chemical and biological weapons and medium-
> range missile programs. Despite gaps in the UNSCOM knowledge,
> particularly on biological weapons and aspects of the missile pro-
> gram, much of the information had been pieced together. Although
> Iraq still maintained the capability to re-establish its WMD devel-
> opment program, the material and technologies had been destroyed
> and were, to a large extent, still being denied by the supplier states.[71]

As Lewis also points out, UNSCOM was never intended to continue for very long: "Following the end of the Gulf War, most states
and analysts believed—naively perhaps—that following Iraqi declara-
tions and some minor cat and mouse play, the work would be all but
over within one to two years."[72]

However, the inspections dragged on, and correspondingly the
sanctions remained in force. This gave rise to international pressures
that something had to be done to alleviate the suffering of the Iraqi
people. Therefore, on April 14, 1995, the UN Security Council adopted
an "Oil-for-Food" program through Resolution 986. Iraq finally, in
December 1996, agreed to implement the resolution. One of the provisions of Resolution 986 was that the program had to be approved
for renewal every six months by the Security Council.[73]

Under this program, goods purchased by Iraq in return for Iraqi
oil output were provided on the basis of contracts let by the Iraqi government, and these contracts were initially awarded mainly to Russian
and French business clients. The process was supervised by the United
Nations, which controlled the disbursements out of an escrow fund
based on receipts from Iraqi oil sales. Out of this fund also came payments for the expenses of UNSCOM activities in Iraq.[74]

Gradually, the Oil-for-Food program developed into the idea of
"smart sanctions," a proposal the Clinton administration put forward
(and the Bush administration continued). The smart sanctions plan
established a Goods Review List consisting of those items, mainly of a
military or dual-use (i.e., military and civilian) nature, that a special
UN sanctions committee, known as the Committee of the Whole, had

to review and endorse before the Iraqi government could award contracts. Transactions on all other items outside the military or dual-use category could take place automatically.[75]

Australian diplomat Richard Butler took over as executive chairman of UNSCOM in 1997, replacing Rolf Ekeus, a Swedish diplomat who later became ambassador to Washington. From that point onward, relations between UNSCOM and the Iraqis deteriorated sharply. The French, the Russians, and others reproached Butler for failing to consult them, for his high-profile contacts with the U.S. leadership, and for the cowboylike intrusiveness of some of his inspectors. But in truth, as Butler's former deputy, U.S. civil servant Charles Duelfer, points out, UNSCOM's role was exceedingly difficult: a mission of "coercive disarmament" carried out by "an international staff in the absence of a military occupation."[76]

French Interests in Iraq

U.S. officials, and the informed public in general, seemed uniformly fixed in the notion that France was interested in Iraq primarily for the purpose of commercial gain. According to the former number-three official in the Clinton White House, Ambassador Nancy Soderberg, speaking in early 2002, "The French are in part driven by commercial interests in Iraq. If the sanctions were lifted, France would be in a position to obtain substantial contracts."[77] (This statement refers to the large, if unsigned, contract for oil exploration in the Bin Umar and Majnoun fields in southern Iraq, estimated to contain thirty billion barrels[78] and earmarked for the French oil conglomerate TotalFinaElf. The French had arranged this contract with the government of Saddam Hussein before the sanctions went into effect following the Gulf War of 1990–91.)

The widespread U.S. presumption that France's interest in Iraq was mostly commercial makes the French bristle, even those with a history of dealing closely and amicably with U.S. officials. In January 2002, Jean-David Levitte, former diplomatic adviser of Jacques Chirac in the Élysée, former ambassador to the United Nations, and now ambassador to Washington, made the following observation:

> I have always found unjust the idea that the French have only commercial aims in mind regarding Iraq. We have economic interests, as

does the United States and everyone else, but the fact is that Iraq is a very minor trading partner of France. Two-thirds of France's foreign trade is with the European Union; three-quarters of it is with the European Union and the other states of the Organization for Cooperation and Development in Europe [OCDE]; and the last quarter consists of imports of raw materials, but Iraq represents very little in this respect.[79]

As Levitte says later, "In all, France's trade with Iraq represents only 0.2 percent of its worldwide trade."[80]

Kenneth Pollack, director of Persian Gulf affairs at the National Security Council at the time and author of *The Threatening Storm*,[81] takes a different view:

> The French claim of low economic interest in Iraq is an obfuscation. France is the second-largest purveyor of Oil-for-Food contracts; the Russians only recently passed them on this score. France is Iraq's second-largest trading partner. The French export to Iraq raw materials, agricultural products, and oil machinery.[82]

According to *Le Monde*, French exports to Iraq amounted to 660 million euros in 2001, divided mainly among capital goods (50 percent), automobile parts (20 percent), and agricultural products (6 percent). France went from having been the largest beneficiary of the Oil-for-Food contracts, with 10 percent, to being the eighth, behind Russia and a number of Arab countries.[83] (Levitte says that by early 2003 France was down to thirteenth place on the list.)[84] According to Dennis Halliday, a former UN official and an expert on Iraq, at the end of the war pending contracts under the Oil-for-Food program amounted to $1.5 billion for Russia and $300 million for France.[85]

In the middle between Ambassador Levitte and Kenneth Pollack is Bruce Riedel, who was the White House official in charge of the overall Middle East dossier at the time of the negotiations over the creation of UNMOVIC in 1999:

> Business interests were a part of the French concern, but I think only a part. Their leadership wanted to show distance from American policy toward Iraq for both global and Arab reasons, and their domestic politics was much more affected by Iraqi propaganda about the impact of sanctions [on the Iraqi population], given the fact that there are almost five million Arabs resident in France now.[86]

After the Six Day War of 1967, which began when Israel launched a preemptive military attack on Egypt and Syria despite Charles de Gaulle's warning not to do so, France ended its arms relationship with the Jewish state and embarked on a pro-Arab policy that has continued to this day. The French government drew up arms contracts with various Arab governments, including Iraq. A France-Iraq Friendship Association sprang up, led by the hypernationalist Jean-Pierre Chevènement, who advanced the notion that Saddam Hussein, being a secular leader, constituted a bulwark against Islamic fundamentalism in the region, particularly that coming from Iran. Chevènement was later to resign as defense minister in protest against France's participation in the 1991 Gulf War against Iraq. (Before the war against Iraq in March-April 2003, in which France did not take part, the French government provided the United States and the United Kingdom with lists of weapons systems that it had sold to Iraq before the embargo.)[87]

Resolution 1284: 1999

On December 15, 1998, Richard Butler ordered the UNSCOM mission out of Iraq for what turned out to be the last time. The following day he submitted a report to the United Nations to the effect that his mission could not be carried out because of Iraqi obstruction. A four-day Anglo-American bombing campaign, named Operation Desert Fox, began on the same day, December 16. The French reaction to this sudden turn of events was extreme chagrin, as Levitte describes:

> Butler, with the agreement of the Americans, in the midst of a crisis that was a little more serious than the others, but not much more, took the initiative to inform the inspectors that they should leave Iraq. It was he, and not the Iraqis, who asked for their departure. The Security Council had not been informed or consulted by Butler, though I think that the Americans were completely informed. One could understand the withdrawal of the inspectors at the moment that significant bombing was resumed, as otherwise some of the inspectors might be killed. And this is why President Chirac telephoned regularly to President Clinton to warn him about this spiral of events, which logically would lead to the departure of the inspectors. But we very much hold it against Butler because, since he had not consulted us, we did not have the time for a final telephone call to President Clinton. And when daybreak came, the departure of the

planes was already under way and the bombing began. As a result, during the following three years there were no inspections in Iraq, and Saddam Hussein was in a position to develop more freely his programs of arms of mass destruction.[88]

After the Anglo-American bombing in December 1998, it was apparent that Iraq would have nothing further to do with UNSCOM. Accordingly, negotiations began in the UN Security Council over the issue of abolishing UNSCOM and creating a new inspections regime, with the British taking the lead in putting together a resolution. Extended negotiations followed, in which the British made concessions to the French that they then took to Washington for approval. The British resolution (No. 1284) was put to a vote on December 17, 1999. It passed in the Security Council, 11-0, but with four abstentions: Russia, China, Malaysia, and, surprisingly, France. Despite a phone call from President Clinton to President Chirac, the French abstained, apparently, in the U.S. view, because they did not want to be less of a friend to Iraq than the Russians, who were expected to abstain. The French point of view, on the other hand, was that the United States pushed the resolution to a vote precipitously. The Americans wound up thinking that the French had been stringing them along.[89]

In the view of French civil servant Gilles Andréani, the affair of Resolution 1284 was a "near miss." Although the French in the end abstained, they were within "two or three small changes" of voting for the resolution when the U.S. ambassador to the United Nations, Bill Richardson, suddenly left New York for Washington and the compromise fell through.[90] Bruce Riedel contests this notion that the United States was pushing too hard for a vote:

> These negotiations took place over a very long period of time, months, not weeks. Thus it is hard to argue there was insufficient time to reach agreement. We went back and forth between Washington, London, Paris, etc. over quite a prolonged period. Both sides had an excellent understanding of the other's viewpoints.[91]

The verdict of Kenneth Pollack is harsh:

> The British were running the technical aspects of the resolution and were dictating the rhythm of the negotiations. They had brokered a

deal between the U.S. and the French and considered they were ready to put it to a vote. They were disappointed with the outcome. They had wanted a 13-0-2 vote. They had expected Russia and China to abstain. A French yes vote would have been a huge plus. The U.S. would then have been able to say to the French, "It's your responsibility to get Saddam to comply." Overall, the feeling was that the U.S. had been betrayed by the French, as the French had told the U.S. beforehand that they would vote for the resolution.[92]

Riedel believes that the negotiation was long and difficult and the outcome was uncertain:

> I would describe the endgame as neither too fast nor a double cross. We all knew from the beginning that the issues dividing Paris and Washington (and London) were serious, and that agreement might not be possible in the final analysis. We went as far as we felt we could and then said to the rest of the UN Security Council, this is what we think is the bottom line. We knew we would have a majority because we worked the ten nonpermanent members very hard. We were disappointed the French did abstain but not shocked. We were fundamentally satisfied with the status quo and UNSCOM, so if others wanted change, we had to be convinced of its wisdom.[93]

Both Riedel and Pollack detected a difference in the French point of view, depending on which part of the Quai d'Orsay they were dealing with. In Riedel's account:

> What became clear to us very early on was that the French were somewhat divided on how to proceed. The section of the Quai that dealt with international organizations [IO], was much more sympathetic to our view that the new rebadged inspection regime, UNMOVIC, had to have all the rights and powers of its predecessor, UNSCOM, and the right to go anywhere anytime. The NEA [Near East] section of the Quai was much more sympathetic to the Iraqis, indeed its Assistant Secretary equivalent had just returned from a tour as Ambassador in Baghdad and wanted a toothless regime with the power to recommend early sanctions relief. We tried to use this division to our advantage by working most closely with the IO section.[94]

On Resolution 1284 itself, the French persist in the view that the Anglo-Americans precipitated the vote, which might otherwise have resulted in the French endorsing the text. According to Levitte:

Resolution 1284 [was preceded by] a very long negotiation which lasted for nearly a year, on each paragraph, on each comma, and we came almost to the end. At that point the British and the Americans wanted to bring it to a vote because they were fed up with the length of the negotiation. We, the French, wanted to vote in favor of the resolution but we wanted the resolution to be sufficiently clear, so that it could be applied.

Unfortunately the vote was precipitated. President Chirac telephoned to President Clinton and Tony Blair to say to them, "Don't push this to a vote. Give us a little more time, give us another week, and we should be able to clarify the ambiguities" But the Americans did not want to clarify the ambiguities. I think they honestly did not want to see the inspectors return to Iraq, for the simple reason that when the inspectors are in Iraq, it is a recipe for repeated crises. And when the inspectors are not in Iraq, one is less well informed but one is freer to act in the military domain.

Perhaps I am too Machiavellian, but I think that the U.S. did not want to have a favorable vote by France, Russia, and China, because that could have convinced Saddam Hussein to accept the return of the inspectors. What the U.S. sought was not the return of the inspectors but the support of the international community for the next stage of bombing. If France had said that the clarifications were sufficient, the other two, Russia and China, would have voted in favor. Not because they "follow" us but because they were thinking along the same lines [on this issue].[95]

Ironically, Levitte added, a follow-on Security Council resolution, No. 1382, which was adopted at the end of November 2001 and passed unanimously, was for the purpose of ameliorating the Oil-for-Food program and of clarifying the ambiguities in the preceding Resolution 1284: "And so, two years later the Americans themselves proposed [that there be a clarification]."[96]

In his memoir on his experience as executive chairman of UNSCOM, Richard Butler provides a markedly different version than Levitte's:

A vote on adoption of [Resolution 1284] was scheduled for the week of December 13, 1999. . . . Russia had finally settled on a strategy of abstention. . . . When Russia's strategy became known, France asked that the vote be delayed for further consultations. It was a

> move inspired by French panic. France had planned to approve the
> resolution. But it was crucial, in its view, to leave no daylight
> between France and Russia on any question related to Iraq. . . . The
> major French oil [conglomerate, TotalFinaElf], had signed massive
> contracts with the Iraqi oil industry; in addition, only two weeks ear-
> lier articles in the Iraqi government press had threatened to void
> those contracts if France didn't support [the Iraqi position].
>
> Thus the French couldn't afford to let the Russians posture as
> Iraq's only true friend on the Security Council. They used the time-
> out to try to convince the Russians to vote in favor of the resolution.
> . . . However, Russia decided not to budge, so France made its choice
> and went along with Russia (and Iraq).[97]

Putting aside accusations of bad faith and even a "double-cross,"
one is tempted to ascribe this difference of views between France and
the United States on what to do about Iraq as not merely a common
desire to be on opposite sides of an issue but, more importantly, a
divergence in strategic culture between the United States and Europe
that several authors have recently discerned. Bruce Riedel illustrates
this divergence with what he calls the "line of force" argument:

> The tension between Washington and Paris was over how much
> incentive to build into the new [UNMOVIC] system to encourage
> Iraqi cooperation. Our view was to keep the incentives minimal,
> given the past record of the Iraqis in exploiting any loopholes and
> in overall noncompliance. By 1999, if not much earlier, Washington
> believed Saddam would never comply with the inspection regime
> and thus we needed a more robust policy.[98]

Riedel's "line of force" argument contrasts with what could be
called the "rationalist" approach of the French, as Levitte observes:

> [In the bilateral dialogue between the United States and France],
> there were periods of crisis that were rather severe, and periods of
> calm. Our theme was always the same. First, one must not be per-
> fectionist in the inspections to the point where it becomes unrealis-
> tic. Iraq is as large a country as France. Once 95 percent of Iraqi
> arms have been destroyed, with a leader like Saddam Hussein who
> cheats, it is very difficult to find the remaining five percent, which
> are in little bottles, in little reservoirs, of chemical and biological
> weapons which can be concealed under an armchair. This is why it

was important to maintain in Iraq the teams of inspectors and all the ongoing control mechanisms. Such a solution was certainly not ideal, but it was better than having no control at all over Iraq's programs. Furthermore, the inspectors destroyed between 1991 and 1998 more weapons of mass destruction than was the case during the Gulf War itself.[99]

The French, with their implacable logic, did not see Resolution 1284 leading to a negotiated solution with Iraq because it left open too many questions, particularly on the timing of the lifting of the sanctions, which was unclear. Therefore, the resolution offered little incentive for the Iraqis to comply with the inspections. Here we come back to the French preference for political over military solutions in international relations, and the increasingly opposite proclivity of the Americans; and this in turn leads us back to the Robert Kagan formula (cited in chapter 3): "Europeans have stepped out of the Hobbesian world of anarchy into the Kantian world of perpetual peace."[100] The French, not possessing the military means (or will, in this case), saw Saddam Hussein as being in the stronger position, able to manipulate and confound the inspectors, who were in Iraq without the benefit of an occupying force. The U.S. view was that if force was necessary to make Saddam comply with UN resolutions, it should be applied; force had been sanctioned before against Iraq and therefore it could be used again.

Resolution 1441: September–November 2002

On November 8, 2002, the UN Security Council passed Resolution 1441, imposing a tough inspection regime on Iraq that Baghdad proceeded to accept, albeit grudgingly. The vote was unanimous, 15-0. It was a far cry from Resolution 1284, passed nearly three years earlier, which set up UNMOVIC as the new inspection body replacing UNSCOM. Then the vote was 11-0, but with four abstentions: France, Russia, China, and Malaysia.

What made the difference? Obviously it was the change in U.S. administrations. According to Levitte, what was new was the manifest determination of President Bush to use force if necessary to obtain the return of the inspectors. Philip Gordon and Justin Vaïsse writing in *Le Monde* echoed this view on November 13, 2002, five days after the passage of Resolution 1441:

Paradoxically, if one wants to be honest about it, it was nevertheless the unilateralist wing—the Rumsfelds, the Cheneys, the Wolfowitzs—to whom one owes the mobilization of the international community. It was their threats to act without consulting the United Nations that made possible an agreement on the inspections, and likewise it is their threats to go to war that today renders credible these inspections.[101]

Following President Bush's presentation of his Iraq strategy to the United Nations on September 12, 2002, the United States prepared a resolution for the Security Council. In Levitte's account, the U.S. draft, first presented to the French during a visit to Paris by Marc Grossman, under secretary of state for political affairs, on September 27, would have given a blank check to the United States, to the effect that if the Iraqis were found to have committed a "material breach," the United States could undertake military action against them without referring back to the Security Council.[102]

From the outset, Levitte recommended that the U.S. text not be made public, so as not to produce a "crystallization" around this first version, which gave the French, and others, problems, in that it opened the way for the United States to go to war without further deliberation by the Security Council. To withhold the text would facilitate its evolution; otherwise, if the text were made public, the press would comment on each paragraph, and the positions of the parties would harden. Despite the fact that there were leaks, the text itself was not officially made public.

The French, continues Levitte, let it be known that they had a text of their own but preferred to keep it "in the pocket," while concentrating instead on what should be put into the U.S. text (which was also a British text) and what should be taken out.

Although the Americans wanted to focus on the five permanent members of the Security Council, the French took the position that it would be better to know the requirements of all fifteen members of the council. In the deliberations, a polarization developed around the Americans and the British on one side and the French, Russians, and Chinese on the other, but with the Chinese remaining in the background. The French objective was to focus on what was acceptable to Hans Blix, head of UNMOVIC, for an enhanced mandate of the inspectors, and what was necessary for France: preserving the role of the Security Council as the supreme authority governing international behavior.

President Chirac presented the French negotiating position in an interview with the *New York Times* on September 9, 2002. He proposed a démarche in two phases: first, a resolution would be passed by the Security Council on a revised inspection regime; second, if Iraq were found in violation ("material breach") of the inspection terms, the Security Council would immediately meet to consider the situation and take appropriate measures, including the use of force.[103]

At no time, says Levitte, did the French threaten a veto. Instead, the French strategy was to build a blocking majority on the council around the French position. With France, Russia, China, Mexico, Ireland, Cameroon, Syria, and Guinea together on one side, the United States was not in a position to obtain a majority vote in the fifteen-member council in favor of "automaticity" of military reaction against Iraq in the event of a "material breach." The French-led group remained solid throughout, despite strong pressure from the Americans.

It was fascinating to see, observes Levitte, how the drawn-out negotiations, which lasted more than seven weeks, were conducted at three levels that nevertheless remained coordinated one with the other. First, there was the level of the chiefs of state, conducted by telephone calls between Presidents Bush and Chirac (and also among the other chiefs of state or government concerned). Then there was the ministerial level, with very frequent contacts taking place between Secretary of State Colin Powell and Foreign Minister Dominique de Villepin that often involved discussions on minute details. Finally, there were the continual contacts in New York among the delegations to the United Nations.

During this long period, there was criticism that the Security Council was moving too slowly, but this, in Levitte's view, was mistaken on two counts:

> That the negotiations took so long was because of internal deliberations within the American government in Washington, which took more time than that spent across the negotiating table in New York and in consultations with the capitals of the various countries concerned.
>
> A certain length of time was necessary so that the positions

could evolve, within Washington itself and in the various capitals; and so that an appraisal of the other parties' points of view could be properly made, allowing for adjustments to take place in the negotiating positions.[104]

In sum, and in Levitte's appraisal, the time spent on Resolution 1441 was not lost time. The result was a resolution that was the toughest one since the original Resolution 687 at the end of the Gulf War.

Levitte also points to the role of Jacques Chirac in persuading Syrian president Bashar al-Assad to vote for the resolution. On the day of the vote, both Chirac and UN secretary-general Kofi Annan spoke by telephone with Bashar in an attempt to persuade him. Chirac emphasized that the Syrian vote was very important, as Syria was the only Arab country on the Security Council at that moment. A unanimous vote in the council was the best way to convince Saddam Hussein to accept the resolution, on which depended the issue of peace or war.

The French aim was to bring the resolution to a vote on Friday, November 8, in advance of an Arab League meeting in Cairo that was scheduled to take place during the following two days. The Syrians had initially wanted to hold the vote on Monday, November 11. The French thought this would be dangerous, as it would give the Arab League the chance to suggest amendments, in which case the Syrians would return to New York on November 11 with modifications to propose. The French (and others) instead wanted the Arab League to be faced with a resolution already adopted and therefore to focus on ways and means to convince the Iraqi leadership to implement it.

During the negotiations, several members of the Security Council remarked to the French that their tough and "rash" position was likely to have negative consequences for French-U.S. relations in the future. On the contrary, according to Levitte, the "frank and constructive" position of the French reinforced this relationship:

> Resolution 1441 was a good result for Paris, for Washington, for the UN, and for the relations between the U.S. and the UN. If the initial text proposed by Washington had been voted on, it would probably have been rejected by a majority; if adopted by a slim majority, it would have been rejected by Baghdad. A unanimous vote on the issue was necessary to convince Baghdad to comply.[105]

Levitte says that there was never a dialogue of recrimination or criticism between the French and the Americans. The discussions were tough but always constructive and focused on getting a resolution passed. Levitte's counterpart, John Negroponte, U.S. ambassador to the United Nations, was a "very great professional." On the French side, President Chirac and Foreign Minister de Villepin played the key roles. The job of the delegation in New York was, figuratively speaking, to "put to music" what had been decided.

According to a senior State Department official, French negotiating behavior during the debate over Resolution 1441 reflected the fact that Chirac could forge a more coherent foreign policy because he was no longer "cohabiting" with a socialist prime minister, as had been the case when Resolution 1284 was the issue.[106] Though others question whether cohabitation made that much of a difference,[107] it is certainly true that because Foreign Minister de Villepin not only was of the same party as President Chirac but had been an intimate counselor of the president since early in the previous decade, coordination between the two was virtually seamless. And Jean-David Levitte had been Chirac's diplomatic adviser and sherpa in 1995–97.

This ease of coordination was particularly important because, as both Americans and French agree, the negotiation over Resolution 1441 was a very different kind of negotiation, in that it was largely conducted in the capitals of the countries involved. The diplomatic missions at the United Nations in New York played an ancillary role: while making some adjustments here and there, they had to be careful not to make any concessions that their ministers were unwilling to, or did not intend to, give.

In the bilateral French-U.S. context, the negotiation consisted mostly of detailed discussions between de Villepin and Secretary of State Colin Powell, described by a senior State Department official overall as "difficult but serious discussions. They moved in and out of agreement but finally came together." All told, and in the bilateral context, Powell made 150 phone calls to counterparts at the ministerial level in the course of the negotiations over the resolution. President Bush was also involved in phone calls to other chiefs of state and government, but Powell was the lead negotiator on the U.S. side.[108]

The difference in the negotiating tactics between the Americans and the French were quite distinct, according to the same senior State Department official. The Americans sought to work through the Permanent Five of the Security Council (the United States, the United Kingdom, France, Russia, and China). The French frequently consulted outside the Permanent Five. The French were mainly responsible for details of the negotiations that leaked out to the press.

The protracted debate, the official continues, developed into a battle for the hearts and minds of the nonpermanent representatives in the fifteen-member Security Council. Since a resolution requires nine affirmative votes and no vetoes in order to pass, and since four countries (France, Russia, China, and Syria) were not satisfied with the U.S. resolution as initially presented, with three more votes the resolution could be blocked. The United States was not concerned about the possibility of a French veto, since there had been no French veto unilaterally since the 1970s. Besides, anyone who vetoed had to know this would trigger military action against Iraq.

The United States, the State Department official continues, expected all along to retreat from its initial draft; its aim was to find where in the draft adjustments would have to be made. The U.S. tactic was to engage in what were lengthy discussions about the draft, without introducing new pieces of paper that would have provided fresh targets for the others to aim at. The first French initiative was to make available a nonpaper that was in fact a threat. By implicitly threatening to table the nonpaper as an alternate text, the French aimed to deprive the U.S. text of support while accumulating support for their own position.

A UN official familiar with the negotiations provides a similar but slightly different version of the unfolding negotiations.[109] The French sought to secure the main point: to prevent the interpretation of the resolution as itself authorizing the use of force. It was clear to the United States from the beginning that almost all the other members had problems with the possibility that the automatic use of force could emerge from this resolution. This was a false issue, as the way the United States had cast the debate was such that the United States came to a compromise very early. The problem then became working on the language in such a way as to overcome the suspicions of the French and the Russians, that is, how to create a formula of language that would give sufficient assurance that the United States would not automatically go to war against Iraq.

For its part, the UN official continues, the United States decided to accept the idea of a second meeting of the UN Security Council. The going-in U.S. position had been that a resolution should be passed and then, if the Iraqis breached it, force should be used. The French for their part came to agree that there did not have to be two resolutions, but there had to be two steps, which meant that if the Iraqis were in material breach, a second meeting of the Security Council would have to decide what steps to take.

In the UN official's view, the French could have been more helpful, as the United States had tremendous difficulty closing out the deal. The United States had put a lot on the table, in terms of concessions, compared with its going-in position. At the point where the United States said it could not go further, the French then began moving toward the U.S. position.

Early on in the negotiations, according to the UN official, the French had quickly occupied the center of gravity in the council on a range of issues that the other members were concerned about, such as an automatic resort to war. To the French assertion that "You don't have the votes," the Americans would rejoin that they were not counting votes; their objective was to bring the other members of the council on board with regard to their own position. Once the other members recognized how much the United States had moved from its original position, the French came to realize that they were losing the center of gravity in the council.

According to the State Department official cited earlier, the United States on November 6 came to closure with the French on the revised U.S.-British draft. At this point, the French, having decided to vote yes, did not want anyone else to vote no. The French immediately began urging the Russians to sign on. The French also were instrumental in persuading the Syrians to vote yes, and the 15-0 vote came two days later, on November 8. Following the vote, the French, Russians, and Chinese issued a tripartite declaration separate from the statements they had each made at the time of the voting. However, according to the State Department official, the declaration was not materially different from the statements at the time of the voting. The official concludes, "It [Resolution 1441] was a different resolution [than the one originally proposed], but it was finally voted. It represented everything we needed to accomplish and more."[110] The UN official has a somewhat different view on the tripartite declaration: "Nobody paid attention to it except the Iraqis. This was a good reason for not having done it. The objective was a strong and clear message. To circulate a statement afterwards blurred the message."[111]

The long debate over UN Resolution 1441 illustrates, in schematic terms, a contrast between the U.S. emphasis on moral judgments and the French emphasis on logic and rationality. U.S. insistence that "we were not counting votes," which was a "false issue," but rather attempting to persuade other members to come around to its point of view betrays a characteristic self-righteousness that others, particularly Europeans, tend to perceive as sanctimoniousness and/or hypocrisy. The French, with their insistence on the logic of "nonautomaticity" (i.e., no carte blanche for going to war) and seeking endlessly to close any loophole that would undermine such a logic, lend themselves to perceptions of posturing for national self-importance, or what is subsumed, for Americans, under the term "grandeur."

Resolution 1441 contained the wording that it was "decide[d] that Iraq has been and remains in material breach of its obligations under relevant [UN] resolutions" and that Iraq was being afforded a "final opportunity" to comply with these obligations. Iraq's failure to cooperate fully with the implementation of the resolution would constitute a further material breach and would be "reported to the [Security Council] for assessment." The resolution concluded with a reminder that "the Council has repeatedly warned Iraq that it will face serious consequences as a result of its continued violations of its obligations."[112] ("Serious consequences" is a euphemism for military action.)

The passage of Resolution 1441 by a unanimous 15-0 vote seemed a great triumph at the time, especially for Secretary of State Colin Powell. As Levitte observes, "The vote was a success of Colin Powell. He was the artisan of this long negotiation."[113] The outcome also seemed to demonstrate that, after weeks of painful negotiations, the French and the Americans could indeed work together. But as Corinne Lesnes points out in *Le Monde*, the battle had not taken place; it had only been put off.[114]

In truth, Resolution 1441 had been left in a state of what is known in diplomatic parlance as "creative ambiguity." The resolution contained an implicit, open-ended threat of military action stemming from a material breach of which Iraq was continuously guilty. Yet a further material breach was to be reported to the Security Council for "assessment." For the French, this meant that there was no "automaticity" in terms of going to war, in that the Security Council would have to meet again. For the United States, there was no requirement for a second resolution in order to go to war; it was only specified that the council would meet to assess a further material breach. As time went on, and as the British ambassador to the United Nations, Sir Jeremy Greenstock, puts it, "We entrenched ourselves in different interpretations of what the wording of Resolution 1441 meant."[115]

The Road to War

In the wake of the unanimous vote on Resolution 1441, the French government's expectation was that Saddam Hussein would commit a blunder in making life difficult for the returning inspectors and/or that weapons of mass destruction would be found in Iraq. Instead, however, Saddam Hussein went into a mode of "passive cooperation," agreeing on "process" while stringing the situation out as long as possible until the hot weather would make military campaigning in Iraq more difficult. At the same time, no significant finds of weapons of mass destruction were made. In light of these unexpected developments, the French concluded that the new inspections regime was useful, in that the inspectors' presence constrained Saddam from using such weapons, and that therefore a war was not necessary.[116]

But the French did not come to this conclusion early on. Initially, there was a seeming harmony between the U.S. and French viewpoints. On December 9, 2002, when Jean-David Levitte presented his credentials to President Bush as the new French ambassador to Washington, he was congratulated on France's action in the United Nations over Resolution 1441. According to Vincent Jauvert of *Le Nouvel Observateur*, a French general visited the Pentagon on December 21, 2002, and announced that, in case of conflict, the French were prepared to contribute fifteen thousand troops and one hundred aircraft or, in other words, about the same level of participation as during the Gulf War of

1990–91. But the general made plain that no deployments would take place until the chief inspectors made their first report.[117] This was scheduled to take place on January 27, to conform with the sixty-day time limit following the start of the inspections, as specified in Resolution 1441.

On January 7, President Chirac, presenting his New Year's wishes to the French armed forces at the École Militaire, told them to get into a state of military readiness. However, several days later in a similar reception for the *corps constitués* (constitutional bodies of the state), he seemed to contradict himself. Greenstock offers this explanation:

> Jacques Chirac, when he made his speech telling the French mili-tary to get ready for a possible conflict, soon realized his speech had been misinterpreted as indicating an intention to go to war. In sub-sequent statements, he "overcorrected." This started a vicious cycle, as the reaction from the American side to the overcorrection was severe. On January 20, de Villepin made his statement that war could not be justified. This worsened the atmosphere and it made it difficult to recover from it. The French had the growing assumption that the U.S. had already decided to go to war, regardless of the out-come of the inspections. Diplomacy seemed only for show. The U.S. began advancing different reasons for going to war: weapons of mass destruction, wickedness of Saddam, etc.[118]

But while the French had gradually been turning to a "logic of peace," as the case for war continued to elude the United States, the latter had all along been pursuing a "logic of war." Strangely, this did not become apparent to the French until early January, through the U.S. Mission to the United Nations. Up until then, the French were continuing to credit Secretary Powell with trying for a peaceful reso-lution through the United Nations, although at the same time they considered that the military buildup in the Persian Gulf area being carried out by Defense Secretary Donald Rumsfeld was undermining what Powell was trying to do.[119] This was also the view, though put somewhat differently, of Richard Holbrooke, who had been U.S. ambassador to the United Nations in the Clinton administration: "In retrospect, the military buildup and the diplomacy were out of sync with each other. The policies were executed in a provocative way that alienated our friends."[120]

In fact, President Bush's decision to go to war seems to have been made possibly as early as the spring of 2002. In early July 2002, National Security Adviser Condoleezza Rice told State Department policy planning chief Richard Haass that the decision to go to war had already been made.[121] Thus, to Haass, when Colin Powell had his famous dinner with the president in early August 2002, at which Powell successfully made the plea to take the Iraq matter to the United Nations, it was already the case that "the agenda was not whether Iraq, but how."[122]

When the French finally woke up to what was the real U.S. intention, they made the decision to threaten a veto rather than remain with an option of abstention, as had been the case over Resolution 1284 in December 1999. This decision, and its subsequent management, was the work of a duet, with Chirac as the maestro and de Villepin as the first violin. The hierarchical, or pyramidal, nature of the French state was again at work: according to a French defense official, the rest of the French bureaucracy and the military were largely cut out of the play.[123]

The reason behind this fateful decision to threaten the veto, in Ambassador Greenstock's view, was that "Jacques Chirac did not wish to set a precedent whereby the UN Security Council would be put in a position of rubber-stamping a United States decision."[124] Thus one is led to the conclusion that Jacques Chirac considered that even an abstention would be taken as a rubber-stamping of a U.S. decision.

As noted elsewhere in this study, the French are loath to get involved in situations over which they have no control, especially when the United States is exercising such control. Moreover, the French like to undertake actions with panache, to create an *effet d'annonce*. According to Vincent Jauvert, Chirac and de Villepin began to become wary of U.S. intentions after a speech by Colin Powell on December 19, 2002, in which he declared the Iraqi declaration on the weapons of mass destruction, issued six days earlier, a "tissue of lies" that put Iraq in "material breach" of its commitments.[125]

According to Jauvert, Chirac and de Villepin decided to make a dramatic and surprise gesture that would rally the undecideds on the Security Council to the French point of view. France, being the temporary chairman of the Security Council, called for a special open meeting on January 20, 2003, to discuss terrorism, to which Powell and the other foreign ministers agreed. During the meeting, but much more pointedly and emphatically afterward in a press conference that as council chairman he was entitled to hold, de Villepin declared that "nothing" could justify a war against Saddam and for the first time held out the possibility that France might veto a new resolution sanctioning such an action.

Powell was offended, feeling he had been sandbagged into coming to a meeting to discuss terrorism. The United States could hardly argue that Saddam Hussein was not a fit subject for discussion in a meeting on terrorism. Notwithstanding, and in the words of a senior State Department official, "Things went downhill [in the relations between the U.S. and France] after January 20."[126]

In February the French took another step in an attempt to counteract the U.S. "logic of war" by refusing, along with Germany and Belgium, contingent military aid to Turkey in the event the latter was attacked by Iraq. This impasse was overcome on February 19, 2003, when NATO's Defense Planning Committee (which does not include France) approved the U.S. proposal, with German acquiescence.

Another fissure in the European position appeared on January 30, 2003, when, persuaded by Tony Blair, leaders of eight NATO countries (Spain, Italy, the Czech Republic, Denmark, Hungary, Portugal, Poland, and the United Kingdom) came out in support of the United States in an open letter that appeared in the *Wall Street Journal*. This was followed on February 5, 2003, by a separate statement of support for the United States from the "Vilnius Ten" countries in Eastern and Central Europe, all of them candidates for membership in the European Union.

Opening and Closing Moves

Ironically, the French and the U.S. positions on the issue of a second resolution became reversed over the course of the debate in the United Nations that reached its climax in early 2003. The U.S. going-in position, following President Bush's having referred the issue to the United Nations in his speech of September 12, 2002, was that no second resolution was required. The French going-in position was that a second resolution would be necessary before any military action. In a meeting with a group of foreign ministers at the Hotel Pierre in New

York, also in September, Colin Powell became uneasy when he heard Dominique de Villepin lay out the French position: a first resolution demanding that Iraq disarm had to be followed by a second resolution authorizing war, if Iraq refused. "Be sure about one thing," Powell told de Villepin. "Don't vote for the first unless you are prepared to vote for the second." De Villepin gave his assent, according to officials who were present.[127]

As the negotiations proceeded during the fall of 2002 over what became Resolution 1441, the French dropped their insistence that a requirement for a second resolution be included in the text before hostilities could be engaged. The French agreed that the text needed only to specify that a further *meeting* of the Security Council should be held in the event Iraq was found in "material breach."

Later, in order to help Tony Blair, whose pro-war policy was being contested in the British Parliament, and also to help some other members of the Security Council,[128] the United States agreed to introduce a second resolution giving Saddam Hussein an ultimatum for compliance. In taking this action, the United States was going against its long-held contention that a second resolution was not necessary and that 1441 was all that the United States needed to undertake military action.

The United States having changed its position on a second resolution, the French did as well, but for different reasons. On Thursday, February 20, President Bush and Prime Minister Blair agreed to table the second resolution the following week. The next day, Ambassador Levitte went to see Stephen Hadley, the deputy national security adviser, in the absence from Washington of Condoleezza Rice. Levitte urged that the second resolution be dropped, as it would cause unnecessary damage. The suggestion was rebuffed; the United States had to go for a second resolution because Tony Blair needed it.[129]

In Levitte's own account,[130] the French proposed to the United States that the second resolution be dropped and that if the United States was going ahead with war, it should do so on the basis of Resolution 1441, which Washington had initially claimed was all that was necessary; if the second resolution was rejected, it would split the Security Council and would make it patent that the United States was going to war illegally. The solution proposed by the French was that of

"agreeing with friends to disagree." The U.S. side declined the proposal, taking the position that it had enough votes, that the Chinese
and Russians would abstain, and that then France would be in an
extremely uncomfortable position. Moreover, the United States felt
committed to Tony Blair to go through with a second resolution.

On February 26 the United States, the United Kingdom, and
Spain sponsored the second resolution and presented it to the
Security Council. It stated that Iraq remained in material breach, that
Saddam had lost his last chance to fulfill Resolution 1441, and that
severe consequences would follow. On March 6 President Bush was
still pushing for a vote in the Security Council. It was time, he said,
for the members to take a stand. However, with the second resolution
still encountering hesitation within the council, the British consulted
with the inspectors and, on the basis of a report the latter submitted
on March 7, drew up a list of six tests for Saddam Hussein to fulfill in
order to show full cooperation. As Blair explained it to the House of
Commons on March 18:

> [On March 10] we were getting somewhere [with the second reso-
> lution]. We very nearly had majority agreement. . . . There were
> debates about the length of the ultimatum. But the basic construct
> was gathering support. Then on [that] night, France said it would
> veto a second resolution whatever the circumstances. Then France
> denounced the six tests. Later that day, Iraq rejected them. Still, we
> continued to negotiate. [On March 14], France said they could not
> accept any ultimatum.[131]

The French position was that, since a majority of Security Council
members were in favor of continuing the inspections, the question of a
French veto did not arise; if it did, however, the French would "fully
assume all our responsibilities,"[132] which was an allusion to a veto. Also,
the French point out that Jacques Chirac's March 14 threat to veto was
not with regard to any resolution but only with regard to any resolution
containing an ultimatum, contrary to a British spokesperson's claim that
Chirac had threatened to veto any resolution before having seen the
text. Nevertheless, in the view of Ambassador Greenstock, "The French
threat to veto the second resolution was key. Until this became absolutely clear, the Anglo-Americans were having some success: 'we were
at eight [of the nine votes required].'"[133]

According to the UN official cited earlier, the French implicit threat to veto upset U.S. plans, which were based on the assumption that if a new resolution were introduced, the French would abstain. This had been the case, as we have seen earlier, with Resolution 1284 in 1999. If this assumption had held true, the United States considered it would have been able to gain the nine votes for a majority on the Security Council. Instead, the French went around saying to the unde-cideds, in effect, "Since we're going to veto a new resolution, why risk political damage at home by voting for it?" This French action not only took the pressure off Iraq but helped to tip the scales against the United States when the new resolution was proposed. Although the U.S. actions in the Security Council were regarded as cavalier, the French on the other hand seem not to have fully realized that President Bush considered it in the U.S. vital national interest to threaten to go to war with Iraq.[134]

Another compromise proposal, floated by President Ricardo Lagos of Chile on March 15, for a thirty-day deadline for Iraq to com-ply fully with UN resolutions, was accepted by President Chirac but disregarded by the United States.[135] By this time the United States was locked into a "meteorological imperative," on the basis that military action would have to be started in mid-March before the hot weather set in. After a suddenly arranged meeting in the Azores on March 16, George Bush, Tony Blair, and Spanish prime minister José María Aznar withdrew their resolution, and the road to war was open.

Conclusion

As the official at the United Nations put it, the level of damage from the March 2003 imbroglio in the UN Security Council has yet to be assessed.[136] In a sense, this crisis was a heaven-sent opportunity for France to stand for a principle and at the same time maintain its rep-utation of being able to stand up to the United States, in this case threatening the use of a powerful diplomatic tool at its disposal, the veto in the UN Security Council. The crisis that landed in the UN Security Council represented a unique way for France to assert its "difference" from the United States, which it had been seeking to do, with varying degrees of success, since de Gaulle's time. The French could hardly be expected to pass up such an opportunity, especially since, as they saw it, the issue was crystal clear from the point of view of logic: the United States had failed to make a case for invading Iraq that had any contemporaneity to it: Resolution 687 was twelve years old. The characteristic French approach of finding a solution based on reason and sticking to it was evident throughout the crisis: war was the worst of all solutions, Jacques Chirac argued, and therefore all other alternatives had to be explored first.

Thus the French pressed their case, arguing that this crisis was not about oil or trade but about principle. As Jean-David Levitte remarks in the aftermath, "If this were not a matter of principle, don't you think we would have jumped on the bandwagon of war?"[137]

But in another sense, the veto power was also a problem from hell for France as, with politically uncertain allies, Germany and Russia, it risked becoming isolated in the wake of the successful Anglo-American war in Iraq. As Patrice de Beer observes in reference to the fragility of the French position in the aftermath: "A policy is worth only the means that one has to carry it out. And here lies the rub. It is not enough to consider oneself as a power that counts in order to be accepted as such—in particular by the United States, especially sensitive to power relationships."[138]

The crisis, fought out in the UN Security Council and then taken outside the council by George Bush and Tony Blair, revealed the weaknesses and the structural anomalies of the council, namely, that small countries such as Guinea, Angola, and Cameroon should be among the fifteen voting on matters of such vital importance, and that only Britain and France are permanent European members of the council. France's threatened use of the veto served to bring into relief such anomalies, increasing Washington's wariness of the council in general and prompting the neoconservatives in the United States to advocate removing France from the permanent membership of the council.

France has a deserved reputation for fighting above its weight in diplomatic negotiations, particularly within the European Union. France's long diplomatic tradition, its careful selection of elites, its habits of logical argumentation, its educational system—all help explain this reputation. But the need to match means and ambitions becomes critically important when the power disparities are great, as between the United States and France, and when, as de Beer points out, power considerations play heavily in U.S. calculations. Yet France continued to act in the crisis with a culture of authority in dealing with others and in defending the interests of the French state. This was evident in the public diplomacy of Chirac and de Villepin, practiced with panache by the latter, to the extent of seemingly getting carried away with his own rhetoric, and at times to excess by the former with his heavy-handed public criticism of the Vilnius Ten for having supported the United States.

Although no provable operational relationship between Saddam Hussein and al Qaeda was established, the Bush administration, for reasons of its own, had launched into a war against Iraq and in this had the support of a large part of the American people, who, in a rage reminiscent of the reaction to Pearl Harbor, were anxious to strike back at the Islamic world after the September 11 attacks. The depth of this rage, and the cold determination of President Bush to respond with a full-scale war, were clearly underestimated in Europe. As Dominique Moïsi of the French think tank L'Institut Français des Relations Internationales (IFRI) characterizes it:

> I would say that French diplomacy is certainly well thought out and structured, but it has not sufficiently absorbed the changes that have taken place in the international system. In opposing the United States in a flamboyant manner, [it] did not integrate the emotional reality of the 11th of September. . . . And in the final analysis, the question is twofold: First, has our foreign policy increased our stature, our role, our prestige? Second, has France's action favored the emergence of a future diplomacy [for] Europe? To both of these questions, I am afraid that the response is not positive.[139]

Because France not only opposed the U.S. move toward war with Iraq but also lobbied other members of the Security Council against it, France was singled out as the main target of the U.S. administration's wrath. Although in the aftermath French officials point out that every country can be expected to lobby others to its point of view, Washington took it as a French betrayal on an issue of national security. Here again the U.S. passion for unanimity, remarked upon by Tocqueville, stood in the way of a more detached view.

In this unfortunate turn of events, both U.S. and French officials misread each other. The Americans thought that, ultimately, the

French would abstain in a second resolution that would have opened the way for an attack on Iraq. The French thought initially that without a casus belli the United States was unlikely to go to war, and then, after realizing that the United States intended to go ahead anyway, acted as though the weight of international opinion, as reflected in the UN Security Council, could deter or postpone the U.S. attack.

One weakness in Jacques Chirac's position was that, while he had the majority of international opinion with him, he did not have all the European leaders with him. Thus, just as it was Jacques Chirac who ruined George W. Bush's quest for UN approval of his invasion of Iraq, so it was Tony Blair who ruined Chirac's attempt to have Europe condemn a U.S. action taken outside and in spite of the United Nations.

Another weakness in Chirac's position was that in opposing the United States, notwithstanding the logic of his position, he appeared to be giving support to Saddam Hussein. In this context, Dominique Moïsi has this comment in the aftermath:

> The paradox is that, with the war over, the legality appears increasingly doubtful, with the absence of weapons of mass destruction, whereas the legitimacy seems all the greater, with the discovery of the extent of the crimes committed by the regime of Saddam Hussein.[140]

Chirac, whose personal stamp was all over the French opposition to war against Iraq and France's siding with Russia, seemingly has no regrets: "I do not have the feeling of having committed an offense nor of having been wrong," he declared in May 2003.[141] Nevertheless, one cannot help but be reminded of the dictum of Raymond Aron, France's leading public intellectual of the post-World War II period: "The French are continually surprised by what they have just done."

CASE 3: TRADE AND CULTURE NEGOTIATIONS: FRANCE AT THE URUGUAY ROUND

Overview

The third case study in this work deals with French actions aimed at affecting the Uruguay Round negotiations, held under the framework of the General Agreement on Trade and Tariffs (GATT). At the climax of these negotiations in late 1993, the persistent differences between the United States and the European Union on agriculture were holding up prospects for a successful ending to the talks.[142]

Although not a direct party per se in the negotiations that took place in Washington, Brussels, and Geneva, France played a decisive role in restricting, to a certain degree, the liberalization of trade in the agricultural sector and took the lead in the European Union's refusal to make specific commitments in the audiovisual sector during the Uruguay Round. Agriculture was the major subject of contention in the negotiations, and the "cultural" issue came up only toward the very end.

This case study—which, it should be noted, focuses narrowly on French actions and pays relatively little attention to the views of the other states involved—vividly demonstrates France's ability to get its way much of the time in the European Union. Although France's occasional rough tactics are unsettling, in the final analysis other EU members are unwilling to isolate France because it is too important historically in the European Union, as well as too central, politically and geographically, to ignore. At the same time, this case also illustrates that the French, though seemingly intransigent, will compromise if they conclude that the deal on the table is the best that they are likely to achieve.

Background to the Uruguay Round

The Uruguay Round traces back to the post–World War II era and to the impulsion to open up international trade and thereby undo the protectionist measures of the 1930s, considered to be, in part at least, responsible for the Great Depression. A package of trade rules and tariff concessions, under the name of the General Agreement on Trade and Tariffs (GATT), went into effect in January 1948.[143] The GATT, a provisional agreement and organization, was replaced in January 1995 by a permanent institution, the World Trade Organization (WTO).

With the creation of the GATT, a series of international negotiations called "rounds" were held under its auspices. These rounds, or extended negotiations, ended in agreements, each of which was intended to serve as a new stage in the gradual elimination of trade barriers. And, in fact, the growth in international trade under the period of the GATT was phenomenal, rising, for example, from $129 billion in 1960 to $3,485 billion in 1990.[144]

Up to the Kennedy Round (1964–67), negotiations had concentrated on lowering tariffs (customs duties) on imported goods. A system developed whereby when countries agreed to open their markets for goods and services, they would "bind" their commitments. For goods, these bindings would amount to ceilings on customs tariff rates, referred to as "bound tariffs." A country could change its bindings, but first it would have to negotiate with its trading partners, and this could result in compensating them for their loss of trade.[145]

This system of bound tariffs spreads itself throughout the international trading system through one of the cardinal rules of the GATT—the Most Favored Nation (MFN) clause:[146]

> What makes the GATT unique and a great force for liberalization is that any concession negotiated laboriously by direct trading partners must be extended automatically and unconditionally to all other GATT members. . . . This is purely and simply the [MFN] clause at work. . . . It is this snowball effect of multilateralization—or the effect of the MFN clause—which made it possible to reduce the industrialized countries' tariffs from an average of over 40% in 1947 to less than 5% after the Uruguay Round.[147]

Starting with the Tokyo Round (1973–79), the focus of attention shifted to nontariff barriers to trade, including subsidies for exports and dumping practices.[148] There was a reason for this change of focus, and part of it was the very success of the GATT in lowering tariffs. According to the WTO, this success "drove governments to devise other forms of protection for sectors facing increased foreign competition. . . . [Notably they sought] bilateral market-sharing arrangements with competitors and embark[ed] on a subsidies race to maintain their holds on agricultural trade. Both these changes undermined GATT's credibility and effectiveness."[149]

In the Tokyo Round agriculture issues had been aired, notably the practice of subsidizing agricultural exports, but the GATT had proved unable to place any limits on such subsidies.[150] Although agriculture had come under the GATT from the beginning, as it is considered a trade in *goods* (as contrasted with a trade in *services*), it had a "special status": any "farm, forest or fishery" product was exempted from the prohibition against export subsidies and "any agricultural or fisheries product" was exempted from limits being placed on imports.[151] The resultant distortion of free trade was especially conspicuous in the European Union. As Alice Landau relates:

> Over the years, agriculture [had] become a subject of conflict between the United States and the EU. The quarrel was based on a simple fact . . . the disequilibrium between supply and demand for agricultural products. [When] demand stagnates, supply explodes. . . . The resulting agricultural surpluses accumulate, and they have to flow into foreign markets often with the aid of subventions.
>
> The agricultural dispute is focused on market share. In 1985 the U.S. share of agricultural exports worldwide was 14%, that of the EU was 31%, and that of the Cairns Group [of fourteen agricultural exporting countries not including EU members or the United States] was 26%.[152]

This meager U.S. share of total exports translated, according to Landau, into an estimated loss to the United States of $65 million a year from the 1960s onward. She adds:

> The quarrel involves internal policies and commercial practices with, at the heart of the discord, the [EU's Common Agricultural Policy (CAP)]. . . . The use of price supports and export subsidies . . . produces distortions in worldwide trade in agriculture. The CAP results in important losses for the agricultural exporting countries [outside the EU].[153]

France and the Common Agricultural Policy

When General de Gaulle returned to power in 1958, to the surprise of those who knew of his hostility toward supranational institutions, he agreed to endorse the European Economic Community (EEC), established the previous year by the Treaty of Rome. In agreeing to support the EEC, de Gaulle had to face two inherent difficulties. The first was that in the economic area (what is now known as Pillar One), decisions are "communitarian": they are made by the system of qualified majority voting (QMV) rather than by unanimity, and thus they take away a measure of sovereignty from the member countries. The second difficulty was that an EEC agricultural policy, the principal aim of which would be to subsidize for European farmers, had not been included in the Treaty of Rome. Although the broad principles of a CAP for the EEC were established in January 1962, internal agreements on financing the CAP had yet to be accomplished.[154]

De Gaulle threw down a marker on both the QMV system and the nonfinalization of an agricultural policy during the so-called empty chair crisis, in which France boycotted the EEC for eight months until the Luxembourg Compromise was arrived at on January 29, 1966. Part of the compromise was that it would remain informal and would not be incorporated into the European Union's treaty corpus. It allowed for a member-state to invoke the need for a unanimous vote, even on a communitarian or Pillar One subject, if its vital interests were at stake. (The shadow of the Luxembourg Compromise, and thus the threat of a French veto, couched in terms of the need for "unanimity," was to hang over the later stages of the Uruguay Round negotiations in the dispute over agriculture.)

Four months after the Luxembourg Compromise, internal arrangements for financing the CAP had been completed and the CAP was fully incorporated into the EEC.[155] Since France is Europe's largest agricultural exporter, this policy of EU aid to agriculture has been of benefit first and foremost to French farmers, and France has adopted a hard line on maintaining CAP levels.[156] For example, in the year 2000, of a total of 40,436,000,000 euros dispensed under the CAP, France received 8,982,000,000 euros, or 22.2 percent. This figure was significantly higher than the percentages received by the other major EU countries: Germany, 14 percent; Spain, 13.5 percent; Italy, 12.4 percent; and the United Kingdom, 10 percent. Furthermore, in the same year France's contribution to the overall EU budget was significantly lower (16.7 percent) than Germany's (25.2 percent).[157] Back in the 1980s, when the Uruguay Round was launched, the CAP accounted for 70 percent of the European Union's overall budget.[158] In arguing that any agreement on agriculture in the Uruguay Round had to be compatible with the European Union's CAP, France was thus endeavoring to protect its privileged position as the largest single recipient of CAP subsidies.

The Uruguay Round Begins

The Uruguay Round was officially launched on September 20, 1986, at Punta del Este, Uruguay. Even though some of the provisions of the previous Tokyo Round, which had ended in 1979, had not been put into effect, the United States wanted a fresh negotiation that would cover agriculture, services, and intellectual property. The latter, involving traded inventions, creations, and designs,[159] had been indirectly raised in the Tokyo Round, under the rubric of controlling the counterfeit trade, but no concrete results had emerged.[160] As for services, although they were included in the Uruguay Round, the negotiations were conducted outside the formal framework of the GATT[161] and emerged as a separate agreement under the WTO, known as the General Agreement on Trade in Services (GATS). This was also the case with intellectual property (Agreement on Trade-Related Aspects of Intellectual Property Rights [TRIPS]).[162] A third agreement, on trade-related investment measures (TRIMs), which states rules for investment-related measures and sets a framework for future action, was also part of the Final Act of the Uruguay Round.[163]

According to the WTO, the overall purpose of the Uruguay Round was "to extend the trading system into several new areas, notably trade in services and intellectual property, and to reform trade in the sensitive sectors of agriculture and textiles. All the original GATT articles were up for review. It was the biggest negotiating mandate on trade ever agreed to."[164]

The European Commission's deputy director general for trade, Roderick Abbott, says that the aim of the Uruguay Round was to install a real discipline on agriculture. Heretofore, the emphasis had been on tariffs. Internal subsidies to producers in the member countries, and subsidies for export, were to be introduced on the agenda. The so-called variable levies, which were devices aimed at curbing imports, were to be done away with and converted into tariff negotiations.[165] Also called nontariff measures, these devices included licenses, excessive formalities, and various administrative taxes.[166] This process of conversion into tariffs became known as tariffication.

To summarize, then, as far as the GATT negotiations on agriculture were concerned, liberalization was focused on three areas in which trade was subject to "distortion": internal supports (e.g., price supports,

subventions for agricultural research, and direct payments to farmers);
export subsidies; and import barriers (tariff and nontariff measures).

The planners of the Uruguay Round aimed to complete the work
in four years' time. There was to be a midterm review conference in
Montreal in December 1988 and a "final" conference in Brussels in
December 1990—designated the "determination session"—at which
an agreement would be signed. But the Montreal conference was
inconclusive, and the Brussels conference broke down, with the issue
of subsidies to agriculture as the main stumbling block.[167]

It took another three years until the agricultural issue was settled
and an accord was finally reached among the GATT membership, on
December 15, 1993. The accord depended on an agreement in the first
instance between the United States and the European Union, with the
former representing a major force behind trade liberalization in agriculture, and the latter, spearheaded by France, the leading resistant.[168]

The European Commission as the
European Union's Negotiator on Trade

In the area of trade and its international regulation, France as a member
of the European Union has ceded a significant degree of sovereignty to
the European Commission; ever since the beginning of supranational
Europe, it has been the commission that is uniquely charged with presenting EU positions in trade negotiations with countries and regional economic institutions outside the European Union.[169] In the EU context,
therefore, foreign trade is supranational in that it is run by the European
Commission, representing the community as a whole, and it is part of
Pillar One, or the economic area. Foreign policy and defense (Pillar Two)
remain intergovernmental and under the authority of the Council of
Ministers, representing the interests of the individual member-states. As
Hugo Paemen and Alexandra Bensch put it:

> Trade and agricultural policies are among the most integrated of all
> the European Community's areas of responsibility. The member-
> states have transferred all their rights of action to the Community.
> Decisions are taken not unanimously but according to the Qualified
> Majority Rule . . . Article 113 . . . is the Treaty provision which estab-
> lishes a common policy among the Member-states in the area of for-
> eign trade—the "common commercial policy."[170]

Thus, in matters of trade, French negotiating behavior becomes *internal* to the European Union in that France participates as one of fifteen member countries in putting together a common position. France has no negotiating role *externally*. There are informal country-to-country contacts that take place in the background of trade talks, as between the United States and France, but in a formal sense trade negotiations are black-and-white: the commission negotiates for all EU members in matters of trade.[171]

The commission, then, is on its own to a large extent while conducting trade negotiations. However, it has to report back regularly to the Council of Ministers because the commission receives its mandate to negotiate trade issues from the council, that is, the member governments. When the Council of Ministers meets to consider a trade matter, it is known as Committee 113.[172] However, policy matters regarding trade are the purview of another incarnation of the council, the General Affairs Council (GAC), composed of the foreign ministers of the member-states. Other sectoral councils meet regularly (economic/financial affairs and agriculture) or as the occasion requires (transport, energy, culture, justice/home affairs, etc.).[173]

Paemen and Bensch describe the arrangement between the European Commission and the Council of Ministers this way: "The European Commission is an independent, central body which has the power of initiative and to execute decisions. However, its proposals must first be approved by the Council of Ministers of the European Community."[174]

The process of trade negotiations is in three parts: the commission receives a mandate from the council to negotiate; the commission then negotiates; and the commission comes back to the council (normally the GAC) for ex post facto approval.[175] There is a considerable gray area surrounding the "mandate" that the commission receives, which helps explain why in the later stages of the Uruguay Round negotiations some member-states—France in particular—alleged that the commissioner for external trade, Sir Leon Brittan, had exceeded his mandate. On this issue, Jean-David Levitte, then French ambassador in Geneva, where day-to-day negotiations in the Uruguay Round were conducted at the headquarters of the GATT, comments:

> In the Uruguay Round, one had a reduced negotiation: Sir Leon
> Brittan was the negotiator for the whole European Union, on the

basis of a mandate that was conferred on him by the Council of Ministers—that is, the fifteen ministers of foreign affairs. And frankly, we did not have a great deal of confidence in Sir Leon. We found him too open toward American preoccupations and to the transatlantic outlook, and not attentive enough notably to French preoccupations, and particularly in the area of agriculture.[176]

Behind this issue of the "mandate" lies the deeper one of the relationship between the Council of Ministers and the European Commission, which reflects the difference between those who hold to the tenets of supranationalism and those who prefer strict control by the national governments, otherwise known as intergovernmentalism. The fault line here lies generally between the smaller countries, who are in favor of supranationalism, and the larger ones, particularly France and Britain, who are in favor of intergovernmentalism. In terms of the role of the commission, as Remco Vahl observes, "there are basically two approaches: one that views the Commission as an independent, autonomous actor, capable of leadership in the processes of European integration and [EU] decision-making, and one that sees the Commission as a subservient actor that serves the interests of governments in the Community."[177] Generally in EU matters, it is the second approach that the French pursue, and in this the Uruguay Round experience not only was not an exception but was emblematic. Thus, not only were the French reluctant to have agriculture subject to negotiations in the GATT in the first place; they were not wholly pleased by how they were being represented through the commission.

The Agriculture Dossier: From "Blair House I" to "Blair House II"

Following the breakdown of negotiations at the Brussels conference in 1990, at which agriculture was the main stumbling block, no more plenary conferences were held. However, negotiations continued on at GATT headquarters in Geneva. Levitte describes the actual process of these negotiations as they took place in Geneva in the following terms:

When the negotiation got under way, [although] the commission's team led by Leon Brittan was alone in the room [with officials of the GATT], everything became known. Alongside Brittan's team, behind the door, so to speak, there were the representatives of all the fifteen countries. I lived through this when I was ambassador in Geneva, where one met every morning in what was called the "bunker," which was the building of the European Union, with the representative of the European Commission, to verify that he had his instructions, and that he understood what the fifteen [countries] expected of him, etc. After that he left to [conduct] the negotiations. And then he returned and gave us a report of what had happened, and the instructions for the next day were verified [with him]. Although the GATT was located at Geneva, the most critical part of the Uruguay Round negotiations took place at Brussels, at the level of the Council of Ministers and Sir Leon.[178]

After the failure of the Brussels "final" conference in December 1990, the director general of the GATT, Arthur Dunkel, put together a compromise draft of a final legal agreement and introduced it at Geneva on December 20, 1991. It did not include lists of commitments, country by country, for reducing import duties and for opening markets in services. On December 18, 1991, even before the document was circulated, French prime minister Edith Cresson denounced it as an American diktat—not just the agricultural part but most of the rest as well.[179]

The document that was circulated on December 20, 1991, became, albeit with a number of changes, the basis for the final agreement,[180] which, however, was still two years away. Known as the Dunkel Draft, or the Draft Final Act (DFA) of the Uruguay Round, the document became the basis of an agreement between the United States and the European Union worked out at Blair House a year later, on November 20, 1992.[181] This agreement, which was a modification of the Dunkel Draft in important respects in its agricultural component, became known as the Blair House Accord.[182]

This Blair House compromise, based on a modified and weakened version of the Dunkel Draft,[183] was brought back by the commission negotiators to Brussels for submission to the Council of Ministers, where the French representation pronounced it as unworkable.[184] In the French view, the Dunkel Draft was not compatible with the CAP. With the French in the lead, work began on a new draft, intended to replace the original version worked out at Blair House. The revised draft was taken back to GATT headquarters and was fed into the negotiating process.[185]

Between the discarding of the original Blair House agreement (which came to be called Blair House I) and the consideration of the revision (which became the basis for the final agreement of the Uruguay Round in December 1993 and thus known as Blair House II), a change of actors occurred all around: in the U.S. administration, in the French government, in the European Commission, and in the GATT. George Bush, defeated as president, ceded power to Bill Clinton on January 20, 1993, and in the same month Mickey Kantor replaced Carla Hills as U.S. trade representative (USTR). The Right triumphed in the French legislative elections of March 1993, and a new government came in, headed by Edouard Balladur as prime minister and Alain Juppé as foreign minister. In the European Commission, Sir Leon Brittan succeeded Frans Andriessen in the external trade portfolio in January 1993. And in the GATT, Peter Sutherland took over from Arthur Dunkel as director general in July 1993.

According to Pierre Vimont, former French ambassador to the European Union, who in 2002 became cabinet director of the foreign minister, the perception in Brussels was that with the change of government in France a decision could be forced through on agriculture while France was in this state of transition.[186] This did not, however, turn out to be the case, exemplifying the theme, evoked elsewhere in this volume, that the machinery of government in France continues on more or less independent of change in the political authority.

As noted, the dissatisfaction of the French was focused on the person of Sir Leon Brittan, who, they contended, was not following the mandate given to him by the member-states concerning trade in agriculture. However, Brittan came relatively late into the picture. As Roderick Abbott points out:

> French observers tend to blame Brittan as if he alone were responsible for the whole affair. In fact, through the important earlier stages of negotiations at the Brussels meeting (1990) and through the 1992 CAP reform discussions and Blair House I, it was the work of Andriessen [external trade commissioner] and [Ray] Mac Sharry [agriculture commissioner]. Sir Leon then had the difficult task of picking up the whole process and moving it forward; and then in the autumn [of 1993] carrying the negotiations on services as well as agriculture.[187]

In the fall of 1993, the French, supported by Germany, succeeded in convoking a "Jumbo Council," composed of ministers of foreign affairs, European affairs, foreign trade, and agriculture, with the intent of obtaining a renegotiation of the original Blair House draft. The meeting was convened on September 20, 1993, in Brussels under the Belgian presidency of the European Union.

According to a French official close to the scene at the time, Brittan had said to the French before the Jumbo Council meeting that he would consider their position. But in the council meeting he said the contrary—that the commission was following its mandate and knew exactly how to proceed. French foreign minister Juppé expressed sharp opposition, and the Belgian president suspended the meeting. The French then leaked to the press words to the effect that if the commission had wished to sabotage the negotiations, it could not have done a better job of it. In response, Brittan protested that this was not his intention, and the Jumbo Council resumed, with Brittan exhibiting a changed attitude.[188]

"What is interesting in the Uruguay Round and the 'Jumbo Council' at Brussels," comments the same French official,

> was the inflexible position of the French Government when it considered that its essential interests were at stake, in this case our agricultural exports. This attitude, of course, was in keeping with the famous Luxembourg Compromise. This episode demonstrates also the dialectic between confidential negotiations—the meeting with Brittan before the opening of the "Jumbo Council," and the recourse to pressure through the media which enabled the French to reverse the direction of the way things were going.[189]

In the view of another key French actor at the time, Jacques Andréani, then ambassador to Washington:

> Leon Brittan had overstepped his responsibilities in the agriculture dossier. He made concessions that were biased in favor of the Americans. There was confusion and a lack of clarity on the EU side. In 1993 there was a change of government in France, and the Balladur government did good work on this dossier. Alain Juppé defended brilliantly the French position, and the commission had to reopen the dossier and change the terms of the Blair House accord. Brittan went back [to Washington in late September 1993] with new instructions for negotiation.[190]

However, the "new instructions" Brittan received from the Jumbo Council did not call for renegotiating the Blair House agreement, which the French had wanted. At the end of the meeting, the Jumbo Council decided to seek "clarification," not renegotiation, of the Blair House deal.[191] But the Americans, confronted with this request for clarification, said, in effect, "No. An agreement is an agreement; besides, the Congress has already been informed."[192]

At this point, the role of Ambassador Andréani in Washington was not to negotiate but merely to discuss the issues with his U.S. interlocutors, who were mainly the number-two officials in the State, Commerce, and Treasury Departments. Andréani told them that his role was simply to explain the French position. When the U.S. negotiators suggested a side letter of understanding between the Americans and the French, Andréani said, "No, your interlocutor is the commission." The settlement finally arrived at gave the French partial satisfaction.[193]

France was not a direct party in the negotiations between the United States and the European Commission, which had to be settled before the Uruguay Round could be brought to a close, but this did not prevent Juppé from "marking" closely the European Union's mandatory, Brittan. Levitte describes this process:

> Toward the end of the negotiation, and apart from the meetings of the fifteen ministers in which Sir Leon received his mandate, Alain Juppé telephoned quite regularly to Sir Leon to remind him that France had asked him to do this or that, for it was inscribed in the mandate [that there will be a surveillance exercised by the Council of Ministers]. In effect, Juppé was conveying the message, "We know what you are doing, and we know what you are saying."
>
> As part of the follow-up negotiations, there were bilateral visits of Sir Leon to Washington, to try to find a compromise on a particular point. Sir Leon naturally wanted a mandate that was as vague as possible, to have a maximum margin of maneuver, and we wanted to give him a mandate as precise as possible.
>
> Within the European Union there were the countries favorable to international trade without controls, who tended to be on the side of Sir Leon—the Nordics and the British. And then there were the countries who wanted a close surveillance: for the Portuguese, it was textiles; for France, it was agriculture.

The negotiation resulted in the Marrakesh Agreement [of April 1994], which in our opinion is a good one. We found it balanced, but we had come close, from the French point of view, to a catastrophe, because Sir Leon gave himself a margin of maneuver notably at our expense, that is, on agriculture. And Alain Juppé had to take him in hand very severely.[194]

Abbott, representing the commission and therefore the interests of the European Union as a whole, presents a viewpoint that contrasts with the single-minded French defense of their interests in the negotiations on agriculture:

I see little contradiction in Sir Leon making reassuring noises in private, that he would do his best to take French desiderata into account in further talks with the Americans, and then defending himself in public as operating within his mandate and not seeking any fresh "instructions." Not only did he have a need for flexibility, he had to take equally into account what the views and positions of the other member-states would be if he got into an impasse with the Americans.[195]

According to Vimont, the French had to resort to the threat of veto in order to achieve a modification of the original Blair House agreement:

The French government could not accept the Blair House [I] decision, but it did not have much support in this, and decided to resort to the threat of a veto over the parts of the negotiation other than agriculture. Whereas industrial investment and intellectual property could be decided by qualified majority vote, services had to be decided by unanimity; for, although the commission can negotiate on services, decisions on services have to be acted upon by unanimity. Therefore the French government took the position that the overall Uruguay Round package should be accepted by unanimity because the services part of it had to be decided upon by unanimity.[196]

Abbott presents a contrasting view on the issue of unanimity:

Because of the political importance of the agreements reached, and the uncertainty over the competence issue in trade and services, Sir Leon had already indicated that he would seek a unanimous decision as well as the approval of the European Parliament, neither of which is strictly required by treaty.[197]

Overall, the will of the international community was to finish with these long-overdue negotiations. Other parties to the negotiations, chiefly the Cairns Group, threatened to stall agreements on the other elements of the Uruguay Round agenda if an agreement on agriculture could not be achieved. As Abbott explains:

> The French were persuaded that this negotiation had to be settled. The French had made gains in the industrial, services, and intellectual property spheres. They bit the bullet and made the best deal [on agriculture] that they could.[198]

Abbot emphasizes "the important role of Jacques Delors," the French president of the commission, in "persuading the French government in late 1993 that it had achieved as much as it could and that there was little appetite within the [European Union] for prolonging what had already become a very long negotiation."[199]

The foregoing would seem to bear out Jean-Marie Guéhenno's dictum that the French are more realistic than they like to admit.[200] It also tallies with the observation made by a French ambassador: "From the peasant, our country has also retained a fundamental realism, without which we would not have been able to survive a certain number of historical disasters."[201]

The Nature of the Final Deal on Agriculture

In Geneva on December 15, 1993, Peter Sutherland, who had succeeded Arthur Dunkel as director general of the GATT, announced that the United States and the European Union had arrived at a final deal in Brussels on December 6. Timothy Josling, Stefan Tangermann, and T. K. Warley summarize the deal this way:

> The nature of the final deal (sometimes called Blair House II) was to delay the immediate impact of some of the export subsidy cuts implicit in the Blair House reductions. [That is], countries were allowed to choose a different base year from which to start reductions in those cases where exports had increased significantly since the start of the Round. The final level of export subsidies allowed was not modified.[202]

Hugo Paemen and Alexandra Bensch place particular emphasis on the modifications that the European Union was able to obtain on the reduction of export subsidies, through the change in the afore-mentioned "base year" or "reference period." The change in the reference period was significant because exports had risen sharply in the interim: "most important of all, it was agreed that 1991–1992 could be taken as the reference period instead of 1986–88. For the [European Union], this meant a substantial increase in its export capability." The authors mention the significance of the "peace clause" being extended from six years to nine years in Blair House II. As far as Europe was concerned, the "peace clause" "enabled Europe to obtain a guarantee that the mechanisms of the Common Agricultural Policy, which it had been seeking in vain to 'Gattify' since 1962, would be deemed compatible with the rules of the [GATT] for a period of [the duration of the clause]."[203] In other words, all disputes on agriculture pending before the WTO would be suspended for the period of the "peace clause," which would expire at the end of 2003, having been extended from six to nine years as a result of the Blair House II adjustments.

For the French government, the "unacceptable" Blair House I agreement had been successfully transmuted into Blair House II, which, it stated, "continues the process of reform of the Common Agricultural Policy and safeguards the exporting vocation of the European Union."[204]

A U.S. view, as expressed by Rufus Yerxa, then deputy U.S. trade representative, is that the French gained certain significant benefits out of the trade aspects of the Uruguay Round. But they paid a price, and that was accepting the principle of agricultural reform. For example, they are now no longer able, under the CAP, to manipulate agricultural tariffs so that the import price coincides with the domestic price, in effect nullifying imports.[205]

Results of the Uruguay Round: Trade in Services

As noted earlier, trade in services took the form of a separate accord (the General Agreement on Trade in Services [GATS]), which became part of the World Trade Organization Agreements signed at Marrakesh on April 15, 1994. What emerged from the services negotiation was a framework of principles that all signatories endorsed. It was then left to individual countries to make commitments in specific sectors.

The specific sectors in the GATS agreement are the following: movement of persons, air transport services, financial services (banking and insurance), maritime transport services, and telecommunications.[206] The most important aspect of the GATS agreement was that services for the first time were brought under the purview of an international trade regime—the WTO—and that the signatories had committed themselves to future rounds of negotiations.

Under great pressure from the U.S. film industry, the United States, in the very last stages of the Uruguay Round negotiations, sought to include an audiovisual dossier. But the French, with strong backing from the European Union, took the lead in demurring on such discussions, invoking the need for an "exception" for the protection of culture; Mickey Kantor, the U.S. trade representative, was forced to back down on the issue.[207] As Levitte explains the French position:

> We asked that culture be excluded from the Uruguay Round. We believe that culture is not a merchandise. This is a French point of view. You have in Hollywood powerful industrialists who consider that a good film is a merchandise that brings in a lot of money and sells very well. We [on the other hand] plead in favor what of we call the "cultural exception," that is to say, the preservation of cultural diversity, by [providing] protection in the face of a disequilibrium in the relative weight between the American cultural industry, notably the cinema, and the European [cultural] industry.[208]

Protecting and promoting culture is a Europewide concern, not just a French one, although the French have taken the lead on the issue. According to Abbott, the French were less isolated within the European Union on the audiovisual issue than in the agricultural negotiations and in fact obtained considerable support for their position, particularly from the Spanish, the Italians, and the Germans.[209] In pushing this more "politically correct" issue, France was able to take some of the onus off itself as having been an intransigent defender of the CAP in the agricultural negotiations.[210]

Since its creation in 1949, the Council of Europe has spearheaded an initiative to recognize, promote, and preserve European culture. The council in 1954 promulgated a European Cultural Convention pledging "concerted action in promoting cultural activities of European interest."[211] France seeks to reinforce its own cultural policy by having it reflected in regulations and directives of the European Union, using as a juridical basis the conventions promulgated by the council.[212] The European Union's audiovisual policy statement includes an endorsement of "external measures, in particular the defense of European cultural interests in the context of the World Trade Organization."[213]

One of the EU provisions is the "Television without Frontiers" Directive, which was introduced as part of the Single European Market.[214] It provides for any member-state to have access to the television products of another member-state. It also allows member-states to reserve a portion of broadcast time for works produced within the European Union. The size of the quota varies, but it is highest in France, at 60 percent.[215] (The French further stipulate that 50 percent must be in the French language and they use a narrower definition of what constitutes a European production.)[216]

The audiovisual dossier, particularly as regards the cinema, is a uniquely neuralgic issue between France and the United States that goes back to the Blum-Byrnes loan agreement of May 28, 1946, named after the French prime minister, Léon Blum, and the U.S. secretary of state, James Byrnes. This agreement contained a provision, which became very controversial in France, whereby the United States obtained the right to bring U.S. films into France without an import quota, contrary to what had been the case in the 1930s. At the same time the French were limited on the number of French films that could be shown in France. This was a so-called screen quota: "starting from July 1, 1946, the screen quota reserved for French films will not exceed four weeks every four months," the agreement stipulated.[217] The intention was that these quotas were not to remain indefinitely: once France had recovered economically, they would be abolished entirely.

The United States sees this issue from a free-trade point of view, of course, while the French are bent on protecting their cultural patrimony from what they regard as an invasion of U.S. culture. In terms of the cinema as it exists today in France, the government supports its film industry by direct financial aid for the production and distribution of French films, and by a tax on cinema receipts, including those from U.S. films shown in France.[218] The amount of this tax is 10 percent, which to a large extent is a tax on U.S. films, given their domination of the market.[219] While U.S. films are extremely popular in France, the other side of the coin is that France, along with Britain, has the most thriving film industry in Europe. The other European countries are not even close.

Since services are based on the unanimity rule as far as the European Union is concerned, the French during the Uruguay Round were able to persuade their fellow members of the validity of the contention that audiovisual "products" (films, videos, etc.) should not be up for negotiation.[220] The Americans reacted sharply to the European Union's obduracy on this issue, with the result that the services part of the Marrakesh Agreement was limited to a statement of principles, with the various sectors left over for future consideration.

The French view is that audiovisual products remain off the WTO's table. The subject was not raised at the launching of the new negotiating round at Doha (called the Doha Development Agenda) in November 2001.[221] At the European Commission, the view is somewhat different:

> We consider that the audiovisual sector is *not* outside the GATS agreement but is fully covered by the framework of principles and rules that the GATS text represents. What is true is that the EU (and many other parties) did not make any specific commitments in this sector; but in that respect the sector is not different from many others where there were no, or only a few, such commitments in the individual schedules of the parties.
>
> The audiovisual sector is, like any other, subject to the commitment for further negotiation, as foreseen in Article XIX of the [GATS] agreement, and these [negotiations] did begin in January 2000. The [audiovisual] sector is the subject of requests in the current Doha context and offers will be made at a later stage.[222]

As someone who has been on both sides of the barricades, so to speak, first as an economic adviser to Prime Minister Balladur and then as a European commissioner for financial and monetary affairs, Yves-Thibault de Silguy has this view, perhaps untypically nuanced, of the French negotiating style at the Uruguay Round:

The French are not fully at ease discussing trade liberalization in international gatherings, and in this they have a certain fear of the outside world *(le grand large)*. The reason behind this is the strong tradition of state intervention in economic affairs dating back to [Louis XIV's finance minister, Jean-Baptiste] Colbert and the notion that the state regulates everything. Along with this goes the French preference for the supremacy of the political over the economic. A culture of economics, as well as the knowledge of economics, is relatively less developed in France.

The French approach tends to be overcautious and nervous *(frileux)*, more so than is warranted by the results on the ground, where the French do not come off any worse than the others do. In fact, France is one of the great beneficiaries of the [GATT/WTO] system.

The French approach is like that of the Paris street urchin *(gavroche):* he who complains the loudest is likely to be heeded. This attitude disconcerts our partners, who become apprehensive about the French attitude. [Leon] Brittan and his team were convinced they were working in the French interest, which was true.

Unquestionably, the Uruguay Round had positive effects for France, especially in terms of the favorable trade balance which resulted from it. Furthermore, the Uruguay Round put in place a dispute regulation system in a truly multilateral framework.[223]

Most of the Uruguay Round changes to tariffs and levels of subsidies were to be implemented over six years (at least for developed countries), starting in 1995. Therefore, and despite the failure of the Seattle conference in 1999, new negotiations on agriculture and on trade in services began in January 2000, and these have now been folded into the Doha [Development] Agenda.[224] It is projected that this new negotiating cycle will be completed by early 2005.[225]

Conclusion

In this case we see French brinkmanship put to work in the defense of the national interest. France, as "the key [EU] member-state in matters agricultural,"[226] and as the very embodiment of the "cultural exception" in the face of the Hollywood juggernaut, was the leading European player behind the scenes in both of these dossiers, finding, however, more support in the EU ranks on the audiovisual than on the agricultural issue.

French combativeness and indeed inflexibility were fully on display on two subjects that are at the heart of the French patrimony—the peasant tradition and French culture. The "culture of authority" was brought into play: the French harassed the principals in the European Commission who were mandated to conduct trade negotiations on behalf of the European Union, stretching the surveillance function of the European Council over the commission to the limit. They focused their attacks, in private and in public (including in the press), on Sir Leon Brittan, who came in at the later stage of the protracted negotiation. At the same time, a degree of realism crept in at the end: the principle of including agriculture as part of an international trade regime was accepted by the French (who, however, continued to resist the United States on discussing audiovisual issues).

This was far from a zero-sum game, whether as regards France with respect to its EU partners, the European Union with respect to the United States, or the forces of intergovernmentalism with respect to those of supranationalism within the European Union; though France, in calling for unanimity in voting, raised the specter of a veto and the Luxembourg Compromise,[227] it achieved only partial satisfaction in the end,[228] acceding to the enormous worldwide pressure to finish the agricultural negotiations and thereby bring the Uruguay Round to a long-overdue close. But owing to the sharpness and effectiveness of the French tactics, and the publicity this received, the outcome was even more favorable to France in the public relations sense than it was in the real one.

Although the French position on the agricultural dossier frequently isolated France from many of its EU partners, the French-German alliance held firm. As Alice Landau points out, France was able, in the final stages, to gain the support of Germany in demanding a "clarification" of the agricultural dossier, which resulted in a modification of the terms in what became the eventual agreement.[229]

In the final analysis, France is too big, and too central, to be left as the odd man out in European Union deliberations. The other Europeans want to get along with France and do not like to see the French isolated, according to Yerxa: "It's amazing how effective the French are in the EU in getting their own way."[230] This effectiveness is largely due to the fact that the French over the recent decades have become more adept at dealing in multilateral settings, as in the European Union.

On the other hand, and as Abbott points out, it would be too *simpliste* to see the French as "having matters their own way" in the Uruguay Round, even if their EU partners were ready to meet their concerns to a point:

> True, the French were hinting that they would block agreement to the final deal if it did not suit them; but they too have to measure what is negotiable with other partners and assess the consequences of taking unreasonable positions in terms of their relations with EU colleagues.[231]

Nevertheless, the Uruguay Round is a textbook example of France fighting above its weight, particularly following the arrival on the scene of Edouard Balladur's government in 1993, when Foreign Minister Alain Juppé spearheaded the French case on agriculture—the perfect image of the tough, elegant, and in-control *énarque*.[232]

6

Negotiating
with the French

THIS CHAPTER OFFERS VARIOUS SUGGESTIONS for negotiators who wish to make their encounters with French officials more productive.[1] These suggestions are aimed in particular at negotiators from the United States, but they should prove useful for diplomats from any of the major Western powers. Each section of the chapter highlights one of the key elements of French negotiating behavior analyzed in the preceding chapters and marries it to one or more suggestions for countering or accommodating that behavioral trait.

The ideas presented here will not, of course, transform the character of negotiations with the French, which are shaped above all by differing national interests—or at least by differing perceptions of those interests—and by the policies governments adopt to defend and promote them. However, to the degree that negotiations with the French have been impeded by the mist of incomprehension that seems so often to envelop U.S.-French encounters, this chapter may help to give U.S. diplomats a clearer view of their French counterparts and a better idea of how to reach agreement with them.

At the same time, it is important to bear in mind that this mist of incomprehension is rarely as dense as it seems to be. Despite occasional overheated rhetoric from both sides to the contrary, France and the United States both belong to the same—Western—civilization; despite wide differences in language and culture, both operate within the context of the Western set of values and have numerous mutual interests. Dealing with the French is quite different from interacting with people from an entirely different civilization, such as that of China, Japan, India, or Iran.

It is also important to recognize that France's voice has been an alternative to that of the United States for almost fifty years or, as Stanley Hoffmann puts it, "France has been fighting against unipolarity since Charles de Gaulle came to power."[2] In other words, though intimately a part of the West, France is less than a perfect ally of the United States, and therefore one cannot expect that an agreement between the two countries is automatic, or even possible.

LA GRANDE NATION—SHOW RESPECT

French pretensions to a global role may no longer be matched by French power in the international arena, but the tradition of *la Grande Nation* endures nonetheless. The French are well versed in the glories of their long history. Moreover, the spirit of the French Revolution still resonates in terms of France's conviction that it presents a uniquely admirable and yet universally applicable model of a just and well-ordered political system and society. France may no longer possess vast colonies—and those that remain are called, appropriately, "confetti"—but it maintains links to many of its former domains and retains much of the self-importance of a major metropolitan power. The power and the trappings of the French state also play a large part in sustaining the idea of *la Grande Nation*.

This abiding sense of French greatness is evident among the French diplomatic corps and often comes across as arrogance. Foreign interlocutors encounter at times an almost unbelievable degree of French *suffisance* (smugness) backed up by all the subtleties of language that they find hard put to match. Certainly, many foreign negotiators would agree that de Gaulle's scathing description in November

1967 of Jews as "an elite people, sure of themselves and domineering" might equally well be applied to the French themselves. In fact, de Gaulle was taken aback by the adverse public reaction to his words, probably thinking that, in addition to chastising the Israelis, he was giving them a backhanded compliment.[3]

Yet, while French diplomats may seem to exaggerate the role that France plays on the contemporary international stage, France's negotiating partners would be wrong to dismiss all French claims as bombast. France is a key element in the international system. Its universalist mission and its appeal to the oppressed have a global resonance; its language is widely spoken and its culture admired throughout the world; it is a major trading partner, having the world's fifth-largest economy after the United States, Japan, Germany, and Great Britain;[4] it has a permanent seat on the UN Security Council and thus the power of veto; it possesses an arsenal of nuclear weapons; and it has often demonstrated its willingness to intervene abroad militarily. In short, France counts: it is a key factor in the political equilibrium of the West and in the balance of power in Europe.

In light, then, of both the French attachment to the myth of *la Grande Nation* and the reality of France's international standing, it is important that French negotiators not be made to feel that they are being slighted by their foreign counterparts. The French want to be considered as a major power and to be taken seriously. They have an acute sensitivity concerning a European pecking order with respect to the United States and the outside world. They note with a sort of mordant irony that never in the twentieth century or beyond has the United States treated them on the same plane as the British, despite the facade of the Big Three Western powers and their periodic tripartite meetings since World War I.

Americans should resist thinking reflexively about the French in terms of pretensions of grandeur. Just as the French individual has been brought up to have an opinion on everything, in the tradition of *l'honnête homme*, so France as a collective identity is in the habit of making policy pronouncements on a very wide range of subjects of global concern. Sometimes this comes across as pretentiousness, as France often does not have the power to influence events outside Europe. But the fact is that France still looks upon itself as a major power with worldwide influence.

Behind a facade of logical certitude, the French are highly emotional and are quick to perceive slights, real and imagined. A U.S. pronouncement that emphasizes the United States' position as the sole superpower may seem to U.S. officials to be little more than a statement of fact, but to French officials, and depending on how it is put, it may well appear to be a calculated insult, intended to underline France's second-class status.

At the same time, U.S. diplomats should not pretend that the United States is weaker than it is. With their own nation having been built through conquest, the French respect power, they recognize the United States as a superpower, and they expect the United States to act like one—perhaps, however, not to the extent that the United States did in the war on Iraq in the spring of 2003. As Jacques Juillard wrote in his column in *Le Nouvel Observateur:*

> Not only was the French position on the Iraqi crisis just; it was the only one not to insult the future. What everyone underestimated was the cold American determination to push ahead with force, to flout all legality, even if it meant destroying all international institutions [and] supplanting them with alliances on a case-by-case basis.[5]

French officials are almost unique within diplomatic circles for saying that if France were a superpower, it would act in the same way that the United States does. A certain negative confirmation of this can be found in the following observation of Hubert Védrine, who advocates adopting

> a certain way of acting toward others that is antithetical to some of our national reflexes, be they chauvinistic or even universalistic. Thus we [shouldn't] keep acting like a great power that thinks its job is to pass on its "message" to others. That remains true in certain important cases. But we've got to be careful lest our European partners end up saying that if by chance the French were to find themselves in the same position as the Americans today, they'd be even more unbearable than the Americans! Many Europeans think this already.[6]

In short, U.S. negotiators should demonstrate U.S. self-confidence while showing respect for French self-worth. Such respect can be dis-

played in numerous ways. For instance, the French have a highly developed sense of, and an interest in, history and France's place in it—what
Pierre Nora characterizes as "the national hegemony of history"[7]—
whereas Americans are widely regarded as being profoundly ignorant of
history. Thus, a French diplomat might be pleasantly surprised to hear
a U.S. counterpart recall events in U.S. history in which the French
played a positive role such as the French combined land and naval contribution in the battle of Yorktown, which was decisive in the defeat of
England in the Revolutionary War. The French remember this; not
many Americans do.

It is also important for foreign diplomats to show respect for the
French language, by either speaking it well or not at all. To the French,
their language is a thing of beauty, a uniquely versatile instrument for
conveying ideas with clarity and elegance, especially in conversation. (As
Voltaire put it, "Of all the languages of Europe, French should be the
most generalized, because it is the most suitable for conversation.")[8] The
French thus bristle to hear this instrument being mishandled by inex-
pert players.

AN AGGRESSIVE UNDERDOG—SHOW YOU'RE LISTENING

The other side of the French coin from the tradition of *la Grande
Nation* is the culture of the underdog—emphasized by the string of
French defeats that have alternated with periods of glory. Clearly
linked to this state of alternation is what French political scientist
Pierre Bréchon has characterized as "the strong pessimism of the
French with respect to their society and their institutions."[9]

France has long seen itself as a nation struggling against the dominant power in Europe. This is deeply ingrained in French history, as in
this description of "The Plenipotentiary" by the seventeenth-century
philosopher and moralist Jean de la Bruyère: "He intimidates the strong
and the powerful, he encourages the weak. He unites in common interest several of the weak against the more powerful one, to make the
scales equal."[10] Often the dominant power happened to be an empire,
and this mind-set has developed, as noted in chapter 3, into a "culture
of opposition to the dominant norms."[11] Today, even though the period

of epic nation-state wars seems to have passed, the French still harbor a sense of being overwhelmed by the Anglo-Saxons, which sustains their sense of being an underdog. The fact that the "Anglosphere" powers—meaning the United States, the United Kingdom, and Australia—carried off a swift war in Iraq in 2003[12] can only have increased the French feeling of having been left behind, particularly in the military area.

The "culture of opposition to the dominant norms" is not only related to the role of the underdog that France has had to play following the period of its ascendancy in Europe; it is also related to the straitjacket quality of French political culture and the reaction that has developed against it. As Nora describes this curious phenomenon:

> France by its history and its civilization has developed a reflex of revolt, linked to the formalistic and hierarchical style of authority inherited from the "divine right" monarchy, maintained by a statist and bureaucratic centralization, and which has invaded from top to bottom the institutions, the army, education, and business, and which has impregnated social relations down to couples and families. France: the land of command. There has resulted a latent anarchism, a dialectic of order and subversion which is at the base of France's political as well as intellectual history.[13]

As an underdog, France has grown accustomed to disasters and to rebounding from them, as was the case with Charles de Gaulle following the worst military defeat in French history. "Whether one emphasizes the realism of the de Gaulle policy or its intensive use of myths," comments Nora, "it remains the case that, through thirty years of national presence, the historical genius of de Gaulle consisted of enveloping the real diminution of French power in the vocabulary of grandeur; [and] of transforming magically that most crushing of military defeats of France into a manner of victory."[14]

This Gaullist performance on the world stage employed a technique that combined the high-minded and the bloody-minded. The French, deeply humiliated by the experience of World War II, are grateful to de Gaulle for showing them how to overcome, or sublimate, this black spot in their memory: by acting like a great power still, by preserving independence of action, by being willing to say no, and by accepting and even taking a mordant pleasure in being isolated. French statesmen who deferred to Britain's lead in the 1930s have now been reincarnated as tough and truculent negotiators, modeling themselves, consciously or not, on the tall French general who gave them back their honor—though not their glory. France, "which loves glory,"[15] has, in Nora's words, withdrawn from the course of great history: "It was the change, by stages and shocks, from a great world power to a middle power and its grating adjustments: 1918, 1945, 1962, each of these dates carry[ing] its weight of mutilating reality and compensatory illusions."[16]

The result can be seen today in French interlocutors, who alternate between a superiority complex and an inferiority complex. Although the former may seem more evident to foreigners, the latter is very much in the mind of the French. A soupçon of this tendency can be found in the concern of the French business community about possible U.S. reprisals in the wake of the disagreement over the Iraq war. As Juillard comments:

> Should we apologize for having been against the war? I find it amusing that we see in the United States, but especially in France, a group that invites us to do [just] that. This group we know well. One only has to read our history. Each time that France is attacked, there emerges in our bourgeoisie and among our elites a debate, always the same, as to the best way of capitulating.[17]

Such defeatism, however, is anathema to the keepers of the Gaullist flame, who are easy to find at the Quai d'Orsay, and who present themselves as self-confident and unbending. To quote Juillard again, this time commenting on the consequences of Jacques Chirac's behavior in the crisis over Iraq in 2003: "From now on, everything will depend on the ability of Jacques Chirac to manage, in a Gaullist fashion, a situation à la de Gaulle which he set about [creating] with an incredible impetuosity."[18]

The inclination to play the underdog is accentuated in negotiations with the United States because France and the United States are hardly equal partners. Painfully conscious of the United States as the sole superpower, the French enter a negotiating session with the Americans with a sense of apprehension and suspicion. It takes time to overcome this sentiment and thus open the possibility of reaching a mutually satisfactory agreement. One way of doing so is for U.S. diplomats to accept what negotiations expert Roger Fisher calls "the duty of the powerful" by showing respect and recognition to the side that is at a disadvantage; in other words, the U.S. side can accept the asymmetry in power between the two nations by exhibiting "unilateral constructive behavior" even if the French side is displaying a truculent approach.[19] When disagreement arises, Americans can usefully respond, says Fisher, by "active listening." Instead of stating the U.S. position as a means of reacting, the U.S. negotiator can draw out the French interlocutor by asking why he or she disagrees and by showing an interest in the latter's way of thinking. U.S. negotiators should be careful to acknowledge dissenting opinions as legitimate and to treat them with respect. Too often, U.S. diplomats proclaim, rather than carefully lay out, their negotiating position, as if they expect no significant contradiction but instead an act of ratification.

Negotiations experts Robert Mnookin, Scott Peppet, and Andrew Tulumello posit a dialectic between *empathy* ("demonstrating an understanding of the other side's needs, interests and perspective, without necessarily agreeing") and *assertiveness* ("advocacy of one's own needs, interests and perspective"). In their view, the goal of a negotiator is "combining empathy and assertiveness in negotiation."[20] Tactically, this can be done by "turning back on the other his responses, in seeking to clarify them, and in [thus] showing that one is listening."[21] In the case of the French, like other peoples who are especially taken with the beauty and instrumentality of their own language, they are most comfortable being listened to rather than the reverse. Therefore, and in particular with the French, it is extremely important not to neglect empathy. The U.S. negotiator should be a good listener as well as a good speaker. It is even more important to *show* that one is listening and that one gets the point of what the French are trying to say, even though there may not be an agreement in the end. Without *empathy*, exchanges with the French are liable to be confrontational.

Even with empathy, it should be admitted, negotiations are unlikely to be entirely cordial. In France there is a marked taste for confrontation and aggressiveness in verbal exchanges. One has only to watch talk shows and debates on French television to appreciate the degree to which the speakers hector and insult one another. This tendency, which is fostered by the fiercely competitive French school system, has long extended into the negotiating arena. The recent introduction of the subject of negotiations and negotiating technique into the curricula of ENA and other higher-level educational institutions is motivated in part by a recognition of the counterproductive results of this aggressive style.

For their part, U.S. and other negotiators should learn to distinguish between private and public displays of rhetorical ferocity by their French counterparts. What is said behind closed doors is a better indicator of the real French mood than what is presented for public consumption. Foreign officials are often irritated to discover that a mild and consensual conversation with their French counterparts is followed by the release of a French statement sharply critical of the other side. This pattern, however, signifies little more than a French tradition of combative public rhetoric, a tradition spurred by a need to display one's forensic powers, to assert the authority and independence of the French state, and, often, simply to restate French principles. France's interlocutors should not take such statements too seriously, for in many cases public disagreement turns into private agreement, echoing the oft-repeated phrase "The French say no and do yes." For instance, despite the fierce rhetoric exchanged between the United States and France over the issue of war with Iraq, France permitted U.S. military overflights of France to the Middle East during the crisis—something that Switzerland, for example, did not.

RESISTANCE TO COMPROMISE—BE PATIENT, BUILD RELATIONSHIPS, AND DON'T ALWAYS EXPECT TO REACH AGREEMENT

As noted in chapter 4, Couve de Murville declared that "the objective [of a negotiation] is not to arrive at a negotiated solution; it is to defend one's point of view."[22] This remarkable approach, so unlike the businesslike style of U.S. diplomats, goes a long way in explaining the tenacity with which French negotiators stick to their opening position and their disinclination to countenance compromise. A French delegation usually enters a negotiation with long-range goals, and typically it would rather eschew the chance of reaching agreement than sacrifice those goals.

Agreement can sometimes be reached if the French president, or at a lower level the prime minister or foreign minister, decides to intervene just as the talks appear to be collapsing, but such intervention usually occurs only after a lengthy middle game, often characterized by French intransigence. This was the case with two protracted negotiations: in the Uruguay Round in 1993, when President Mitterrand intervened after being persuaded that the French had obtained as much as they could hope for;[23] and in 2002 during the drafting of Resolution 1441 on Iraq, when, according to a UN official familiar with the negotiations, the French sensed they were losing the center of gravity in the Security Council and came to an agreement with the Americans.[24] Whether or not the latter is an accurate reflection of what actually occurred, what seems often to take place is a sobering reappraisal of the French power position, at which point the French side comes to closure—a reflex, as some have termed it, of "peasant realism," also described as the French "solidity" based on a long-standing peasant tradition.[25] It is this peasant tradition, as Armand Frémont characterizes it, that is the "cradle of French conservatism" and the "matrix of continuity in the face of change."[26]

For France's negotiating partners, patience is vital. For Americans especially, given their focus on rapid achievement, impatience must be kept on a tight rein. Even at mealtimes patience is important. For the French, a meal is part of the negotiation itself in that it is an instrument or an accoutrement, and if France is hosting the talks, a meal gives the French an opportunity to display the sophisticated culinary skills they prize so highly. Remarks by U.S. and British officials to the effect "Why didn't they just serve sandwiches?" are thus sure to offend.

Patience, however, should not be inexhaustible. Rather, it should be tempered by realism. Americans and others who set great store by reaching an agreement should keep in mind that many negotiations with the French may not result in a conclusion, or not in a satisfactory one at any rate. Americans should also have a self-awareness of what Tocqueville called their "passion for unanimity,"[27] which can lead them, especially in dealing with the French, into thinking that an opposing viewpoint, rather than being sincerely held, is designed soley to injure or obstruct U.S. interests.

Furthermore, France's negotiating counterparts should make some effort to accommodate the French preference for establishing a relationship before getting down to business. Even in a single meeting it is helpful to allow sufficient time to establish some degree of personal rapport before discussing the substantive issues at hand. If one must cancel a meeting with a French counterpart, one should send an explanatory note to demonstrate that one values the relationship. In most circumstances, it is likely to be better if one is less direct and less up-front about advancing concrete positions. With the French, it is better to wait until some rapport develops. The low-context U.S. approach is to declare bluntly, "I want to talk about such-and-such." The high-context French approach is to intimate, "I want to know what is going on between the two of us."[28] The up-front approach, combined with the reflexes of a superpower conditioned over half a century of dominance in NATO, can be decidedly counterproductive in encounters with the French.

For the French, the emotional tenor of negotiations is important, not perhaps as important as the interests at stake, but certainly of more consequence than it is to U.S. negotiators. It is helpful to try to build a friendly, personal relationship with French counterparts, for instance, by inquiring about the French official's hobbies and personal interests. French officials generally appreciate being invited to join their counterparts in private settings. Brent Scowcroft, the national security adviser under President George H. W. Bush, noted in a memoir (written with Bush) that the personal relationship between the president and his French counterpart, François Mitterrand, was set on the right track early on in the administration when, in 1989, Bush invited Mitterrand to visit him at his summer home in Kennebunkport, Maine: "The Kennebunkport meeting was the President's personal style of diplomacy at its finest. The relationship established over that weekend played a great role in the way some of the momentous events of the next three years worked out. Despite deep differences on occasion, this personal rapport was able, in most instances, to allow sufficient cooperation for resolving issues satisfactorily."[29]

THE GODDESS OF REASON—
RECOGNIZE THE FRENCH RESPECT FOR LOGIC

French negotiators are conspicuously devoted to what has been referred to as the goddess of Reason. Drawing on the work of Descartes, the *philosophes* of the Enlightenment and, later, the ideologues of the French Revolution made reason a substitute for religion. As Claude Langlois has characterized it, the "revolutionary religion" represented a "transfer of sacredness," and the challenge was "to make free citizens adhere to the new system founded on reason."[30] And the precursor figure behind this transformation, Descartes, "completely contaminated" the doctrine of the Church and "remains in history as the one who carried out definitively the split between philosophy and religion."[31] Today, the French negotiator has the sense, perhaps partly subconsciously, of being possessed of the "Cartesian project [whereby] one makes oneself through reason master and possessor of nature."[32]

In addition, and as noted earlier, the French are brought up to have an idea on everything and to express it with clarity. In the words of Madame de Staël:

> In all the classes, in France, one senses the need to talk; speech is not only, as elsewhere, a means of communicating ideas, sentiments and business matters, but it is an instrument that one likes to play, and which revives the spirit, like music with some other peoples, and strong liquor with others.[33]

The habit of French exposition, what is called *dissertation*, tends to follow a similar path: the general theme is announced; a series of points, often three of them ("the sacrosanct division in three points"),[34] is presented; an argument is developed on each of the points, with many detours being taken to pursue various paradoxes and contradictions; and finally a conclusion is reached.[35]

Cartesianism and *dissertation*, combined with a taste for wit, audacity, and panache and an impatience with Anglo-Saxon phlegm, produce a characteristic French style: seizing the floor with a lengthy disquisition that lays out the logic of the French position; sticking tenaciously to that position; and, if necessary, accepting the role of the lone holdout, even to the extent of walking out of, or boycotting, negotiations. Armed with the certitude of having the right solution through a superior exercise of reason, French negotiators are reluctant to retreat from their opening position, especially when pushed to do so by representatives of the Anglo-Saxon world that seems constantly to be trying to overwhelm French culture and disregarding French interests and sensitivities.

This mind-set, needless to say, does not make agreement easy to reach. However, Cartesianism does offer some opportunities for France's negotiating counterparts. In the first place, the "Cartesian spirit" involves what François Azouvi refers to as "the subordination of content to rational form,"[36] a phenomenon that recalls statements by French interviewees cited in earlier chapters that the French can make an equally logical argument for or against a particular point of view, that they enjoy moving from one concept to another as a sort of intellectual game. If a negotiating counterpart can encourage this tendency to explore the logic of the different point of view, a French official may find some rationale for shifting ground.

In the second place, foreign negotiators would do well at some point to enunciate a broad strategy, setting out a statement of goals, so that the French side can understand the overall logic of their counterparts' position. This would fit well the French penchant to form first a general understanding of things, to perceive the overall framework of a discussion. Following talks about European defense with U.S. interlocutors in early 1992, a French official concluded: "They had nothing to say." The Americans, he said, had no overall vision of the future or of any new direction that the Atlantic Alliance might take. They seemed motivated only by a pragmatic need to justify a continuing U.S. troop presence in Europe.[37]

In the third place, the French, sure of the logic of their own position, come to the table with a clear idea of what is to be their final position—but often without a fallback position. This offers their counterparts an opportunity to fill this void with their own proposals. (As seen in chapter 5, this is what the U.S. side attempted to do when it became clear that Jacques Chirac's attempt to have a French officer placed in charge of NATO's Southern Command was a nonstarter. The U.S. suggestions might have succeeded had not a socialist government suddenly taken over in France in the spring of 1997.) At the same time, however, foreign negotiators should be careful not to introduce a new idea that does not fit into the overall logic of things or is inconsistent with what has been decided in the past; to do so will inspire only inflexibility on the French side of the table.

FRANCE VERSUS THE UNITED STATES–
AVOID COMBATIVENESS UNBECOMING TO A SUPERPOWER

"For at least two centuries," notes Jean-Philippe Mathy, "the Gallic and Anglo-American traditions have looked askance at each other."[38] France, like the United States, thinks of itself as a showcase of universal values, and the two nations have long competed to promote their own model of society throughout the world. Despite ostensible similarities, the two models are fundamentally at odds. The French tradition of "state-centered capitalism," where the "citizens count on the state rather than the market to ensure their welfare,"[39] is in sharp contrast with the traditional U.S. view of the minimalist role of the state. Equally sharp is the difference in attitudes toward religion. The French Revolution was aimed at casting off the shackles of the monarchy, the nobility, *and* the Catholic Church. These fundamental differences involving the institution of the state and the exercise of religion within the state mean that U.S. negotiators have long been on opposite sides of the barricades from the French on issues as diverse as abortion, free trade, and protection of the environment.

The competition between the two countries feeds a mutual antagonism. Anti-Americanism has a long history in France, beginning from the time of the U.S. colonies and flowering in the twentieth century, especially in the aftermath of World War II. More recently, the accelerating pace of globalization–a phenomenon that many French equate with the spread of what they see as pernicious U.S. values such as unrestrained capitalism–and the United States' behavior as the preeminent global power have only intensified anti-American feeling and bolstered a readiness to stand up to the superpower. This sentiment is not just confined to the intellectual class but can be found in various other parts of French society. On the U.S. side, ill feeling toward the French is not hard to find. At times of strained French-U.S. relations–as during the debate in 2002–03 within the UN Security Council over whether to sanction a U.S.-led war against Iraq–the depth and viciousness of U.S. Francophobia can–and did–swiftly increase. When, once the war began, it became a question of blood, the mutual hostility reached a peak of intensity never before seen in the bilateral relationship and unprecedented among Western allies.

U.S. interlocutors should treat French anti-Americanism with a certain indulgence, not being quick to recognize it but rather brushing it aside unless it becomes too egregious. They should not let the French get under their skin, as so often happens.[40] Rather they should recognize the deep roots, and the legitimacy, of the French desire to be independent and to maximize their power in relation to others. They should also play up implicitly the enduring aspects of the French-U.S. tie. France *is* the United States' oldest, if now not its best, ally. This requires looking deep into history: while not denying (and certainly the French do not) that the United States twice rescued France in the twentieth century, U.S. negotiators should recognize the enormous French losses in World War I as well as the distinct possibility that the U.S. republic might not have come into being without French intervention. They should invoke subtly the mythology and the symbols of positive episodes in the French-U.S. relationship (Lafayette, Yorktown, Pershing, Eisenhower, etc.) in the knowledge that, if they do not take the lead, few among the U.S. population will, because, as noted earlier in this study, France has no "constituency" in the United States.

France has developed a culture and a tactic of working through multilateral bodies, such as the European Union, the Organization for Security and Cooperation in Europe, and the United Nations, in part as a way to leverage its power with regard to the United States. A French diplomat explains why multilateralism, which is so important for the French, is much less so for the Americans: "They are the strongest. America is a great power. It is a sign of a great power that it doesn't need to worry about others. Americans can do it by themselves. We like the multilateral."[41]

U.S. negotiators should expect that the French will characteristically opt for multilateral solutions to international issues. Part and parcel of this multilateralism is a penchant for peaceful solutions to problems, a preference shared by most of Europe. There is a clear and growing divergence between Europe and the United States as regards the willingness and ability to use force. As was seen in the lead-up to the U.S.-led military campaigns against Iraq in 1991 and 2003, France, as a permanent member of the UN Security Council, will characteristically seek to exhaust all peaceful options before endorsing the use of force.

The French attachment to multilateralism is most pronounced in respect to the European Union, of which it was a founder and remains a leading member. Other member-states may at times deplore French pressure tactics, even bullying tactics, within the European Union, but they are generally more in sympathy with France than they may appear or admit to U.S. interlocutors. EU members realize that, given its crucial role in Europe, both historically and at present, France cannot and should not be isolated. U.S. negotiators should not be overly sanguine about the new members of the European Union becoming a counterweight to France, as was the case during the Iraq crisis when the so-called Vilnius Ten candidates[42] for EU membership offered a joint statement in support of the United States. As Steven Erlanger of the *New York Times* has observed: "The new member countries will discover that they have common interests in the EU. It will be easier to repair rifts within the EU than transatlantic rifts."[43]

At the same time, Americans should pay more attention to the French desire for leadership in continental Western Europe. Although France is no longer in a dominant position in the European Union— especially in light of the accession of many new member-states that feel no obligation to defer to France—it still has an ambition to be the "voice" of Europe.

THE HIERARCHICAL STATE—RECOGNIZE THE INFLUENCE OF FRENCH POLITICAL CULTURE

French negotiators are both constrained and empowered by French political traditions and practices. In the first place, negotiators are acutely aware of an overriding obligation to defend the interests of the state, which is venerated in France to a degree almost unimaginable in the other major Western powers. It is, indeed, difficult to exaggerate the role of the French state as it relates to how the French think of themselves and conduct themselves. As Nora observes:

> It is the State, in France, that has oriented both the practice and the concepts of the economy, even [the] liberal [economy], and has painfully and incompletely penetrated them; [it is] the State that created the great academic and university institutions, even conferring on them the instruments of their autonomy; [it is] the State that

> spread the language codes that were considered good and suppressed the dialects; [it is] the State that civilized the society. No other country has established such appropriateness between its national State and its economy, its culture, its language and its society.[44]

Duty-bound to protect the state, French negotiators are tenacious in their defense of the French position, yet also limited in their room for maneuver insofar as they dare not agree to any concession to their negotiating partners that might weaken the power of the state, if only marginally. A French negotiator can go only so far in cooperating with any foreign counterpart.

The hierarchy and the longevity of the French state, and the concept of *la raison d'État* (a concept that is all but absent in U.S. political culture), have also sustained a tradition of secrecy. This reflex produces a general reluctance to give out information. In many (though not all) cases, an exchange of information with the French means that the other party winds up with the short end of the stick.

In some ways, the job of French negotiators is made easier by the discipline of their political system. In France, as the French are fond of remarking, "the state acts as one man." This is especially evident in the realm of foreign affairs, in which the executive can design a policy and entrust it to the bureaucracy to conduct without fear of interference from the legislature. Whereas the White House must always contend with interference from Congress and numerous pressure groups, the Élysée has little fear that the French parliament will act as a brake on its foreign policy. Even in periods of cohabitation, with the presidency and the government in the hands of different political parties, virtually no difference appears internationally in the presentation of French foreign policy. For French officials at the negotiating table, this coherence means that they are unlikely to be embarrassed by a sudden switch in government policy or contradicted by dissenting voices at home.

Moreover, because they do not have to respond to multiple constituencies represented in the legislature, French negotiators enjoy greater latitude in terms of their behavior at the negotiating table. They can throw tantrums, stage walkouts, and deploy other dramatic techniques, safe in the knowledge that they will not be exposed to wounding criticism in the National Assembly or from a press that has

less influence on foreign policy than in other countries. France's negotiating partners should take care, therefore, not to let themselves
become provoked by theatrics and histrionics, but they should also be
prepared to respond firmly at an appropriate moment, for example, by
walking out of negotiations themselves. It should also be borne in
mind that behind the histrionics often lurks cold calculation. One
French diplomat observes that the French negotiator has to concen-
trate on being nonemotional: "Don't let your passions carry you away;
it is the other delegation that should become unnerved."[45]

French officials are on the lookout for, and happy to benefit
from, a lack of discipline on the other side of the negotiating table. For
instance, the French are entirely familiar with the more cumbersome
and decentralized decision-making system in the United States, where
various outside constituencies come into play and can prompt switches
or reverses in U.S. policy. The impression of U.S. inconsistency is reinforced by the fact that U.S. officials come and go much more frequently than in France, where government service is less politicized.
French negotiators may sincerely bemoan the changeability of the
U.S. stance, but they are pleased to profit from the damaging press
leaks that U.S. interagency squabbles can sometimes generate in the
middle of negotiations.

Differences between the U.S. and the French systems exist also at
the level of negotiating personnel. Americans should be very careful not
to attribute to their French interlocutors the same authority or political
inclinations that U.S. negotiators typically possess. For instance, U.S.
negotiators should not consider that an agreement reached with the
French military will necessarily be endorsed by the French civil authority; the French military does not enjoy the same authority that its U.S.
counterpart has. Also, it should not be assumed that the *énarque*,
although a member of the French elite, is naturally going to be conservative. As Ezra Suleiman has points out, the French system of state-
created elites works for both the Right and the Left. As *énarques* rise in
the bureaucracy, they usually are assigned to a ministerial cabinet and
thus are labeled either "Left" or "Right," depending on the political coloration of the minister.[46]

The French are hard to place ideologically. Taken as a whole,
they may be said to embrace "state-centered capitalism," but they are

deeply divided on many issues, some of which even predate the Revolution.[47] Cited earlier was Nora's description of "new France against ancient France, secular France against religious France, the France of the Left against the France of the Right."[48] In part because of this lack of an easily identified ideology—for example, de Gaulle's "ideology" was that of the nation-state of France—Americans do not know exactly what to expect from French negotiators. The French judge issues on their own merits, as they see them through the lens of their Cartesian philosophy.

7

Looking Ahead

CHANGES IN ATTITUDES

The characteristics of French negotiating behavior described in this volume are going through a process of attenuation and change. Certain characteristics will remain constant: the centralized and pyramidal character of the French state; French Cartesianism—the emphasis on logic and reason, and the style of *dissertation;* the dialectic between a sense of superiority and a sense of inferiority; and the French preference for building a relationship before getting down to the business at hand.

It is in the area of positional negotiations—coming to the table with a fixed, carefully reasoned position and sticking to it—that one is liable to see greater flexibility. This is partly due to a generational change. The new French negotiators are less the uniform products of the *grandes écoles* than their predecessors were; they are more pragmatic and less rigid; they have greater international experience and are more open to the world; in some cases they have had an education outside France; and, last but not least, they have a facility in English much greater than their forebears.[1]

257

What is speeding this change in the profile of French negotiators is the process of globalization, a phenomenon that makes the French apprehensive, but one with which they are coping better than others, and better than they themselves realize or admit—as Philip Gordon and Sophie Meunier point out in *The French Challenge: Adapting to Globalization*.[2] In their work, Gordon and Meunier produce figures to show that during the past twenty years or so France has been moving away from its traditional model of state control *(dirigisme)* and toward a greater degree of market capitalism and a more open economy. One such statistic is that the number of shareholders in the French stock market has increased from 1.5 million in 1978–82 to 5.6 million in 2000, or about 10 percent of the adult population (which is, however, still less than the comparative figures of 22 percent and 15 percent for the United States and Britain, respectively).[3] Even more impressive, the number of Internet users in France increased from 540,000 to three million between January 1998 and January 2000.[4]

These changes do not mean that the system by which France shapes its elites will cease to function; the odds are that foreign interlocutors will continue to face what one U.S. diplomat has characterized as "the most cohesive and homogeneous foreign-policy elite in the business."[5] Nonetheless, that elite will increasingly display a more flexible, less nationalist, and more multilateral attitude in international arenas. French negotiators have come to act, and will do so increasingly in the future, more consensually, huddling closer to their European partners. In the words of Pierre Vimont, cabinet director of Foreign Minister Dominique de Villepin and former ambassador to the European Union, "Little by little we have become accustomed to negotiations within the [European] Community."[6]

Perhaps the most salient long-term trend that is observable is the emerging French tolerance of and penchant for compromise, a trend that, though not always consistent, marks a sharp contrast with the France of a generation ago, marked by the strong-arm, uncompromising approach of Charles de Gaulle, the emblematic moment of which was the "empty-chair" crisis of 1965–66, when France engaged in an extended boycott of the meetings of the European Community.

This trend toward compromise and a desire to work through multilateral institutions, discernible increasingly since the end of the

Cold War, became distinctly more pronounced during the transatlantic and intra-European crisis over the war in Iraq in 2002–03. In a moment not unlike that of the Suez crisis of 1956—when France was at loggerheads with the United States and in the aftermath of which Konrad Adenauer is reported to have said to Prime Minister Guy Mollet and Foreign Minister Christian Pineau that "Europe will be your revenge"—as Paris and Washington moved further apart, so Paris seemed to be moving closer to the European Union. Until this crisis over Iraq, France had seemed to be in a state of immobilism regarding the European Union since the late 1980s and early 1990s, when François Mitterrand and Jacques Delors had taken the lead in directing Europe's agenda. France's long ascendancy in the European Union was slipping away, as two prominent thinkers of the French Left, Pascal Lamy and Jean Pisani-Ferry, observed in early 2002:

> For having too long believed that Europe was being built in its own image, the French suffer today from not recognizing themselves in it: diffraction of state authority, promotion of competition, opposition to state management of public services. They discover with surprise . . . that the movement for the construction of Europe is calling into question several of the pillars of the model of government that they thought they had exported. At the same time, European unification, whose necessity and legitimacy they do not dispute, is going automatically to reduce their weight within the Union. The common future will take place at a distance from its borders, what they alone, or virtually alone, continue to call "Eastern Europe." And finally, they see themselves diminished in the face of a Germany numerically more powerful and an England politically more alert.[7]

Interestingly, it was in the midst of the international crisis of 2002–03 that France arrived at a number of startling compromises, the sine qua non behind which was the restoration of the Franco-German alliance to the functioning state it had known under Chirac's and Schröder's predecessors. Perhaps the most surprising mark of this new trend toward compromise was the softening of the French line on the Common Agricultural Policy (CAP), which costs 40 billion euros a year and takes up approximately half the EU annual budget. Unpopular outside the European Union, as it helps keep non-EU agricultural products out of the European market, the CAP has also been a source of

French unpopularity inside the European Union, as France is the leading beneficiary of EU subsidies to farmers. In a sharp turnaround, France not only agreed that the proposed EU constitution acknowledge the role of the European Commission in deciding on CAP goals but in a meeting of EU agricultural ministers in Luxembourg in June 2003 accepted the principle that, as of 2005, CAP payments will no longer be determined by the quantity of production alone but will take into consideration other factors, notably food security and environmental conditions.

It is also significant that it was a Frenchman—Valéry Giscard d'Estaing—who took charge of forging a compromise on the proposed EU constitution during the year-and-a-half-long exercise of the Convention on the Future of Europe, which has been compared with the Constitutional Convention in Philadelphia that produced the U.S. Constitution. Laying down the principles of diplomatic courtesy and transparency, widening the circle of participants beyond diplomats, and calling for unanimity of agreement rather than for a vote, Giscard managed to come up with a consensus.[8] One wonders if someone other than a Frenchman could have achieved this impressive result, France having played so central a role in the European Community from its beginning.

It is further significant that the recommendations of the Convention on the Future of Europe paralleled closely the Franco-German proposals of January 2003 (which called for an end of the rotating presidency of the European Council, for the creation of a post of foreign minister for Europe, and for the simplification of the qualified majority voting system). Clearly the German and French leaderships have come to realize that they must remain together on issues if they are to maintain a leading role in an enlarged European Union.

Certain long-range trends suggest that these newfound French habits of compromise and consensus might, at least in form, extend to the French-U.S. relationship. Globalization, growing use of the Internet, and greater proficiency in English, for example, will mean that U.S. and French negotiators will experience more functional compatibility.

France's move in the direction of market capitalism and away, to a certain extent, from state-centered capitalism does not necessarily mean, however, that its negotiating behavior will be more compatible fundamentally with the approach taken by "Anglo-Saxon," and partic- ularly U.S., negotiators. A more pragmatic approach and a more outward- looking perspective on the world, characteristics that are stimulated by globalization, remain nevertheless circumscribed by the political posi- tions of the French state. This constraining factor is perhaps stronger in France than in other countries, as French negotiators are bound by an ethos of national and cultural superiority and by the enduring tradition of a powerful and hierarchical state bureaucracy. In other words, it will be the national choices of France that will be decisive, even though French negotiators can be expected to display an increasing flexibility and an increasing awareness of the other's point of view.

In the view of former foreign minister Hubert Védrine, French negotiations of today are far different from the classic negotiations of the past, and this process of change is likely to continue. Today, nego- tiations are more or less continual and nonstop; they are rarely strictly bilateral; they increasingly feature the use of English; and they enter almost invariably into the public domain, thus making the manage- ment of public opinion extremely important. This is evident particu- larly on the issue of the CAP, given France's powerful farm bloc.

According to Védrine, the French negotiator's world today is one of complexity and interaction on a number of levels—national, Euro- pean, and ad hoc—an example of the latter being the Contact Group on the former Yugoslavia. It is often a world of simultaneous negotia- tions and it is one where interactions are taking place even before a negotiation begins.[9]

FRANCE AND THE UNITED STATES

As for the relationship between France and the United States, in Védrine's view:

> There is a French pretension and ambition that goes back to the Enlight- enment and is now marked by jealousy. There is a competition [between France and the United States] over values and principles that is delicate to manage. With other countries it is easier; the French representative can make the claim, "I have my interests but I speak in the name of humanity." What is needed is to conceive a new compromise between the empire [the United States] and the rest of the world.[10]

The Iraq war of 2003 saw the breakup of the Big Three alliance—the United States, the United Kingdom, and France—which can be said to have begun with the U.S. entry into World War I in 1917. It is true that there was an earlier breakup of the alliance, in the Suez crisis of 1956, but that was less serious from the point of view of bilateral French-American relations. Although it was, similarly, a case of two members of the three against one, it was not so much a French-American confrontation, particularly in that the focus of the personal rivalry was between U.S. secretary of state John Foster Dulles and British prime minister Anthony Eden. From the Suez crisis Britain and France drew different lessons: for Britain, it was not to go athwart the United States again in matters of strategic policy; for France, it was to end French dependence on the United States by developing its own nuclear capability.

The Big Three underwent other strains in the twentieth century, as when Germany in 1940 knocked France off its pedestal as a great power, when de Gaulle dropped out of NATO in all but name in 1966, and when Britain and France refused (vociferously in France's case) to join in the U.S. war in Vietnam. Although unsatisfactory in some respects for France, which the United States has never treated on the same plane as it does Britain, this loose alliance persisted through trilateral meetings held episodically. As noted in chapter 3, Germany entered the picture through the medium of the Quad meetings, but as the strategic picture evolved away from the static defense of Europe, it became clear that Germany was not disposed to undertake military interventions abroad—at least not for the immediate future.

It took the end of the Cold War and the removal of the Soviet threat to loosen the tie among the Big Three. It did not happen right away, and in fact the Big Three came together in the first Gulf War in 1990–91. But the second Gulf War—the war against Iraq in 2003—broke the association decisively; whether it also broke it permanently remains to be seen.

As noted earlier, in the debate that preceded the Iraq war, Jacques Chirac told the French military on January 7, 2003, to prepare for action. But in the end the competing strategic visions of the two countries came into sharp relief and thus conflict: one vision, that of the United States as leader of the Western alliance assuming that its allies would support it on a matter of going to war; and the other, that of national independence and a multipolar world, long promoted by French leaders.

These two competing strategic visions that have constituted the stuff of the French-U.S. debate over the past forty-odd years are complemented by two diverging visions of what the transatlantic relationship should be: one is that of NATO, representing an Atlantic community of equals, but with the United States in the lead, as expressed by John F. Kennedy; the other, inspired by Charles de Gaulle, is that of a resuscitated Europe acting as an independent and equal partner of the United States—a Europe under strong French influence with France, in the phrase of Maurice Vaïsse, "seeking at the same time a solidarity and a superiority over its partners."[11]

In the aftermath of the dispute over the Iraq war in 2003, Presidents George W. Bush and Jacques Chirac met at a G-8 summit in France on June 1–2, 2003, and, with a handshake and discreet pats on the shoulders, made a superficial attempt to patch up the relationship.

In Paris, however, the end of the Iraq war ushered in a "morning-after" atmosphere. For the first time since de Gaulle departed office, French leaders had stood up to the United States on a matter of principle and on an issue of peace and war—and yet it had gained them little: the French threat to veto was insufficient to prevent a war. European public opinion was with the French (and German) position, but the European Union, as represented in the European Council, was divided. Most fundamentally, France had taken on the burden of leading the opposition to the United States, despite the great power imbalance between the two countries.

After the Iraq war, a major, if not an overriding, concern in France has been its relationship with the United States. The crisis heightened awareness on both sides of the Atlantic that something fundamental and damaging had happened to the relationship. On an individual level, French and U.S. negotiators began to approach each other with a new measure of wariness as a result of the crisis. Clearly the tone of negotiations between the United States and France underwent a change, despite the restoration of surface amicabilities.

Furthermore, as regards the United States, there is something intangible but nevertheless real that colors French perceptions, a sort of received wisdom or *pensée unique* that emanates from French officialdom

and prevents an open-minded view of the United States from expressing itself. Védrine identifies a "discomfort" in French elites when it
comes to seriously analyzing the United States:

> This discomfort is due to the past, a past so charged with primitive
> anti-Americanism from the Marxist and Soviet period that it inhibits
> today's elites. They are so afraid of going off in a [different] direc-
> tion that they become wary of engaging in any serious critique of the
> United States.[12]

In this regard, it is striking just how few French intellectuals and
public figures challenged the *pensée unique* in France that the Iraq
war was ill-advised and morally wrong.

In many aspects of strategic culture, the United States and Europe,
and particularly the United States and France, have diverged. Robert Kagan
attributes to Robert Cooper the idea that Europe is now living in a "post-
modern system," which rests no longer on the balance of power but on "the
rejection of force" and on "rules of behavior that each one imposes on himself. . . . In the postmodern world, the reason of state and the amorality of
the theories of Machiavelli on the art of governing . . . have been replaced
by a moral conscience" in the context of international politics.[13] As was
seen in the Iraq crisis, French negotiators will generally hold out for a
peaceful solution, either out of optimism that this can be achieved or, at a
minimum, out of hope that hostilities can be avoided or, at least, put off.

However, as French officials constantly emphasize, France has
not renounced the use of military force. France and Britain are the two
Western European powers most inclined toward military interventions
abroad when the situation demands it or when their own national
prestige requires it. Therefore French, as well as British, help is needed by the international community when crises break out in Asia and
Africa and in situations in which the United States is unable, or
unwilling, to send forces to stabilize the area. This was pointed up in
June 2003, when French troops led an intervention force to stop the
killings in Bunia, in eastern Congo. Colin Powell complimented the
French on this publicly, thus acknowledging France's continuing role
in helping assure world peace. In the future, France's capability, along
with its willingness, to undertake military interventions abroad will be
a strong card in its relationship with the United States, as will its effi-
ciency and know-how in combatting terrorism.

Of concern in Paris, however, is the gap in military capability that opened up between Britain and France in the 1990s. As noted earlier in this study, France has made a concerted effort to close this gap. Not only was the British military equipment budget 1.6 times higher than the French one in 2001, but also, as Jacques Isnard notes, "the lead of Great Britain over France is even more established when one compares the budgets for research and technological development. This puts the British in a better position to prepare the future and to play the role of leader in the organization of European security and armaments in the coming period."[14] And as Britain proved in the Iraq war, it has the military means to match its policies.

*   *   *

As should be abundantly clear from previous chapters, French officials enter negotiations with Americans distrustful and suspicious—an outlook that has its counterpart on the U.S. side. This legacy of mistrust is often ignored—perhaps because it is easier to do so and perhaps, as far as the United States is concerned, because of its ahistorical outlook. Ultimately, however, the weight of history makes itself felt; one learns that the rancors of the past cannot be swept aside easily. When new disputes arise, this troublesome past reemerges—and in the case of the Iraq war it reemerged with unprecedented vituperation, particularly on the U.S. side.

In contrast to the generally ahistorical Americans, the French are very conscious of their history, including their long tradition of diplomatic negotiations, and of the fact that, particularly since 1940, the bilateral relationship has been less than ideal. In any encounter with Americans, therefore, French negotiators are prepared for difficulties. French officials generally look behind U.S. pronouncements, often couched in what the French see as a moralizing tone, searching for deeper, darker U.S. motives and suspecting that the United States is intent on duping France or demolishing French objections. These suspicions are not without foundation, considering what Stephen Rosen has described as "the American ability to generate principles that are in reality self-serving."[15] Still, conspiracy theories have a more flourishing life in French than in Anglo-American culture.

Reminiscent of French defense expert Nicole Gnesotto's formula that "the discourse of autonomy often contradicts the practice of cooperation,"[16] French-U.S. relations in the military area are reasonably amicable and productive. The two nations have undertaken a range of joint operations that stretch from the first Gulf War to parallel missions in Afghanistan to train a new Afghan army following the defeat of the Taliban. There are, of course, some exceptions to this constructive record, notably French-U.S. operational differences regarding the air war over Serbia in 1999. But the respect among the U.S. military for French units on the tactical level is such that the French have become useful military partners for the United States, whether in the NATO context or in that of "coalitions of the willing."[17] According to a French defense expert, the general reaction within the French military at being left out of the Iraq war in 2003 was one of dismay.[18]

Overall there is an awareness, both in Paris and Washington, that this is a dysfunctional relation between supposed allies. There are different schools of thought on how to proceed in the future. For example, John Kornblum considers it futile to play up to the French, to believe in their sense of logic, or to try to change their point of view. Rather, states Kornblum, "it is best to give it to the French straight, recognizing that they will not like you for it."[19]

Most U.S. administrations since World War II have come into power with the idea of improving relations with France. Yet outgoing administrations, more often than not, have concluded, with some bitterness, that this was a useless exercise. Each new administration has learned to its chagrin that new problems crop up or old ones reappear. For instance, at the outset of the second Clinton administration in 1996, Madeleine Albright, the incoming secretary of state, was determined to develop a good relationship with her French counterparts, believing that her knowledge of French and her family's European background would help to bring about an improvement. By the end of her tenure, Albright had decided otherwise.

An incoming U.S. administration typically criticizes the previous administration for becoming unnecessarily quarrelsome with the French and declares its intention to improve the relationship. The same pattern appears on the French side, as indicated by Jacques Chirac's initial moves toward a rapprochement with NATO after taking power in 1995. Later, when after a period of cohabitation Chirac resumed full power with the defeat of the socialist-led government in the legislative elections of April–May 2002, the colorful, stinging rhetoric of the outgoing foreign minister, Védrine, gave way to the more benign approach of Védrine's successor, Dominique de Villepin, who made explicit France's new "positive" attitude to U.S. officials during his initial visit to Washington.[20] Such episodes of bonhomie are usually short-lived, as proved to be the case when French-U.S. tensions began to mount in 2002 over U.S. plans for a war with Iraq.

FRANCE AND EUROPE

The problem for the future for France lies not only with its clouded relationship with the United States but also with the European Union and all the promise and uncertainty of that institution, with which France's future is now inextricably linked. With the reunification of Germany in the 1990s and the expansion of the European Union in the new century further undermining France's accustomed ascendancy, France is showing signs of adapting itself, of coming to terms with the post–Cold War Europe. The voices of the anti-Maastricht guardians of the national sovereignty in France (the *souverainistes*), so strident in the 1990s, have become subdued and even virtually eclipsed.

As we saw in the case study on the Uruguay Round, France is constrained in its international policies by its membership in the European Union, especially in global trade negotiations. At the same time, because France is a member of the European Union, the United States, in the trade area but in some other areas as well, cannot deal with France apart from the European Union. Thus France's EU membership not only constrains France's freedom of maneuver but also protects France: the United States has to think not only of France's negotiating behavior but also of Europe's negotiating behavior. Michael Brenner and Guillaume Parmentier, authors of *Reconcilable Differences*, point to the fact of "France's strategy of embedding its interests within a common European position [in order to] strengthen its hand while creating disincentives for the United States to attack Paris-inspired initiatives."[21]

But France's policy of multilateralizing its relationship with the United States in order to maximize its leverage with what is by far the stronger partner can also carry some disadvantages. As the same authors also note:

> France's choice in making the EU the centerpiece of its foreign policy places a premium on shaping new modes of EU–U.S. consultation and coordination. The absence of a permanent transatlantic institution dealing with nonsecurity issues is a particular liability for France, because it enjoys neither the closeness of its partners' networks of U.S. contacts nor a sense of full membership in the NATO structures that facilitate dialogue beyond military matters, narrowly defined.[22]

If France's aim of being the driving force in making the European Union a world power equal to the United States is to be realized, EU members must exhibit a relatively high degree of unity and coherence. In the climax of the Iraq crisis in the spring of 2003, however, Europe fell into disarray and division, rendering the European Union's Common Foreign and Security Policy (CFSP) devoid of meaning. In the future, France in particular but also the other leading member-states will have to make a greater effort to come together if the European Union is going to possess the kind of political and economic power that the United States now wields. It is the unanimity rule that impedes the development of a strong European foreign policy. The proposed EU constitution has brought a degree of coherence to this very opaque and diffuse institution, but unless the qualified majority voting system can be applied to decisions on foreign policy and defense, the cacophony that the European Union presents to the world will persist and indeed grow louder as the number of member-states grows larger.

French negotiators will find themselves not with split loyalties but with split responsibilities. They will be dealing at the national level bilaterally and at the EU level multilaterally. If the European Union develops a unified foreign policy, they will also be dealing with the foreign minister of the European Union and the personnel of that office.

That *la Grande Nation* is no more does not mean that French greatness has disappeared. French contributions to philosophy, literature, and art are matters not just of the past but of the present as well. But France's reduction in the twentieth century from the status of a great power to that of a middle power has left the country with a painful choice: that Gaullist formula with a tautological ring—"France to be great must be France"—has now become "France to be great must be Europe." France's policy toward the European Union has been marked by a fundamental, and debilitating, contradiction. If France, as a middle power, wants to enhance its influence in the world, it can do so most effectively through a stronger and more united Europe. Yet Europe can achieve this status only through more supranationalism or communitarianism and less intergovernmentalism. But France and Britain—the oldest nations in Europe, representing "the two constitutive histories of the European identity"[23]—are among the most reluctant to relinquish the elements of national sovereignty that are necessary for the creation of a federated Europe that could, at least theoretically, become a new great power alongside the United States. The challenge for France in the future will be to give up some of its cherished sovereignty in return for achieving greater consensus among its European partners—thereby strengthening the stature of the European Union while maintaining French influence in the European Union and in the world.

Whether Europe will become a political power in its own right will depend in no small part on a strong and continuing will to cooperate on the part of the French and the Germans. France and Germany can be compared to a married couple of a certain age who decided to take a long weekend apart to assess the changes in their attitudes. This "long weekend" occurred at the turn of the century. At the end of the weekend, reason prevailed, and the two marriage partners decided they had to cooperate more closely and effectively. But although the relationship has been reaffirmed politically and symbolically—most visibly by the joint meeting of the two parliaments in Versailles in January 2003 to mark the fortieth anniversary of the Élysée Treaty—it still suffers at the level of emotion and culture from a continuing, if not increasing, incompatibility. For instance, there is a decline in both countries in the study of the other's language.

Sooner or later Germany's larger population will have the effect of eliminating altogether the French ascendancy that existed after World War II, though not to the extent that France will have to accept the role of junior partner in their relationship. Both countries will also have to acknowledge that the enlargement of the European Union will reduce the influence of their relationship. To be sure, the French-German "locomotive" will continue to exert a strong pull on the European Union (assuming this machine continues to function well), but it will be less able than before to carry along the other members. Two countries of Europe, however important, cannot control twenty-three others.

Even if France and Germany continue to cooperate and act as the locomotive of the European Union, this alone will not make the European union a world power. Remaining an economic giant and a political and military dwarf will not make the European Union felt throughout the world.[24] And in order for the European Union to develop a military arm, it is necessary for the British and the French to come together again in close cooperation aimed at the building of a European defense force. For the time being, at least, Germany cannot be considered a significant player in this area of conducting military interventions abroad.

CONCLUSION

Védrine describes the position of the French negotiator today as "delicate" and "unstable"—quite different from the situation facing, for example, Chinese diplomats, whose country is sure to be more important twenty years from now, or from that enjoyed by American negotiators, with U.S. hegemony assured for a long time. Védrine characterizes France as "ill at ease with itself: it has an attachment to the symbols of French grandeur, but it also has a depression syndrome."[25]

What seems to be on the horizon for French-U.S. relations is a dialectic between greater comity, resulting from globalization, and a growing divide in political perspectives, spurred by the end of the Cold War and the events succeeding September 11. The French have adapted to globalization to a surprising degree, making much greater use of the Internet, privatizing some state enterprises, and becoming much more fluent in English. In the latter area, while the French have not conceded that English is the global lingua franca, they have accepted the need to handle English well if they are to make their way in foreign negotiations. Globalization has also encouraged a more flexible approach among French negotiators and a greater penchant for compromise.

Ultimately, however, negotiations and negotiating behavior are determined by national interests and political decisions. While the

United States has shown an increasing readiness to act unilaterally, preemptively, and aggressively in its "war on terror," France has chosen to engage its future with that of the European Union, which is to say that the French preference for acting through multilateral institutions will not only endure but grow stronger. Although the European Union has made impressive progress toward the establishment of a collective economic entity, its political and military institutions are little more than an idea at this point. Until and unless this state of affairs changes, the power imbalance between the United States and Europe is such that the divide in political and strategic perspectives, most notably on the question of war versus peace, will continue.

France's relationship with what Védrine (and others) call "the Empire" is not a satisfactory one, and Védrine suggests that a new arrangement is necessary. Whether France will want to continue its struggle to make itself and Europe into an equal partner of the United States remains to be seen. The prevailing view within the French government, according to one French political analyst, is that the current problems in the bilateral relationship will be largely rectified when the Bush administration leaves the scene.[26] This, though, is less than certain given the depth of the rift that occurred in 2003.

In the face of these uncertainties, although American and other interlocutors will continue to encounter a tough, talented, and well-educated individual in the person of a French negotiator, the base from which he or she operates can be expected to remain for some time, to use Védrine's word, "unstable."

Notes

PREFACE

1. Richard H. Solomon, *Chinese Negotiating Behavior: Pursuing Interests through "Old Friends,"* with an interpretive essay by Chas. W. Freeman Jr. (Washington, D.C.: United States Institute of Peace Press, 1999); Jerrold L. Schecter, *Russian Negotiating Behavior: Continuity and Transition* (Washington, D.C.: United States Institute of Peace Press, 1998); Scott Snyder, *Negotiating on the Edge: North Korean Negotiating Behavior* (Washington, D.C.: United States Institute of Peace Press, 1999); W. R. Smyser, *How Germans Negotiate: Logical Goals, Practical Solutions* (Washington, D.C.: United States Institute of Peace Press, 2003); and Michael Blaker, Paul Giarra, and Ezra Vogel, *Case Studies in Japanese Negotiating Behavior* (Washington, D.C.: United States Institute of Peace Press, 2002).

2. These include Kevin Avruch, *Culture and Conflict Resolution* (Washington, D.C.: United States Institute of Peace Press, 1998); Raymond Cohen, *Negotiating across Cultures: International Communication in an Interdependent World* (Washington, D.C.: United States Institute of Peace Press, 1997); and Chas. W. Freeman Jr., *Arts of Power: Statecraft and Diplomacy* (Washington, D.C.: United States Institute of Peace Press, 1997).

3. *French Negotiating Style*, United States Institute of Peace Special Report (Washington, D.C.: United States Institute of Peace, 2000).

4. Commissariat Général du Plan, *Organiser la politique européenne et internationale de la France,* report of the group presided over by Admiral Jacques Lanxade, rapporteur Nicolas Tenzer (Paris: La documentation française, 2002).

1. INTRODUCTION

1. "We are all Americans," trumpeted the publisher of the left-of-center *Le Monde* (September 13, 2001) in the aftermath of the attacks on the Pentagon and World Trade Center.

2. Timothy Garton Ash, "Anti-Europeanism in America," *New York Review of Books*, February 13, 2003, 32.

3. Charles de Gaulle, *Avec le renouveau, 1958–1962*, vol. 4 of *Discours et messages* (Paris: Omnibus/Plon, 1993), 692. De Gaulle used the phrase in a press conference on September 5, 1960.

4. Garton Ash, "Anti-Europeanism in America," 32.

5. Jean Birnbaum, "Enquête sur une détestation française," *Le Monde*, November 25–26, 2001, 15. The reference is to Philippe Roger, *L'Ennemi américain: Généalogie de l'antiaméricanisme français* (Paris: Seuil, 2002).

6. Birnbaum, "Enquête sur une détestation française." Denis Lacorne is the author of *L'Amérique dans les têtes* (Paris: Hachette, 1986).

7. Tony Judt, "America and the War," *New York Review of Books*, November 15, 2001, 4.

8. Alfred Grosser, *The Western Alliance* (New York: Continuum, 1980), xv.

9. John Kornblum, interview by author, Berlin, March 8, 2002.

10. Senior British diplomatic official, interview by author, London, April 25, 2002.

11. "La France est-elle un pays d'exception?" interview with Theodore Zeldin, *Le Monde*, April 14–15, 2002, 20.

12. Richard Bernstein, "Allies Once Again? But That Could Be the Rub," *New York Times*, April 5, 2003, B7.

13. Gilles Andréani, chief of the Analysis and Forecasting Center, French Ministry of Foreign Affairs, interview by author, Paris, December 12, 2002.

14. Dominique Decherf, French diplomat and author, interview by author, Cambridge, Mass., May 10, 2001.

15. Gérard Araud, e-mail to author, January 3, 2002.

16. Commissariat Général du Plan, *Organiser la politique européenne et internationale de la France*, report of the group presided over by Admiral Jacques Lanxade, rapporteur Nicolas Tenzer (Paris: La documentation française, 2002), 92–93.

17. Interview by author.

18. Ibid.

19. German diplomat, interview by author, November 28, 2001.

20. *Le Monde*, December 9, 2000. The quotation is from an article by Dirk Schümer in the *Frankfurter Allgemeine Zeitung* on December 7.

21. Jean Carpentier and François Lebrun, eds., *Histoire de France* (Paris: Seuil, 1987), 249.

22. Jacques Godechot, *La grande nation: L'Expansion révolutionnaire de la France dans le monde de 1789 à 1799*, vol. 1 (Paris: Aubier, 1956), 11.

23. Anne-Line Roccati, "L'UMP mirage de la droite?" *Le Monde*, September 20, 2002, 19.

24. Alain Lempereur, preface to Critical Edition of François de Callières, *De la manière de négocier avec les souverains* (Geneva: Librairie Droz, 2002), 22.

25. Philippe Burrin, "Vichy," in *Les lieux de mémoire*, vol. 2, ed. Pierre Nora (Paris: Gallimard, 1997), 2478.

26. Charles de Gaulle, *The Call to Honor, 1940–1942*, vol. 1 of *The Complete War Memoirs of Charles de Gaulle*, trans. Jonathan Griffin (New York: Simon and Schuster, 1964), 242.

27. Jean-Louis Crémieux-Brilhac, *La France libre: De l'appel du 18 juin à la libération*, vol. 1 (Paris: Gallimard, 1996), 629.

28. Interview with René Rémond, *Le Monde*, January 9, 2001, Section *Horizons*.

29. Ambassador Nancy Soderberg, telephone interview by author, January 9, 2002.

30. Henry Kissinger, interview by author, New York, October 23, 2002.

31. Pierre Mélandri and Justin Vaïsse, *L'Empire du milieu: Les États-Unis et le monde depuis la fin de la guerre froide* (Paris: Odile Jacob, 2001), 464.

32. Birnbaum, "Enquête sur une détestation française," 15.

33. www.cbsnews.com/stories/2002/08/29/september11/main520058.shtml.

34. Stanley Hoffmann, "Deux universalismes en conflit," *La Revue Tocqueville* 21, no. 1 (2000): 65.

35. Dominique Schnapper, *La communauté des citoyens: Sur l'idée moderne de nation* (Paris: Gallimard, 1994), 14.

36. President Jacques Chirac, speech at the opening of the Thirty-first General Conference of UNESCO, October 15, 2001, reported in *Le Monde*, October 16, 2001, 17.

37. Corine Lesnes, "Hubert Védrine dénonce le 'simplisme' et l'unilateralisme 'utilitaire' des Américains," *Le Monde*, February 8, 2002, 3.

38. Elaine Sciolino, "France Mutes Its Criticisms of U.S. Stance toward Iraq," *New York Times*, August 29, 2002, A14.

39. Senior U.S. diplomat, interview by author, August 24, 2002.

40. Philip Gordon and Sophie Meunier, *The French Challenge: Adapting to Globalization* (Washington, D.C.: Brookings Institution Press, 2001), 24.

41. Ibid., 26.

42. Ibid., passim.

43. Hubert Védrine with Dominique Moïsi, *France in an Age of Globalization*, trans. Philip H. Gordon (Washington, D.C.: Brookings Institution Press, 2001), 29.

44. Schnapper, *La communauté des citoyens*, 66.

45. Ibid., 132.

46. Eugen Weber, *Peasants into Frenchmen: The Modernization of Rural France, 1870–1914* (Stanford, Calif.: Stanford University Press, 1976).

47. Kissinger, interview by author.

48. Ibid.

49. A French ambassador posted to Brussels, interview by author.

2. The Cultural Context

1. Robert D. Kaplan, "Looking the World in the Eye," *Atlantic Monthly*, December 2001, 73.

2. The bust of Marianne (modeled since 2000 by Laetitia Casta and Evelyne Thomas) is found in mayoralties throughout France. The unofficial emblem of the French Revolution, she wears the Phrygian bonnet, the revolutionary headdress. In the nineteenth century she served as a counter-model to the Virgin Mary in the rivalry between Catholics and secularists. Claude Langlois, "Catholiques et laïcs," in *Les lieux de mémoire*, vol. 2, ed. Pierre Nora (Paris: Gallimard, 1997), 2333.

3. Roselyne Chenu, *Paul Delouvrier ou la passion d'agir* (Paris: Seuil, 1994), 126.

4. Jacques Bainville, *Histoire de France*, vol. 1 (Paris: Plon, 1933), 212.

5. Alain Plantey, former president of the Institut de France, interview by author, Paris, May 25, 2002. Ambassador Plantey is the author of *La* *négociation internationale au XXIe siècle* (Paris: CNRS Éditions, 2002). *Intendants* were royal officials, generally trained in finance, who were sent to the provinces to assure that the royal writ was observed.

6. *Le Petit Robert* 1, *Dictionnaire de la langue française* (Paris: Robert, 1990), 701.

7. Henry Kissinger, *Diplomacy* (New York: Simon and Schuster, 1994), 60.

8. Chenu, *Paul Delouvrier ou la passion d'agir*, 137.

9. Ibid., 139.

10. Olivier Schrameck, *Matignon Rive Gauche, 1997–2001* (Paris: Seuil, 2001), 31. "Ancien régime" refers to the period of the traditional monarchy in France, which preceded the French Revolution at the end of the eighteenth century.

11. Jacques Revel, "La cour," in *Les lieux de mémoire*, vol. 3, 3144.

12. Daniel Vernet, "Hubert Védrine célèbre Madeleine Albright, Joschka Fischer vante la France," *Le Monde*, January 13, 2001, 1.

13. Pierre Nora, "La génération," in *Les lieux de mémoire*, vol. 2, 2998.

14. Andrew Knapp and Vincent Wright, *The Government and Politics of France*, 4th ed. (London: Routledge, 2001), 202–203.

15. Philip H. Gordon, director of the Center for the United States and France (CUSF) at the Brookings Institution (lecture presented at Harvard University, Cambridge, Mass., November 19, 2000).

16. Jacques Andréani, *L'Amérique et nous* (Paris: Odile Jacob, 2000), 291.

17. Stanley Hoffmann, "Deux universalismes en conflit," *La Revue Tocqueville* 21, no. 1 (2000): 65.

18. Ibid., 65–66.

19. Jacques Godechot, ed., *Les constitutions de la France depuis 1789* (Paris: Garnier-Flammarion, 1970), 34.

20. Alain Lempereur, e-mail to author, May 4, 2003.

21. François Furet (lecture presented at the seminar "The Revolution of 1789 and Us," Fondation Saint-Simon, Paris, January 24, 1989).

22. Hubert Védrine with Dominique Moïsi, *France in an Age of Globalization*, trans. Philip H. Gordon (Washington, D.C.: Brookings Institution Press, 2001), 17.

23. Ibid., 17–18.

24. To add to the semantic confusion, discourse in France, particularly on the Left, has come to equate "democracy" with multiculturalism, in contrast to resolutely secular and unitary French republicanism. In the words of

Régis Debray, "In [a] Republic, everyone defines himself as a citizen, and all the citizens together make up the 'nation,' this 'associated corps living under a common law and represented by the same legislator.' . . . In [a] Democracy, everyone is defined by his 'community' and the ensemble of communities makes up the 'society.' Here men are brothers because they have the same rights, and there because they have the same ancestors." Régis Debray, *Contretemps: Éloges des idéaux perdus* (Paris: Gallimard, 1992), 22.

25. Raymond Aron, *Essai sur les libertés* (Paris: Calmann-Lévy, 1965), 17.

26. Edgar Morin, interview, *Le Monde*, December 23–24, 2001, 13.

27. Furet (lecture presented at Fondation Saint-Simon).

28. Jean Starobinski, "Rousseau and Revolution," *New York Review of Books*, April 25, 2002, 55. Napoleon's quotation is from the memoirs of Madame de Staël.

29. Bainville, *Histoire de France*, vol. 2, 225.

30. Nora, "La nation mémoire," in *Les lieux de mémoire*, vol. 2, 2210.

31. Stanley Hoffmann (lecture presented in the course "French Thought about Politics and Society," Harvard University, Cambridge, Mass., spring 1991).

32. David A. Bell, *The Cult of the Nation in France: Inventing Nationalism, 1680–1800* (Cambridge, Mass.: Harvard University Press, 2001), 24.

33. Furet (lecture presented at Fondation Saint-Simon).

34. William Pickles, *The French Constitution of October 4, 1958* (London: Stevens and Sons, 1960), 14.

35. Ibid., 4.

36. Ibid., 8.

37. Hoffmann, "Deux universalismes en conflit," 66–67.

38. Ibid., 67.

39. See, for example, figures for percentage share of national income in World Bank, *World Development Indicators, 2001* (Washington, D.C.: World Bank, 2001); and income distribution indicators for France and the United States in United Nations Development Program, *Human Development Report, 2001*, available at www.hdr.undp.org.

40. As indicated in the 1997 figures for public social expenditure as a percentage of GDF in Organization for Economic Cooperation and Development (OECD), *Society at a Glance*, 2001 (Paris: OECD, 2002).

41. Furet (lecture presented at the Fondation Saint-Simon).

42. François Mitterrand (speech delivered at the Socialist Party Congress, Épinay, France, June 13, 1971). This often-repeated phrase is part of a larger one about the power of money: "money that corrupts, money that buys, money that crushes, money that kills, money that ruins, money that rots the conscience of man." See www.psinfo.net/entretiens/mitterrand/epinay.html.

43. François Furet, *Le passé d'une illusion: Essai sur l'idée communiste au XXe siècle* (Paris: Robert Laffont/Calmann-Lévy, 1995), 440.

44. Ernest Mignon, *Les mots du général* (Paris: Fayard, 1962), 57.

45. Sunday attendance at mass has dropped to about 10 percent of the population in France today, but 80 percent of French citizens are nominally Roman Catholics. Dominique Decherf, "French Views of Religious Freedom," in *U.S.-France Analysis* (Washington, D.C.: Center for the United States and France, July 2001), 2.

46. Ezra N. Suleiman, *Elites in French Society: The Politics of Survival* (Princeton, N.J.: Princeton University Press, 1978), 225.

47. Decherf, "French Views of Religious Freedom," 2.

48. Stanley Hoffmann, foreword to *Oldest Allies, Guarded Friends: The United States and France since 1940,* by Charles G. Cogan (Westport, Conn.: Praeger, 1994), viii.

49. Michel Tatu, "Tangage franco-américain," *Le Monde*, May 29, 1992, 1.

50. Mitterrand made these comments in the mid-1990s. See Georges-Marc Benamou, *Le dernier Mitterrand* (Paris: Plon, 1996), 52 ff. Mitterrand's quotation is from Pierre Mélandri and Justin Vaïsse, *L'Empire du milieu: Les États-Unis et le monde depuis la fin de la guerre froide* (Paris: Odile Jacob, 2001), 455, 473.

51. Hoffmann, foreword to *Oldest Allies, Guarded Friends*, viii, ix.

52. Mélandri and Vaïsse, *L'Empire du milieu*, 473–474.

53. Poland also contributed a detachment of special forces troops to the war against Iraq.

54. *"Le grand large"* is from the famous remark Winston Churchill made in a stormy session with Charles de Gaulle at Portsmouth, United Kingdom, on June 4, 1944, before the Normandy landings: "How can you think that we British would take a position separate from that of the United States? We are going to liberate Europe but it is because the Americans are with us in doing it. Because every time we have to choose between Europe and the open seas *(le grand large)*, we will always choose the open seas. And every time I have to choose between you and Roosevelt, I will always choose Roosevelt." Jean Lacouture, *Le rebelle*, vol. 1 of *De Gaulle* (Paris: Seuil, 1984), 770.

55. This phrase is derived from the Arabic *beni* (son of) and denotes a person who is always eager to approve the position of an established authority.

56. Védrine, *France in an Age of Globalization*, 92.

57. *French Negotiating Style*, United States Institute of Peace Special Report (Washington, D.C.: United States Institute of Peace Press, 2000), 3.

58. Jean Birnbaum, "Enquête sur une détestation française," *Le Monde*, November 25–26, 2001, 15. "Liberal" is meant in the European sense of the term: a policy that favors market capitalism.

59. Roger Chartier, "La Ligne Saint-Malo-Genève," in *Les lieux de mémoire*, vol. 2, 2819.

60. U.S. diplomat, interview by author, April 26, 2002.

61. Jean-Marie Guéhenno, interview by author, New York, January 10, 2002.

62. Fons Trompenaars, *Riding the Waves of Culture* (London: Economist Books, 1993), 50. The core of Trompenaars's database is thirty thousand questionnaires sent to managers from multinational and international corporations in fifty-five countries faced with internationalizing their operations. See also the second edition of *Riding the Waves of Culture*, written with Charles Hampden-Turner (New York: McGraw-Hill, 1998), 252.

63. Raymond Cohen, *Negotiating across Cultures: International Communication in an Interdependent World* (Washington, D.C.: United States Institute of Peace Press, 1997), 65.

64. Bell, *The Cult of the Nation in France*, 159.

65. Jacques Revel, "La cour," in *Les lieux de mémoire*, vol. 3, 3177.

66. For more on the *grandes écoles*, see the later discussion in this chapter.

67. Suleiman, *Élites*, 181.

68. Dominique Decherf, interview by author, Cambridge, Mass., May 15, 2001.

69. Jochen Thies, interview by author, Berlin, March 8, 2002.

70. Jacques Lanxade, *Quand le monde a basculé* (Paris: NiL éditions, 2001), 114.

71. Ibid., 139.

72. Jérôme Hélie, "Les armes," in *Les lieux de mémoire*, vol. 3, 3259.

73. Philippe Guelluy, French ambassador to Canada and former French ambassador to NATO, interview by author, Ottawa, April 19, 2002. Chirac turned the situation to practical advantage by persuading the British to put together a Rapid Reaction Force in Bosnia composed of French, British, and Dutch troops so as to prevent the Bosnian Serbs from staging another such provocation. As Jean-David Levitte puts it, the creation of the Bosnian Rapid Reaction Force on June 14, 1995, which was not welcomed by figures in the U.S. legislature, particularly Newt Gingrich and Bob Dole, can be considered as the laying of the cornerstone of an autonomous European defense force. Jean-David Levitte, interview by author, New York, October 12, 2001.

74. *The Political Testimony of Cardinal Richelieu*, trans. Henry Bertram Hill (Madison: University of Wisconsin Press, 1961), 77.

75. Roger-Pol Droit, "Comment Descartes devint la France," review of François Azouvi, *Descartes et la France: Histoire d'une passion nationale* (Paris: Fayard, 2002), in *Le Monde des Livres*, March 15, 2002, 1.

76. Guéhenno, interview by author.

77. Alain Lempereur, interview by author, Cambridge, Mass., September 6, 2001.

78. Guéhenno, interview by author.

79. E-mail to author, April 9, 2002.

80. Jean-David Levitte, interview by author, New York, January 10, 2002.

81. Guéhenno, interview by author.

82. Pierre Vimont, interview by author, Brussels, March 4, 2002.

83. Nora, "La génération," in *Les lieux de mémoire*, vol. 2, 2993.

84. Armand Frémont, "La terre," in *Les lieux de mémoire*, vol. 3, 3048.

85. A French ambassador posted to Brussels, e-mail to author.

86. Ibid.

87. Guéhenno, interview by author.

88. Suleiman, *Elites*, 11.

89. Ibid., 17.

90. Ibid., 29.

91. Gilles Delafon and Thomas Sancton, *Dear Jacques Cher Bill . . . Au coeur de l'Élysée et de la Maison Blanche, 1995–1999* (Paris: Plon, 1999), 196.

92. Henry Kissinger, interview by author, New York, October 23, 2002.

93. Suleiman, *Elites*, 39. The St. Cyr military academy, created in 1802 by Napoleon, was more narrowly focused on the creation of officers as leaders of men, or, to use the current term, warfighters, in contrast to the École Polytechnique, which was more scientifically oriented.

94. Ibid., 36.

95. Ibid., 49.

96. Ibid., 41.

97. From the outset, graduates of the École Polytechnique were supposed to serve in the army but could be exonerated by paying back the cost of their education. In modern times employers in search of talent have often paid this cost.

98. Suleiman, *Elites*, 24.

99. David Bertolotti, École Nationale d'Administration, e-mail to author, April 18, 2003.

100. "The elite corps for generalists are the *Inspection des Finances*, the *Conseil d'État* and the *Cour des Comptes*. Their specialist counterparts include *Ponts et Chaussées* and *Mines*." Knapp and Wright, *The Government and Politics of France*, 281.

101. The Cour des Comptes (Court of Accounts) has as its "essential task . . . to help the government and parliament in controlling the legality of the use of public funds (including, since 1976, those of public enterprises). It is structured hierarchically and comprises some 200 members: the lowest rank of the hierarchy, the *auditeurs*, are all recruited from ENA, while the other ranks have been promoted internally . . . or chosen from outside the court in the government." Ibid., 389.

102. "The Conseil d'État (Council of State) is the supreme French administrative body (it heads a network of regionally based administrative tribunals) and has a host of supervisory and judicial functions. It is also one of the most prestigious of the *grands corps* and a major nursery for the French public and private, political, administrative, and industrial elite." The Conseil d'État also helps draft legislation. Ibid., 388.

103. Ibid.

104. In 1999 the Quai d'Orsay created the Académie Diplomatique (Diplomatic Academy), which offers a three-month course in diplomatic techniques, including negotiation. This course is attended not only by new entrants to the diplomatic corps but also by midcareer officials. Alain Lempereur, interview by author, Cambridge, Mass., November 14, 2001.

105. The Prefectoral Corps, created under Napoleon, is the heir to the *intendant* system of the ancien régime. The *intendants* were sent out to the provinces to collect taxes and generally ensure obedience to royal dictates. Although the prefects, installed in the various French *départements* and *régions*, have in recent years lost some of their power to local elected officials, they constitute an important presence of the central government throughout the country.

106. Bertolotti, e-mail to author.

107. Suleiman, *Elites*, 80.

108. Ezra Suleiman, telephone interview by author, April 15, 2003.

109. Suleiman, *Elites*, 80.

110. Knapp and Wright, *The Government and Politics of France*, 281.

111. David Bertolotti, e-mail to author.

112. Ibid.

113. Laetitia Van Eeckhout, "La commission chargée d'une réflexion sur l'ENA préconise des réformes contre le 'conformisme,'" *Le Monde*, April 24, 2003, 9.

114. Jérôme Lacaille, Harvard Law School student and former ENA student, interview by author, Cambridge, Mass., November 14, 2001. See also Alain Lempereur, "Negotiation and Mediation in France: The Challenge of Skill-Based Learning and Interdisciplinary Research in Legal Education," *Harvard Negotiation Law Review* 3 (spring 1998): 151–174.

3. The Historical Context

1. "Un entretien avec François Furet," *Le Monde*, May 19, 1992, 2.

2. Gilles Delafon and Thomas Sancton, *Dear Jacques Cher Bill . . . Au coeur de l'Élysée et de la Maison Blanche, 1995–1999* (Paris: Plon, 1999), 173. Denis Ross's remarks refer to the unwritten accord of 1993 between Israel and the Hezbollah concluded under the auspices of Ross.

3. Gérard Araud, e-mail to author, January 3, 2002.

4. A French ambassador posted in Brussels, interview by author.

5. De Gaulle took France all the way back to A.D. 496, when Clovis, the Merovingian king, was converted to Christianity.

6. André Alba, "Rome et le Moyen Âge," in *L'Histoire*, ed. Albert Malet and Jules Isaac (Paris: Hachette, 1961), 247. Alba notes that by the middle of the fifteenth century administrative texts began to be published in French instead of Latin.

7. "[France] hardly extended beyond the Somme in the north and the Meuse and the Saône in the east. Lyon was a frontier city; neither Bresse, nor Franche-Comté, nor Nice nor Savoy, were part of the Kingdom." Alba, "L'Âge classique," in *L'Histoire*, 289.

8. Ibid.

9. Alain Lempereur, preface to a critical edition of François de

Callières, *De la manière de négocier avec les souverains* (Geneva: Librairie Droz, 2002), 23.

10. Ibid., 22.

11. Malet and Isaac, *L'Histoire*, 502–503.

12. Jean Carpentier and François Lebrun, eds., *Histoire de France* (Paris: Seuil, 1987), 262.

13. Great Britain's population reached eleven million only in 1801. *Encyclopaedia Britannica, Macropaedia*, vol. 14 (1978), 816.

14. François Furet, "L'Ancien régime et la révolution," in *Les lieux de mémoire*, vol. 2, ed. Pierre Nora (Paris: Gallimard, 1997), 2301–2302.

15. Jacques Godechot, *La grande nation: L'Expansion révolutionnaire de la France dans le monde de 1789 à 1799*, vol. 1 (Paris: Aubier, 1956), 10.

16. Ibid., 11.

17. Carpentier and Lebrun, *Histoire de France*, 257.

18. Malet and Isaac, *L'Histoire*, 736–737.

19. François Furet (lecture presented at the seminar "The Revolution of 1789 and Us," Fondation Saint-Simon, January 24, 1989, Paris).

20. Savoy was added to France in 1860.

21. Lempereur, preface to *De la manière de négocier avec les souverains*, 19.

22. Ibid., 19–20.

23. Ibid., 21. The European Economic Community became the European Community in 1966 and then the European Union in 1993, with the ratification of the Treaty of Maastricht.

24. Ibid., 22.

25. French diplomat, interview by author, May 10, 2002.

26. Régis Debray, *Contretemps: Éloges des idéaux perdus* (Paris: Gallimard, 1992), 97.

27. Henry Kissinger, interview by author, New York, October 23, 2002.

28. Régis Debray, *Les empires contre l'Europe* (Paris: Gallimard, 1985).

29. Kissinger, interview by author.

30. Alain Peyrefitte, *C'était de Gaulle*, vol. 1 (Paris: Fayard, 1994), 153.

31. Interview by author.

32. A French ambassador posted to Brussels, e-mail to author, April 9, 2002. Attempts to distance France from Napoleon are by no means new. For instance, Chateaubriand, a nineteenth-century conservative writer, declared:

"In vain people claim that Buonaparte is not a foreigner. He is in the eyes of all of Europe and of all French people who are not prejudiced; posterity will judge him so. . . . There is nothing French in him, neither in his manners nor in his character. The features of his face reveal his origin. The language that he learned in the cradle was not ours; and his accent like his name reveal his homeland. . . . Buonaparte is foreign to the French." Jean Tulard, "Le retour des cendres," in *Les lieux de mémoire*, vol. 2, 1731.

33. E-mail to author.

34. Henry Kissinger, *Diplomacy* (New York: Simon and Schuster, 1994), 119.

35. John Kornblum, interview by author, Berlin, March 8, 2002.

36. Maurice Vaïsse, *La grandeur: Politique étrangère du général de Gaulle, 1958–1969* (Paris: Fayard, 1998), 676.

37. Daniel Nordman, "Des limites d'état aux frontières nationales," *Les lieux de mémoire*, vol. 1, 1158.

38. Charles de Gaulle, *The Call to Honor, 1940–1942*, vol. 1 of *The Complete War Memoirs of Charles de Gaulle*, trans. Jonathan Griffin (New York: Simon and Schuster, 1964), 10. The Second Empire was that of Napoleon III. The first was that of his uncle, Napoleon Bonaparte.

39. The free city of Strasbourg, in Alsace, did not become part of France until 1681.

40. The First Reich, or empire, was the Holy Roman Empire of the Germanic Peoples (962–1806).

41. Max Beloff, "Tocqueville and the Odd Couple: A Review of Franco-German Relations," *National Interest*, no. 55 (spring 1999): 61.

42. William L. Langer, ed., *An Encyclopaedia of World History* (Boston: Houghton Mifflin, 1948), 951. The number of wounded was 3,044,000 French and 206,000 Americans.

43. Ibid. German wounded were 4,247,000.

44. Stanley Hoffmann, interview by author, Cambridge, Mass., January 10, 2003.

45. Kissinger, *Diplomacy*, 228.

46. It is interesting to note that Marshal Philippe Pétain maintained to Robert Murphy, U.S. chargé d'affaires, in Vichy on August 7, 1940, that Britain had dragged France into the war. Pétain deplored the "brutal self-ishness of Britain" and its disregard of the interests of the continental countries. This had led to its rash declaration of war for which it was not prepared and thus to France's tragedy. *Foreign Relations of the United States*, vol. 2, *1940* (Washington, D.C.: U.S. Government Printing Office, 1957), 380.

47. De Gaulle, *Unity, 1942–1944*, vol. 2 of *The Complete War Memoirs of Charles de Gaulle*, trans. Richard Howard, 665.

48. De Gaulle, *Salvation, 1944–1946*, vol. 3 of *The Complete War Memoirs of Charles de Gaulle*, trans. Richard Howard, 951. This was the so-called Holland solution. The Dutch royal family went into exile in Britain.

49. Ibid.

50. Ibid.

51. Stanley Hoffmann, "The Man Who Would Be France," review of Jean Lacouture, *De Gaulle*, vol. 1, *The Rebel, 1890–1944*, trans. Patrick O'Brian (London: Collins Harvill, 1990), in *New Republic*, December 17, 1990, 36.

52. Jean Monnet, *Memoirs*, trans. by Richard Mayne (Garden City, N.Y.: Doubleday, 1978), 220.

53. François Furet, *Le passé d'une illusion: Essai sur l'idée communiste au XXe siècle* (Paris: Robert Laffont/Calmann-Lévy, 1995), 416.

54. Ibid., 443.

55. Ibid, 443 n. 1.

56. Charles de Gaulle, address at the Hôtel de Ville, Paris, August 25, 1944, *Discours et messages*, vol. 2 (Geneva: Édito-Service, 1970), 92.

57. De Gaulle, *Salvation, 1944–1946*, 871.

58. Christoph Bertram, interview by author, Berlin, May 31, 2002.

59. The reverse alliance *(alliance de revers)*, so called because it was with a country, from the French point of view, at Germany's rear, began in 1893.

60. Monnet, *Memoirs*, 221.

61. Raymond Aron, report of a talk presented at the Association Française de Sciences Politiques, Lyndon B. Johnson Library, National Security File, Country File, France, Box 173 Folder France/Cables, vol. 10 (October 1966–January 1967), Paris 1163, January 26, 1967, 3.

62. *Livre blanc sur la défense nationale* (Paris: CREST, 1972), 14.

63. Vaïsse, *La grandeur*, 381.

64. Henri de Bresson and Lucas Delattre, "Critiques en Europe contre la présidence française," *Le Monde*, December 7, 2000, 3.

65. Alfred Grosser, *Affaires extérieures: La politique de la France, 1944–1984* (Paris: Flammarion, 1984), 196.

66. Ethan Kapstein, University of Minnesota (lecture presented at Harvard University, February 21, 2002).

67. Bruce Bach, Defense Planning and Operations Division of the International Staff of NATO, interview by author, Brussels, March 6, 2002. The views expressed during the interview are Bach's and do not represent those of NATO.

68. Jacques Isnard, "L'armée française revendique sa place en Europe," *Le Monde*, September 29–30, 2002, 14.

69. Under the qualified majority voting (QMV) system, the voting weights in the European Council range from twenty-nine for the largest countries (Germany, France, Great Britain, and Italy) down to two for the smallest (Luxembourg, Cyprus, and Malta). A total of 73.4 percent of the votes are required to form a qualified majority, but the council's decision must also be supported by countries representing 62 percent of the total population of the European Union. This system, however, will change in 2009. See p. 103.

70. Vaïsse, *La grandeur*, 356.

71. Interview by author.

72. Charles de Gaulle, interview by a Mexican journalist, February 23, 1942, *Lettres, Notes et Carnets*, vol. 4 (Paris: Plon, 1982), 213.

73. De Gaulle, *The Call to Honor*, 201.

74. Hoffmann, "The Man Who Would Be France," 34.

75. Lyndon B. Johnson Library, National Security File, Memoranda to the President, Box 2, vol. 7 (October 1–December 31, 1964), account of a meeting in the Oval Office, November 19, 1964, 3.

76. De Gaulle envisioned this formula as a progressive series of stages by which he would normalize France's relations with the Soviets and the Eastern Europeans, and eventually the Chinese. Charles de Gaulle, *Renewal, 1958–1962*, part 1 of *Memoirs of Hope*, trans. Terence Kilmartin (New York: Simon and Schuster, 1970), 202.

77. French diplomat, interview by author, October 11, 2001.

78. Pierre Favier and Michel Martin-Roland, *La décennie Mitterrand*, vol. 3 of *Les défis (1988–1991)* (Paris: Seuil, 1996), 78.

79. The key passage in the Treaty of Maastricht that instituted these political changes is the following: "The common foreign and security policy shall include all questions related to the security of the European Union, including the framing of a common defense policy, which might in time lead to a common defense." Treaty of Maastricht, Article J.4, paragraph 1, www.defense. gouv.fr/europe/traites_fondateurs/maastricht.htm.

80. Rudolph von Thadden, "Un équilibre difficile," *Zeitschrift für Kultur Austausch* 4 (2000): 12.

81. François Mitterrand, *De l'Allemagne, de la France* (Paris: Odile Jacob, 1996).

82. Stanley Hoffmann, "French Dilemmas and Strategies in the New Europe," in *After the Cold War: International Institutions and State Strategies in Europe, 1989–1991*, ed. Robert O. Keohane, Joseph S. Nye, and Stanley Hoffmann (Cambridge, Mass.: Harvard University Press, 1993), 130.

83. A French ambassador possted to Brussels, interview by author.

84. Frédéric Bozo, *La France et l'OTAN: De la guerre froide au nouvel ordre européen* (Paris: Masson, 1991), 195.

85. Declaration of the North Atlantic Council, London, July 5–6, 1990; see www.nato.int/docu/comm./49-95/c900706a.htm, 1.

86. As Hubert Védrine wrote, "We always say 'security' and not 'defense', so as not to alarm the NATO integrationists. But they're already on their guard. The whole problematic of the 1990s is there [in these two terms]." Hubert Védrine, *Les mondes de François Mitterrand: À l'Élysée, 1981–1995* (Paris: Fayard, 1996), 459.

87. Chirac famously recounted that he had spent a summer in the United States in the 1950s, during which he had worked at a Howard Johnson's and had an American girlfriend. Furthermore, Chirac's English is passable; Mitterrand's was not.

88. Kornblum, interview by author.

89. Samy Cohen, ed., *Mitterrand et la sortie de la guerre froide* (Paris: Presses Universitaires de France, 1998), 186.

90. Jean-David Levitte, interview by author, New York, October 12, 2001. According to Levitte, the origins of the French-British defense cooperation go back in particular to British prime minister John Major's invitation to the incoming French president, Jacques Chirac, to make a state visit to London in 1995.

91. In the view of Sir Michael Jay, permanent under secretary in the British Foreign Office, the experience in the Balkans was salutary, as it made the British realize that the French are among the most committed of the European allies over the foreseeable future, and that Britain and France share a common tradition of willingness to undertake military interventions abroad. Had it come to the use of ground forces in Kosovo, Jay believes that

the British and French would have sent troops; the Americans would not have. Sir Michael Jay, interview by author, London, April 25, 2002.

92. Ibid.

93. Britain-info.org/bistext/fordom/defence/4dc98-2.stm, 1.

94. This is not to be confused with the Rapid Reaction Force in Bosnia, which came into being in June 1995.

95. Jacques Isnard, "Défense commune," *Le Monde*, December 12–13, 1999, 3.

96. Claire Tréan, "À Washington, Jacques Chirac souligne l'urgence d'une solution politique," *Le Monde*, November 8, 2001, 4.

97. At the United States Central Command in Tampa, Florida, from which the campaign in Afghanistan was being run, liaison officers from each member country of the gradually assembled coalition were present. Sylvie Kauffmann, "Le nouvel unilatéralisme américain," *Le Monde*, January 2, 2002, 1. The countries joining in the campaign, designated Operation Enduring Freedom, eventually numbered twenty-one and became known as the Global Counter Terrorism Force (GCTF).

98. Françoise Chipaux, "Washington et Paris forment l'embryon d'une armée nationale," *Le Monde*, July 9, 2002, 2. As of August 2003, NATO took over command of the peacekeeping force in Kabul.

99. Jeremy Shapiro, "U.S.-French Relations after Iraq" (paper presented at a conference at Middlebury College, Middlebury, Vt. April 26, 2003). Shapiro is the deputy director of the Center for the United States and France at the Brookings Institution, Washington, D.C.

100. Senior French defense official, interview by author.

101. Ambassador George F. Ward Jr. and Ray Caldwell, interviews by author, Washington, D.C., September 21, 2001.

102. Hubert Védrine with Dominique Moïsi, *France in an Age of Globalization*, trans. Philip H. Gordon (Washington, D.C.: Brookings Institution Press, 2001), 46.

103. Interview by author.

104. Interview with Jean-Pierre Kelche, *Le Monde*, December 9, 2000, 3.

105. President Jacques Chirac, speech at the opening of the Thirty-first General Conference of UNESCO, October 15, 2001, *Le Monde*, October 16, 2001, 17.

106. "L'Europe-puissance: Entretien avec Javier Solana," *Politique Internationale* (summer 2001): 225.

107. Robert Kagan, "Power and Weakness," *Policy Review* (June-July 2002): 3, 10, 11, cited in Rein Müllerson, *Jus ad bellum: Plus ça change (le Monde), plus c'est la même chose (le Droit)*, draft paper, Naval War College Conference on Terrorism, June 2002, 10–11.

108. *Foreign Relations of the United States, 1964–1968*, vol. 1, *Vietnam 1964* (Washington, D.C.: U.S. Government Printing Office, 1996), 469.

109. Ibid.

110. Kornblum, interview by author.

111. Ibid.

112. Rudolph von Thadden, interview by author, Göttingen, March 11, 2002.

113. Senior German diplomat, interview by author, March 7, 2002.

114. Jochen Thies, interview by author, Berlin, March 8, 2002.

115. Daniel Vernet, "Europe, la fin du 'jardin à la française,'" *Le Monde*, December 15, 2000, 1, 19.

116. Arnaud Leparmentier, "Les relations entre la France et l'Allemagne connaissent de nouvelles tensions," *Le Monde*, November 29, 2000, 2.

117. Dr. Karl Kaiser, director of research of the German Council on Foreign Relations and a campaign adviser to Schröder, interview by author, Cambridge, Mass., April 11, 2002.

118. On the eve of the October 25–26, 2002, EU summit at Brussels, Chirac and Schröder made a surprise announcement that they favored extending the CAP until 2013, and that benefits for the incoming countries should be put in place only gradually. For more on the CAP, which benefits French farmers to a greater extent than those of other EU countries, see the third case study in chapter 5.

119. "The stand of German Chancellor Gerhard Schröder against the war shocked President Bush who maintained that [Schröder] had promised him his support." Paul Marie de la Gorce, "Seuls contre tous," *Le Monde diplomatique*, April 2003, 14.

120. Alain Pierret, "Une diplomatie brouillonne," *Le Monde*, May 2, 2003, 14.

121. Delafon and Sancton, *Dear Jacques Cher Bill . . . Au coeur de l'Élysée et de la Maison Blanche, 1995–1999*, 308.

4. THE PROCESS

1. Alan Ryan, "Visions of Politics," review of Sheldon S. Wolin, *Tocqueville between Two Worlds: The Making of a Political and Theoretical Life* (Princeton, N.J.: Princeton University Press, 2002), in *New York Review of Books*, June 27, 2002, 38. *Moeurs* is used here in the sense of customs, habits, and mores, and not in its other two senses of morals and manners.

2. *Webster's New World Dictionary of American English*, 3d college ed., s.v. "process."

3. Alain Lempereur, telephone interview by author, April 3, 2002.

4. German diplomat, interview by author, April 2, 2002.

5. Christoph Bertram, interview by author, Berlin, May 31, 2002.

6. Interview by author.

7. ESSEC is one of three French business schools, generally ranked in the following order: the École des Hautes Études Commerciales (HEC), ESSEC, and the École Supérieure de Commerce de Paris (ESCP). The INSEAD business school at Fontainebleau is not, properly speaking, a French school but an international school.

8. Lempereur, telephone interview by author.

9. Jacques Andréani, interview by author, Cambridge, Mass., March 1, 2002.

10. French diplomat, interview by author, May 10, 2002.

11. Former French academic who is now a senior civil servant, interview by author, Paris, May 23, 2002.

12. Rudolph von Thadden, interview by author, Göttingen, March 11, 2002.

13. Former French academic, interview by author. A comparison of the U.S. and French court systems provides another example of the hierarchical nature of the French state. In the U.S. court system there may be a majority opinion of the court and then some dissenting opinions by minority judges. In the French court system, even if the judges disagree, the final court decision does not show it; it looks unanimous. Alain Lempereur, e-mail to author, July 17, 2002.

14. Commissariat Général du Plan, *Organiser la politique européenne et internationale de la France*, report of the group presided over by Admiral Jacques Lanxade, rapporteur Nicolas Tenzer (Paris: La documentation française, 2002), 89.

15. French diplomat, interview by author, May 10, 2002.

16. Commissariat Général du Plan, *Organiser la politique européenne et internationale de la France*, 114–115.

17. Ibid., 113–114.

18. French defense official, interview by author, Washington, D.C., May 12, 2003.

19. The French government's margin of maneuver, when it comes to the need for budgetary discipline and structural reforms, is very narrow, as was made abundantly clear in late 1995 when strikes and demonstrations against the government's reform proposals paralyzed Paris for weeks, leading indirectly to the defeat of the Right by the Left in the 1997 legislative elections.

20. Jean-Marie Guéhenno, interview by author, New York, January 10, 2002.

21. French diplomat, interview by author, October 11, 2001.

22. Jean-David Levitte, interview by author, New York, January 10, 2002.

23. Stanley Hoffmann (lecture presented at a conference about the French-U.S. rift, Columbia University, New York, May 22, 2003).

24. Senior British diplomatic official, interview by author, London, April 25, 2002.

25. Senior State Department official, interview by author, Washington, D.C., February 7, 2002.

26. Commissariat Général du Plan, *Organiser la politique européenne et internationale de la France*, 60.

27. German diplomat, interview by author, November 28, 2001. An exception to this practice was the appointment to the European Commission of Edith Cresson, whose questionable hiring practices helped bring about the resignation of the entire commission in 1999. But this was a political appointment by François Mitterrand.

28. However, as far as services are concerned, though the European Commission is authorized to negotiate on behalf of the European Union, decisions have to be approved by unanimity in the European Council. Pierre Vimont, interview by author, Brussels, March 4, 2002.

29. Although the European Parliament is now authorized to be a co-introducer for slightly more than 50 percent of EU legislation, when the council makes a decision by qualified majority voting—as for example, in the case of the Common Agricultural Policy—the parliament has no power of co-decision. Pascal Lamy and Jean Pisani-Ferry, "L'Europe de nos volontés," *Les Notes de la Fondation Jean-Jaurès*, no. 27 (January 2002): 26 and n. 7.

30. I am indebted for the statements in this and the following paragraph to Noël Purcell-O'Byrne of the General Secretariat of the European Council. Noël Purcell-O'Byrne, interview by author, Brussels, March 4, 2002.

31. However, the foreign ministers are members of the European Council along with the chiefs of state or government.

32. There are, in fact, two French ambassadors to the European Union; the second is the ambassador to the European Council's Political and Security Committee (the French acronym is COPS). The COPS is chaired by the president of the European Council, who changes every six months as another member country assumes the presidency. The COPS, as a function of the European Security and Defense Policy (ESDP), is in a relationship with the high representative of the Common Foreign and Security Policy (CFSP), who concurrently is the general secretary of the European Council.

33. Vimont, interview by author.

34. Ibid. I am indebted for the statements in this and the following two paragraphs to Ambassador Pierre Vimont.

35. Gérard Araud, e-mail to author, January 3, 2002.

36. Senior British diplomatic official, interview by author.

37. Jay, interview by author.

38. Nicolas Tenzer, interview by author, Paris, December 12, 2001. Tenzer was the rapporteur of the working group within the Commissariat Général du Plan that produced *Organiser la politique européenne et internationale de la France.*

39. Senior German Foreign Office official, interview by author, Berlin, March 7, 2002.

40. French diplomat, interview by author, October 11, 2001.

41. Alain Lempereur, interview by author, Cambridge, Mass., September 6, 2001.

42. Bruce Bach, interview by author, Brussels, March 6, 2002.

43. Alain Lempereur, e-mail to author.

44. Gilles Andréani, interview by author, Paris, December 12, 2001.

45. French diplomat, interview by author, May 10, 2002.

46. Lempereur, e-mail to author.

47. Paul Robert, *Le Petit Robert 1: Dictionnaire de la langue française* (Paris: Le Robert, 1990), 555.

48. A French ambassador posted to Brussels, interview by author.

49. Levitte, interview by author.

50. Araud, e-mail to author.

51. Senior British diplomatic official, interview by author.

52. Araud, e-mail to author.

53. Anthony Blinken, interview by author, Washington, D.C., February 6, 2002.

54. Senior British diplomatic official, interview by author.

55. Louis Menand, "The Principles of Oliver Wendell Holmes," in *American Studies* (New York: Farrar, Straus, and Giroux, 2002), 33–34. Holmes was a justice of the U.S. Supreme Court from 1902 to 1932.

56. Ambassador George F. Ward Jr., interview by author, Washington, D.C., September 21, 2001.

57. A French ambassador posted to Brussels, interview by author.

58. Alain Plantey, interview by author, Paris, May 25, 2002.

59. Andréani, interview by author.

60. Commissariat Général du Plan, *Organiser la politique européenne et internationale de la France,* 37.

61. Lempereur, telephone interview by author.

62. *The Political Testament of Cardinal Richelieu,* trans. Henry Bertram Hill (Madison: University of Wisconsin Press, 1961), 94.

63. Lempereur, telephone interview by author.

64. Jean-Pierre Froehly, German Council on Foreign Relations, interview by author, Berlin, March 8, 2002.

65. Gérard Errera, interview by author, Paris, May 25, 2002.

66. Edward T. Hall, *Beyond Culture* (New York: Anchor Books, 1976).

67. Kevin Avruch, *Culture and Conflict Resolution* (Washington, D.C.: United States Institute of Peace Press, 1998), 64.

68. Cohen, Raymond, *Negotiating across Cultures: International Communication in an Interdependent World* (Washington, D.C.: United States Institute of Peace Press, 1997), 31, 33.

69. Jochen Thies, interview by author, Berlin, March 8, 2002.

70. The phrase comes from the seventeenth century, when the practice, unlike today, was to serve the cheese *after* the dessert.

71. Lempereur, e-mail to author.

72. Roger Cohen, "U.S.-French Relations Turn Icy after Cold War," *New*

York Times, July 2, 1992, A10. According to the *Times*, the remark is contained in an official French transcript of a meeting in Washington on May 11, 1992, between Secretary Baker and Foreign Minister Dumas.

73. Michael Watkins and Susan Rosegrant, *Breakthrough International Negotiation: How Great Negotiators Transformed the World's Toughest Post–Cold War Conflicts* (San Francisco: Jossey-Bass, 2001), 144.

74. Jacques Lanxade, *Quand le monde a basculé* (Paris: NiL éditions, 2001), 74.

75. Fons Trompenaars, *Riding the Waves of Culture: Understanding Cultural Diversity in Business* (London: Economist Books, 1993), 82.

76. Von Thadden, interview by author.

77. Ibid.

78. Robert Hunter, interview by author, Washington, D.C., September 21, 2001.

79. E-mail to author.

80. According to Dr. Karl Kaiser, "Chirac in undiplomatic terms put his foot down and killed the German proposal. It was an enormous setback for Schröder, and his relations with Chirac got off on the wrong foot." Kaiser was an adviser to Schröder during his 1998 campaign. Karl Kaiser, interview by author, Cambridge, Mass., April 11, 2002.

81. Senior British diplomatic official, interview by author.

82. Senior French diplomatic official, interview by author.

83. The Big Three had broken apart in a previous crisis, over Suez in 1956.

84. Philippe Roger (lecture presented at the Center for the United States and France (CUSF), Brookings Institution, Washington, D.C., May 12, 2003). *L'Ennemi américain* is an in-depth study of the historical roots of French anti-Americanism.

85. Senior State Department official, interview by author, Washington, D.C., October 31, 2001.

86. Ward, interview by author.

87. Blinken, interview by author.

88. French diplomat, interview by author, May 10, 2002.

89. Von Thadden, interview by author.

90. The Gallic rooster *(le coq gaulois)* stems from the same Latin word for Gaul and rooster. However, the rooster did not become a popular symbol in France until the seventeenth century and has never been an official symbol. Michel Pastoureau, "Le coq gaulois," in *Les lieux de mémoire*, vol. 3, ed. Pierre Nora (Paris: Gallimard, 1997), 4297–4298, 4305.

91. Ulrike Guérot, e-mail to author, April 8, 2002.

92. This key phrase emerged from the United States Institute of Peace's special report, *French Negotiating Style* (Washington, D.C.: United States Institute of Peace, 2000).

93. John Mearsheimer, *The Tragedy of Great Power Politics* (New York: W. W. Norton, 2001), 461 n. 46. The quotation is from Karl A. Roider Jr., *Baron Thugut and Austria's Response to the French Revolution* (Princeton, N.J.: Princeton University Press, 1987), 327.

94. Stephen Ledogar, interview by author, New York, October 11, 2001.

95. Jay, interview by author.

96. Kaiser, interview by author.

97. Ibid.

98. Thies, interview by author.

99. Araud, e-mail to author.

100. A French ambassador posted to Brussels, interview by author.

101. Jean-Louis Crémieux-Brilhac, *La France libre*, vol. 1 (Paris: Gallimard, 1996), 211.

102. Alain Peyrefitte, *C'était de Gaulle*, vol. 1 (Paris: Fayard, 1994), 333. "Milord" is a continental term of address for an English nobleman and can be a pejorative or mocking reference. *Webster's New World Dictionary of American English*, 3d college ed., s.v. "milord."

103. Charles de Gaulle, *The Call to Honor, 1940–1942*, vol. 1 of *The Complete War Memoirs of Charles de Gaulle*, trans. Jonathan Griffin (New York: Simon and Schuster, 1964), 201.

104. German diplomat, interview by author.

105. Gilles Andréani, interview by author.

106. Ibid.

107. Arnaud Leparmentier and Laurent Zecchini, "Les quinze confient à Valéry Giscard d'Estaing la Convention sur l'Avenir de Europe," *Le Monde*, December 18, 2001, 8.

108. Senior German Foreign Office official, interview by author.

109. Ward, interview by author.

110. Levitte, interview by author.

111. A French ambassador posted to Brussels. interview by author.

112. Pierre Nora, *Les lieux de mémoire*, vol. 2, 1921. The "academic company" is a public institution, the Académie Française, which is charged with compiling the official French-language dictionary. It was founded in 1635 by Cardinal Richelieu.

113. Lempereur, e-mail to author, July 17, 2002.

114. Jean-Marie Goulemot and Éric Walter, "Les centenaires de Voltaire et de Rousseau," in *Les lieux de mémoire*, vol. 1, 379.

115. Pierre Guerlain, *Miroirs transatlantiques: La France et les États-Unis entre passions et indifférences* (Paris: L'Harmattan, 1996), 134. The quotation is from Mort Rosenblum, *Mission to Civilize* (San Diego: Harcourt Brace Jovanovich, 1986).

116. Marc Fumaroli, "Le génie de la langue française," in *Les lieux de mémoire*, vol. 3, 4679. The quotation is from Rivarol, "De l'universalité de la langue française," in *Oeuvres* (Paris: Didier, 1852), 111.

117. Guéhenno, interview by author.

118. François Azouvi, "Descartes," in *Les lieux de mémoire*, vol. 3, 4480.

119. Hunter, interview by author.

120. *The Political Testament of Cardinal Richelieu*, 99.

121. Hunter, interview by author.

122. Guéhenno, interview by author.

123. Jean-Philippe Mathy, *French Resistance: The French-American Culture Wars* (Minneapolis: University of Minnesota Press, 2000), 41. The quotation is from Tony Judt, *Past Imperfect: French Intellectuals, 1944–1956* (Berkeley: University of California Press, 1993), 249.

124. Ibid.

125. Ibid., 253.

126. Guéhenno, interview by author.

127. Mathy, *French Resistance*, 41. Reference is to Julian Benda, *The Treason of the Intellectuals*, trans. Richard Aldington (New York: Norton, 1969).

128. See also Fons Trompenaars's mention of "common ground" in reference to high-context cultures, p. 127.

129. Guéhenno, interview by author.

130. German diplomat, interview by author, November 28, 2001.

131. Ibid.

132. Margaret MacMillan, *Paris 1919: Six Months That Changed the World* (New York: Random House, 2001), 55–56.

133. Gérard Errera, interview by author, Paris, May 24, 2002.

134. Jean-David Levitte, interview by author, New York, October 12, 2001.

135. Admiral (ret.) Jacques Lanxade, interview by author, Paris, May 23, 2002.

136. Plantey, interview by author.

137. Ward, interview by author.

138. John Kornblum, interview by author, Berlin, March 8, 2002.

139. Pascal Ory, "La gastronomie," in *Les lieux de mémoire*, vol. 3, 3750.

140. Ibid. The quotation is from Stephen Mennell, *Français et Anglais à table du Moyen Âge à nos jours* (Paris: Flammarion, 1987), 155–159.

141. Ibid., 3744. The quotation is from Marcel Rouff, *La vie et la passion de Dodin-Bouffant, gourmet* (Paris: Stock, 1984), 18–19.

142. Ibid., 3755. The quotation is from Brillat-Savarin, *Physiologie du goût* (Paris: Flammarion, Édition "Champs," 1982).

143. Senior French civil servant, interview by author, Paris, May 23, 2002.

144. German diplomat, interview by author.

145. Senior U.S. diplomat, interview by author, April 26, 2002. The translation of *traiteur* is "caterer." The French also use the expression *diplomatie des petits fours* (cocktail diplomacy).

146. Levitte, interview by author.

147. Elaine Sciolino, "France Mutes Its Criticism of U.S. Stance toward Iraq," *New York Times*, August 29, 2002, A14.

148. Senior State Department official, interview by author, August 10, 2002.

149. Robert Graham and Haig Simonian, "Chirac Cautions Washington against Unilateral Use of Forces," *Financial Times*, August 30, 2002, 8.

150. Stanley Hoffmann (lecture presented at a conference on the French-U.S. rift).

151. Interview by author.

152. Robert Schneider, "Giscard: Ne m'appelez plus jamais l'Ex," *Le Nouvel Observateur*, June 19–25, 2003, 28.

153. Senior British diplomatic official, interview by author, London, May 25, 2002.

154. Hunter, interview by author.

155. French diplomat, interview by author, May 10, 2002.

156. Andréani, interview by author.

157. Jay, interview by author.

158. Hunter, interview by author.

159. Froehly, interview by author.

160. See chapter 2, pp. 50–51.

161. Lionel Barber, *Financial Times* (remarks at a conference on the French-U.S. rift, Columbia University, New York, May 22, 2003).

162. Alain Lempereur, telephone interview by author, September 25, 2002.

163. Andréani, interview by author.

164. See Gordon and Meunier, *The French Challenge*, 24.

165. *Le grand dictionnaire Larousse*, unabridged edition, 1993, s.v. *"pantouflage."*

166. Public-sector ownership of the French economy has decreased from 10.4 percent in 1985 to 5 percent in 2000, the same level it was at before World War II. See Gordon and Meunier, *The French Challenge*, 21.

167. François Heilbronn, Harvard Business School MBA (1988) and managing partner of the consulting firm of Friedrich, Heilbronn and Fiszer, interview by author, Paris, October 1, 2002.

168. Senior British diplomatic official, interview by author.

169. Ibid.

170. Bach, interview by author.

171. Lanxade, interview by author.

172. Ibid.

173. Ibid.

174. Ezra N. Suleiman, *Elites in French Society: The Politics of Survival* (Princeton, N.J.: Princeton University Press, 1978), 114.

175. Senior French defense official, interview by author.

5. Case Studies

1. Philippe Roger (lecture presented at the conference "The United States and France after the War in Iraq," Center on the United States and France, Brookings Institution, Washington, D.C., May 12, 2003).

2. French diplomat, interview by author, May 10, 2002.

3. Gérard Errera, interview by author, Paris, May 24, 2002.

4. NATO's military headquarters is known as SHAPE (Supreme Headquarters Allied Powers Europe) and is headed by the SACEUR.

5. Errera, interview by author.

6. It may be noted that, as the permanent under secretary of the British Foreign Office, Sir Michael Jay, has observed, the failure of the French return to NATO now appears not as serious a setback as it seemed at the time. Although it would have been better if the return had succeeded, and the military campaign in Kosovo in 1999 would have gone more smoothly, the issue subsequently seemed less important because of the way NATO began to evolve in the 1990s toward conflict resolution and away from its classic collective defense role. Further, the European Union's Security and Defense Policy would sooner or later have had to be backed up by some sort of European defense force: "It is a process that would have happened anyway." Sir Michael Jay, interview by author, London, April 25, 2002.

7. Admiral (ret.) Jacques Lanxade, interview by author, Paris, May 23, 2002.

8. John Kornblum, interview by author, Berlin, March 8, 2002.

9. Ibid.

10. Ibid.

11. Philippe Guelluy, interview by author, Ottawa, April 19, 2002.

12. Kornblum, interview by author.

13. Gilles Andréani, interview by author, Paris, December 15, 2001. As strategic adviser to Foreign Minister Hervé de Charrette, Andréani was a member of the French team and is now the head of the Center for Analysis and Forecasting of the Quai d'Orsay. The reference to the "French team" in the following pages is from Andréani's account.

14. Senior French defense official, interview by author.

15. Rachel Utley, *The French Defense Debate: Consensus and Continuity in the Mitterrand Era* (London: Macmillan, 2000), 173. Chirac's quotation is from R. P. Grant, "France's New Relationship with NATO," *Survival* 1, no. 38 (spring 1996): 63.

16. "France and NATO," Radio France Inter, "Le téléphone sonne," February 8, 1996.

17. Errera, interview by author.

18. Ibid.

19. Gilles Delafon and Thomas Sancton, *Dear Jacques Cher Bill . . . Au coeur de l'Élysée et de la Maison Blanche, 1995–1999* (Paris: Plon, 1999), 185.

20. Andréani, interview by author.

21. www.nato.int/docu/pr/1996/p96-063e.htm, 5–6.

22. U.S. negotiator, interview by author, Washington, D.C., November 30, 2001.

23. Kornblum, interview by author.

24. Jean-David Levitte, interview by author, New York, October 12, 2002.

25. Senior French defense official, interview by author.

26. Errera, interview by author.

27. The air and land forces are under USEUCOM and headquartered respectively at Ramstein (USAFE) and at Heidelberg (USAREUR). The head of USEUCOM is double-hatted. He is also the SACEUR in the NATO context. As of June 2003, the SACEUR took over operational responsibility for both the European and the Atlantic areas.

28. Max Johnson, legal adviser at SHAPE, interview by author, Mons, Belgium, March 4, 2002.

29. Guelluy, interview by author.

30. General (ret.) Klaus Naumann, interview by author, Berlin, March 8, 2002.

31. Errera, interview by author.

32. Delafon and Sancton, *Dear Jacques Cher Bill*, 202.

33. Errera, interview by author.

34. Ibid.

35. Ibid.

36. Joseph Fitchett, "Early Elections in 1997 Halted France's Long Journey Back into NATO," *International Herald Tribune*, July 3, 1998, 8.

37. Naumann, interview by author.

38. Delafon and Sancton, *Dear Jacques Cher Bill*, 204–207.

39. Ibid., 207.

40. Ibid., 214.

41. Ibid., 215–216.

42. Senior French government official, interview by author, May 13, 2000.

43. Delafon and Sancton, *Dear Jacques Cher Bill*, 216.

44. Naumann, interview by author.

45. Gérard Araud, interview by author, Cambridge, Mass., January 27, 2001.

46. Senior French government official, interview by author.

47. Delafon and Sancton, *Dear Jacques Cher Bill*, 185.

48. NATO headquarters official, interview by author, Brussels, March 5, 2002.

49. Araud, interview by author.

50. Kornblum, interview by author.

51. Delafon and Sancton, *Dear Jacques Cher Bill*, 266.

52. Robert Hunter, telephone interview by author, January 2, 2002.

53. Ibid.

54. Ibid.

55. Naumann, interview by author.

56. Ibid.

57. Lanxade, interview by author.

58. State Department official, interview by author, Washington, D.C., April 10, 2002.

59. Louis Gautier, *Mitterrand et son armée, 1990–1995* (Paris: Grasset, 1999), 436 n. 92.

60. State Department official, interview by author.

61. Bruce Bach, NATO official, interview by author, Brussels, March 6, 2002.

62. André Dumoulin, "Les ambitions de l'Europe: De l'après-Kosovo aux indicateurs de cohérence," *Politique Étrangère* (summer 2000): 489–490.

63. Robert Hunter, telephone interview by author, January 2, 2002. See also p. 181.

64. Zbigniew Brzezinski, "Living with a New Europe," *National Interest* (summer 2000): 17.

65. Walter Russell Mead (lecture presented at the conference "The United States and France after the War in Iraq," Center on the United States and France, Brookings Institution, Washington, D.C., May 12, 2003).

66. Patrice de Beer, "Iraq: Fragilité des positions françaises," *Le Monde*, April 24, 2003, 17.

67. Roger (lecture presented at the conference "The United States and France after the War in Iraq").

68. Senior State Department official, interview by author. See also chapter 3, p. 102 and n. 119.

69. The United States objected to the 1997 Kyoto Protocol on carbon dioxide emissions because it considered the protocol an imperfect document, particularly in that it exempted the developing nations from the regime. Washington's objection to the International Criminal Court was based on an unwillingness to have U.S. soldiers abroad subjected to the jurisdiction of an international court.

70. Steven R. Weisman, "A Long Winding Road to a Diplomatic Dead End," *New York Times*, March 17, 2003, A1.

71. Patricia Lewis, "From UNSCOM to UNMOVIC: The United Nations and Iraq," *Disarmament Forum: The Middle East*, no. 2 (2001): 63.

72. Ibid.

73. Charles Duelfer, former deputy chairman of UNSCOM, interview by author, Washington, D.C., January 28, 2002.

74. Ibid.

75. Ibid.

76. Charles Duelfer, interview by author, Washington, D.C., June 24, 2002.

77. Nancy Soderberg, telephone interview by author, January 9, 2002. Ironically, when the French shifted their position more toward the Anglo-Americans in the aftermath of the events of September 11, Iraq awarded most of the contracts under the Oil-for-Food program to the Russians and not to the French. Duelfer, interview by author, June 24, 2002.

78. Josette Alia and Christine Mital, "Les conséquences d'un divorce," *Le Nouvel Observateur*, March 13–19, 2003, 45.

79. Jean-David Levitte, interview by author, New York, January 10, 2002.

80. Jean-David Levitte (talk presented at Massachusetts Institute of Technology [MIT], Cambridge, Mass., May 7, 2003).

81. Kenneth Pollack, *The Threatening Storm: The Case for Invading Iraq* (New York: Random House, 2002).

82. Kenneth Pollack, interview by author, Washington, D.C., January 28, 2002.

83. Babette Stern, "Les échanges franco-italiens ont triplé depuis 1997," *Le Monde*, January 4, 2003, 3.

84. Levitte (talk presented at MIT).

85. Dennis Halliday, statement on *McNeil-Lehrer News Hour*, May 9, 2003.

86. Bruce Riedel, e-mail to author, June 29, 2002.

87. Levitte (talk presented at MIT).

88. Levitte, interview by author, New York, January 10, 2002.

89. Duelfer, interview by author, Washington, D.C., January 28, 2002.

90. Gilles Andréani, interview by author, Paris, December 12, 2001.

91. Riedel, e-mail to author.

92. Pollack, interview by author.

93. Riedel, e-mail to author.

94. Ibid.

95. Levitte, interview by author, New York, January 10, 2002.

96. Ibid.

97. Richard Butler, *The Greatest Threat: Iraq, Weapons of Mass Destruction, and the Crisis of Global Security* (New York: Public Affairs, 2000), 226–227.

98. Riedel, e-mail to author, June 29, 2002.

99. Levitte, interview by author, New York, January 10, 2002.

100. See chapter 3, p. 98.

101. Philip Gordon and Justin Vaïsse, "Une victoire franco-américaine," *Le Monde*, November 13, 2002, 17.

102. Jean-David Levitte, telephone interview by author, November 14, 2002.

103. "French Leader Offers America Both Friendship and Criticism," *New York Times*, September 9, 2002, A9.

104. Levitte, telephone interview by author.

105. Ibid.

106. Senior State Department official, telephone interview by author, November 18, 2002.

107. UN official, telephone interview by author, November 20, 2002.

108. Senior State Department official, telephone interview by author.

109. UN official, telephone interview by author.

110. Senior State Department official, telephone interview by author.

111. UN official, telephone interview by author.

112. www.int/usa/sres-iraq.htm, 1, 2, 4.

113. Levitte, telephone interview by author.

114. Corinne Lesnes, "8 novembre–17 mars: L'Impossible entente aux Nations unies," *Le Monde*, March 19, 2003, 5.

115. Sir Jeremy Greenstock (talk presented at the Center for European Studies, Harvard University, Cambridge, Mass., May 7, 2003).

116. Levitte (talk presented at MIT).

117. Vincent Jauvert, "Quand Chirac se préparait à la guerre," *Le Nouvel Observateur*, March 20–26, 2003, 28.

118. Greenstock (talk presented at the Center for European Studies).

119. Senior French diplomatic official, conversation with author.

120. Weisman, "A Long Winding Road to a Diplomatic Dead End," A11.

121. Nicholas Lemann, "How It Came to War," *New Yorker*, March 31, 2003, 39.

122. Ibid. Notwithstanding, Sir Jeremy Greenstock maintains that the final decision to go to war was not made until February 15, 2003. Greenstock (talk presented at the Center for European Studies).

123. French defense official, interview by author, Washington, D.C., May 12, 2003.

124. Greenstock (talk presented at the Center for European Studies).

125. Vincent Jauvert, "Le blitz de Villepin," *Le Nouvel Observateur*, January 30–February 5, 2003, 33.

126. Senior State Department official, telephone conversation with author, April 15, 2003.

127. Weisman, "A Long Winding Road to a Diplomatic Dead End," A1.

128. UN official, telephone interview by author, April 21, 2003.

129. "The Divided West: Part Three," *Financial Times*, May 29, 2003, 11.

130. Levitte (talk presented at MIT).

131. The text of Blair's speech can be found at www.number10.gov.uk/output/page3294.asp.

132. *Daily Press Briefing*, statements by the Ministry of Foreign Affairs spokesperson, Paris, March 4, 2003, 3.

133. Greenstock (talk presented at the Center for European Studies). Chirac in a television interview on March 10 stated: "Whatever the circumstances, France will vote no" to a second UN resolution authorizing war. "War is always the worst solution." "Against America? Moi?" *Economist*, March 15–21, 2003, 47.

134. Senior UN official, telephone interview by author, April 21, 2003.

135. Levitte (talk presented at MIT).

136. Senior UN official, telephone interview by author. On May 22, 2003, in a certain return to comity after a rapidly concluded war, the Security Council came together again, voting unanimously 14-0 (with Syria not taking part) in favor of Resolution 1483, which lifted the sanctions against Iraq and conferred on the United States and Great Britain the responsibility for running the country. After one year, the Security Council would review the situation.

137. Levitte (talk presented at MIT).

138. Patrice de Beer, "Iraq: Fragilité des positions françaises," *Le Monde,* April 24, 2003, 17.

139. Dominique Moïsi, "Une diplomatie qui n'a pas accru nôtre prestige," *Le Monde,* June 17, 2002, 2.

140. Ibid.

141. Henri de Bresson, "Paris et Berlin redisent en Pologne leur conviction que l'ONU doit jouer 'un rôle central' en Iraq," *Le Monde,* May 11–12, 2003, 5.

142. www.wto.org/english/thewto_e/tif_e/fact5_e.htm, 2.

143. www.wto.org/english/thewto_e/whatis_e/tif_e/fact4_e.htm, 1–2.

144. Hugo Paemen and Alexandra Bensch, *From the GATT to the WTO: The European Community in the Uruguay Round* (Leuven, Belgium: Leuven University Press, 1995), 17.

145. www.wto.org/english/thewto_e/whatis_e/tif_e/fact2_e.htm, 2–3.

146. "The name sounds like a contradiction. It suggests some kind of special treatment for one particular country, but in the WTO it actually means non-discrimination—treating virtually everyone equally." See www.wto.org/english/thewto_e/whatis_e/tif_e/fact2_e.htm, 2.

147. Paemen and Bensch, *From the GATT to the WTO,* 76.

148. Alice Landau, *Conflits et coopération dans les relations économiques internationales: Le cas de l'Uruguay Round* (Brussels: Bruylant, 1996), 82–83.

149. www.wto.org/english/thewto_e/whatis_e/tif_e/fact4_e.htm, 3.

150. Landau, *Conflits et coopération dans les relations économiques internationales,* 84.

151. Paemen and Bensch, *From the GATT to the WTO,* 21.

152. Landau, *Conflits et coopération dans les relations économiques internationales,* 85.

153. Ibid.

154. Timothy E. Josling, Stefan Tangermann, and T. K. Warley, *Agriculture in the GATT* (New York: St. Martin's Press, 1996), 39, 59.

155. The Luxembourg Compromise helped to retard the further integration of Europe for twenty years, until the Single European Act of 1985. This act—which had the stated purpose of creating by January 1, 1993, a single European market for the exchange of goods, persons, services, and capital—stipulated that harmonization measures to bring this about would essentially be decided upon by qualified majority voting.

156. In an EU meeting in Berlin in March 1999, for example, France rejected German attempts to reduce the expense of the CAP. (See also chapter 4, p. 130 and n. 80.) France and Germany came to an agreement in October 2002 to extend the CAP until 2013 and to phase in benefits for the incoming countries only gradually.

In 2003, as noted in chapter 3, France did make some concessions on the CAP, notably that in the future the European Commission should have a role in deciding on CAP goals and that CAP payments should not be tied exclusively to the quantity of production.

157. French Government Draft Finance Law for 2002, Tome II, Installment 2: European Affairs and Article 28: evaluation of French participation in the budget of the European Communities, 6–7, 28–29.

158. Landau, *Conflits et coopération dans les relations économiques internationales*, 89. The PAC now consumes around half of the European Union's budget.

159. www.wto.org/english/thewto_e/whatis_e/tif_e/fact1_e.htm, 1.

160. Landau, *Conflits et coopération dans les relations économiques internationales*, 83.

161. Ibid., 96.

162. www.wto.org/english/thewto_e/whatis_e/tif_e/fact6_e.htm, 1.

163. Paemen and Bensch, *From the GATT to the WTO*, 254–255.

164. www.wto.org/English/thewto_e/whatis_e/tif_e/fact5_e.htm, 1.

165. Roderick Abbott, interview by author, Brussels, March 6, 2002.

166. Paemen and Bensch, *From the GATT to the WTO*, 20.

167. Abbott, interview by author.

168. Remco Vahl, *Leadership in Disguise: The Role of the European Commission in EC Decision-Making on Agriculture in the Uruguay Round* (Aldershot, U.K.: Ashgate, 1997), 218.

169. Abbott, interview by author.

170. Paemen and Bensch, *From the GATT to the WTO*, 94, 96 n. 4.

171. Abbott, interview by author.

172. Ibid. Committee 113 is made up of foreign trade experts from the member-states. The number 113 derives from the European Union Treaty's Article 113, which states that trade negotiations are to be conducted by the commission "in consultation with a special committee appointed by the Council to assist the Commission in this task." Paemen and Bensch, *From the GATT to the WTO*, 135 n. 13.

173. Roderick Abbott, e-mail to author, July 22, 2002. The Council of Ministers is not to be confused with the European Council, which is the forum for regular meetings of heads of state or government for strategic overview of policy and for launching new initiatives. The European Council meets three or four times a year and may make a general statement about GATT/WTO trade negotiations or the need to resolve a specific issue, but it is not executive in this area of policy.

174. Paemen and Bensch, *From the GATT to the WTO*, 94.

175. Jacques Andréani, interview by author, Cambridge, Mass., March 1, 2002; Abbott, e-mail to author.

176. Levitte, interview by author, New York, January 10, 2002.

177. Vahl, *Leadership in Disguise*, 2.

178. Levitte, interview by author, New York, January 10, 2002.

179. Paemen and Bensch, *From the GATT to the WTO*, 202.

180. www.wto.org/English/thewto_e/tif_e/fact5_e.htm, 2.

181. Ibid.

182. Josling, Tangemann, and Warley, *Agriculture in the GATT*, 139.

183. Ibid., 161.

184. Abbott, interview by author.

185. Ibid.

186. Pierre Vimont, interview by author, Brussels, March 4, 2002.

187. Abbott, e-mail to author.

188. French diplomat, interview by author, October 11, 2001.

189. French diplomat, e-mail to author, October 22, 2001.

190. Andréani, interview by author.

191. Vahl, *Leadership in Disguise*, 230.

192. Andréani, interview by author.

193. Ibid.

194. Levitte, interview by author, New York, January 10, 2002.

195. Abbott, e-mail to author.

196. Vimont, interview by author.

197. Abbott, e-mail to author.

198. Abbott, interview by author.

199. Abbott, e-mail to author.

200. Guéhenno, interview by author.

201. A French ambassador posted to Brussels, interview by author.

202. Josling, Tangermann, and Warley, *Agriculture in the GATT*, 162 n. 42.

203. Paemen and Bensch, *From the GATT to the WTO*, 217.

204. Ibid., 243.

205. Rufus Yerxa, interview by author, Washington, D.C., July 22, 2002.

206. World Trade Organization, *The Legal Texts: The Results of the Uruguay Round of Multilateral Trade Negotiations* (Cambridge: Cambridge University Press, 1999), 309–319.

207. Former senior U.S. government official, interview by author.

208. Levitte, interview by author, New York, January 10, 2002.

209. Abbott, interview by author.

210. Yves-Thibault de Silguy, telephone interview by author, July 11, 2002.

211. culture/coe.fr/Infocentre/txt/eng/ecopon.html, 1. The Council of Europe, a loose association of states focused on human rights but also on cultural, social, and legal issues, emerged from the idea of a European Assembly, aired at a May 1948 conference at The Hague of European federalist associations.

212. Vimont, interview by author; Abbott, interview by author.

213. europa.eu.int/comm/avpolicy/intro/intro_en.htm, 1.

214. The Single European Market was the outcome of the Single European Act. See n. 155 this chapter for details.

215. Paemen and Bensch, *From the GATT to the WTO*, 234 n. 1.

216. Philip H. Gordon and Sophie Meunier, *The French Challenge: Adapting to Globalization* (Washington, D.C.: Brookings Institution Press, 2001), 52.

217. Harry S. Truman Library, President's Secretary's File, Papers of John W. Snyder, Secretary of the Treasury, Box 18, Foreign Funds Control (General) Gold: France—September 1946, "Discussions between Mr. Snyder and

Finance Minister Robert Schuman, questions that could be raised by Mr. Schuman," annex 14, 1.

218. Vimont, interview by author.

219. Gordon and Meunier, *The French Challenge*, 52.

220. Vimont, interview by author.

221. Ibid.

222. Abbott, interview by author.

223. De Silguy, telephone interview by author.

224. Abbott, e-mail to author.

225. Vimont, interview by author.

226. Paemen and Bensch, *From the GATT to the WTO*, 33.

227. "The 'Luxembourg Compromise' better known as the 'right of veto,' [is a] political arrangement [that] has no legal state in Community law." Ibid., 143 n. 18.

228. This is confirmed by two French civil servants thoroughly familiar with the case, Jacques Andréani (interview by author) and Pierre Vimont (interview by author).

229. Landau, *Conflits et coopération dans les relations économiques internationales*, 139.

230. Yerxa, interview by author.

231. Abbott, interview by author.

232. Later, however, as prime minister, Juppé came across as unsympathetic to the aspirations of ordinary people.

6. NEGOTIATING WITH THE FRENCH

1. I am particularly indebted to Alain Lempereur for his comments on this chapter.

2. Stanley Hoffman (lecture presented at a conference about the U.S.-French rift, Columbia University, New York, May 22, 2003).

3. As with many famous remarks, the effect of de Gaulle's is attenuated when his words are returned to their original context. The complete sentence is as follows: "Some people feared [at the time of the creation of the state of Israel] that the Jews, still dispersed, but having remained what they had been from time immemorial, that is an elite people, sure of themselves and domineering, would, once reassembled in the site of their ancient grandeur, transform the very moving desires that they had formed for nineteen centuries into an ardent and conquering ambition." De Gaulle made this remark at a press conference on November 27, 1967. The French word *dominateur* is translated as "domineering" when it applies to a person and "dominating" when it applies to a country. Charles de Gaulle, *Vers le terme, Janvier 1966–Avril 1969*, vol. 5 of *Discours et messages* (Paris: Omnibus/Plon, 1993), 1062.

4. *New York Times*, September 21, 2002, A12.

5. Jacques Juillard, "Parlez, monsieur Chirac!" *Le Nouvel Observateur*, May 15–21, 2003, 29.

6. Hubert Védrine with Dominique Moïsi, *France in an Age of Globalization*, trans. Philip H. Gordon (Washington, D.C.: Brookings Institution Press, 2001), 30.

7. Pierre Nora, "L'Histoire de France de Lavisse," in *Les lieux de mémoire*, ed. Pierre Nora (Paris: Gallimard, 1997), 851.

8. Marc Fumaroli, "Le génie de la langue française," in *Les lieux de mémoire*, vol. 3, 4624.

9. "Une enquête européenne," an interview with Pierre Bréchon, *Le Monde*, October 13–14, 2002, 14.

10. Jean de la Bruyère, *Les caractères ou les moeurs de ce siècle* (Paris: Estienne Michaliet, 1689), 245.

11. The phrase is that of a French ambassador posted to Brussels. See chapter 3, p. 61.

12. Poland also contributed several hundred special forces troops in the war against Iraq.

13. Nora, "La génération," in *Les lieux de mémoire*, vol. 2, 2998.

14. Nora, "Gaullistes et communistes," in *Les lieux de mémoire*, vol. 2, 2504.

15. Nora, "L'Histoire de France de Lavisse," 886.

16. Nora, "La génération," 3006.

17. Jacques Juillard, "À genoux devant Wolfowitz?" *Le Nouvel Observateur*, April 17–23, 2003, 35.

18. Juillard, "Parlez, monsieur Chirac!" 29.

19. Alain Lempereur, interview by author, Paris, September 7, 2002.

20. Robert H. Mnookin, Scott R. Peppet, and Andrew S. Tulumello, *Beyond Winning: Negotiating to Create Value in Deals and Disputes* (Cambridge, Mass.: Harvard University Press, 2000), 46–47.

21. Robert Mnookin and Alain Lempereur, "La gestion des tensions dans la négociation," in *Négociation dans l'administration publique: Manuel* *du formateur*, ed. Alain Lempereur, séminaire à l'École Nationale d'Adminis-tration, Strasbourg, May 2002 (Paris: ESSEC IRÉNÉ, 2002), 286.

22. French diplomat, interview by author, May 10, 2002.

23. See chapter 5, p. 228.

24. See chapter 5, p. 203.

25. See chapter 4, p. 152.

26. Armand Frémont, "La terre," in *Les lieux de mémoire*, vol. 3, 3078.

27. Hoffmann (lecture presented at a conference on the U.S.-French rift).

28. Lempereur, interview by author.

29. George Bush and Brent Scowcroft, *A World Transformed* (New York: Vintage Books, 1998), 78.

30. Claude Langlois, "Catholiques et laïcs," in *Les lieux de mémoire*, vol. 2, 2348.

31. François Azouvi, "Descartes," in *Les lieux de mémoire*, vol. 3, 4490.

32. Alain Finkelkraut, "Heidegger," *Le Nouvel Observateur*, August 1–7, 2002, 14.

33. Marc Fumaroli, "La conversation," in *Les lieux de mémoire*, vol. 3, 3620. Madame de Staël's quotation is from "De l'esprit de conversation," *De l'Allemagne*, ed. S. Balayé (Paris: Garnier-Flammarion, 1968).

34. Alain Rey, "Raffarin dans le texte," *Le Nouvel Observateur*, September 12–18, 2002, 52.

35. The *dissertation* reflex is very strong among the French elites. For instance, in writing this book, I sent one of my French interviewees, a senior civil servant, a questionnaire and a chapter plan. When I reached him by telephone, he said he would rather just answer my questions. I put the first question to him, and he responded with a full-blown discourse that lasted about fifteen minutes.

36. Azouvi, "Descartes," 4480.

37. Charles G. Cogan, *Oldest Allies, Guarded Friends: The United States and France since 1940* (Westport, Conn.: Praeger, 1994), 212.

38. Jean-Philippe Mathy, *French Resistance: The French-American Culture Wars* (Minneapolis: University of Minnesota Press, 2000), 24.

39. Philip Gordon and Sophie Meunier, *The French Challenge: Adapting to Globalization* (Washington, D.C.: Brookings Institution Press, 2001), 97.

40. In this regard, see the remarks by a senior British diplomatic official quoted on p. 6 and by Henry Kissinger on p. 15.

41. French diplomat, interview by author, May 10, 2002.

42. See p. 208.

43. Remarks at a conference at Columbia University on the French-American rift, May 22, 2003.

44. Nora, "La nation mémoire," in *Les lieux de mémoire*, vol. 2, 2212–2213.

45. French diplomat, interview by author, May 10, 2002.

46. See p. 56.

47. Gordon and Meunier, *The French Challenge*.

48. Pierre Nora, "La nation mémoire," in *Les lieux de mémoire*, vol. 2, 2210.

7. LOOKING AHEAD

1. Alain Lempereur, e-mail to author, July 22, 2002.

2. Philip Gordon and Sophie Meunier, *The French Challenge: Adapting to Globalization* (Washington: Brookings Institution Press, 2001).

3. Ibid., 23.

4. Ibid., 38.

5. Senior State Department official, interview by author, Washington, D.C., February 7, 2002. Also see p. 116.

6. Pierre Vimont, interview by author, Brussels, March 4, 2002.

7. Pascal Lamy and Jean Pisani-Ferry, *L'Europe de nos volontés* (Paris: Les Notes de la Fondation Jean-Jaurès, no. 27, January 2002), 7.

8. Alain Lamassoure, delegate to the Convention on the Future of Europe, "Aux sources de la negociation européenne: Les penseurs français de la diplomatie a l'époque classique" (speech presented to a conference sponsored by the École Supérieure des Sciences Économiques et Commericales [ESSEC], Paris, June 18, 2003).

9. Hubert Védrine (speech presented to a conference sponsored by ESSEC on the sources of European negotiation, Paris, June 18, 2003).

10. Ibid.

11. Maurice Vaïsse, *La grandeur: Politique étrangère du général de Gaulle, 1958–1969* (Paris: Fayard, 1998), 237.

12. "Que faire avec l'hyperpuissance," interview with Hubert Védrine, *Le Débat*, no. 125 (May-August 2003): 6.

13. Robert Kagan, "L'Europe postmoderne," *Le Monde*, July 28–29, 2002, 8.

14. Jacques Isnard, "La défense française et le modèle anglais," *Le Monde*, July 17, 2002, 12. See also chapter 3, p. 86 for the comments of NATO official Bruce Bach on the French lagging behind the British, especially in new weaponry.

15. Stephen Rosen, "Thoughts on Imperial Strategy" (lecture presented at a seminar, Harvard University, Cambridge, Mass., September 23, 2002).

16. Nicole Gnesotto, *La puissance et l'Europe* (Paris: Presse de Sciences Po, 1998), 113.

17. Bruce Bach, interview by author, Brussels, March 6, 2002.

18. French defense expert, interview by author, Washington, D.C., May 12, 2003.

19. John Kornblum, interview by author, Berlin, March 8, 2002.

20. Senior State Department official, interview by author, August 10, 2002. Also see p. 150.

21. Michael Brenner and Guillaume Parmentier, *Reconcilable Differences: U.S.-French Relations in the New Era* (Washington, D.C.: Brookings Institution Press, 2002), 118.

22. Ibid., 123.

23. François Furet, "L'Ancien régime et la révolution," in *Les lieux de mémoire*, vol. 2 (Paris: Gallimard, 1997), 2316.

24. Stanley Hoffmann, "Pour une Europe puissance complète," *Le Monde*, June 6–7, 1999, 14.

25. Védrine (speech presented to a conference sponsored by ESSEC).

26. Interview by author, Washington, D.C., July 28, 2003.

Select Bibliography

Books

Andréani, Jacques. *L'Amérique et nous*. Paris: Odile Jacob, 2000.

Aron, Raymond. *An Essay on Freedom*, translated by Helen Weaver, 5. New York: World Publishing, 1970.

Attali, Jacques. *Verbatim III*. Paris: Fayard, 1995.

Auduc, J.-L. *L'École en France*. Paris: Nathan, 1997.

Avruch, Kevin. *Culture and Conflict Resolution*. Washington, D.C.: United States Institute of Peace Press, 1998.

Bainville, Jacques. *Histoire de France*. Vol. 1. Paris: Plon, 1933.

Bell, David A. *The Cult of the Nation in France: Inventing Nationalism, 1680–1800*. Cambridge, Mass.: Harvard University Press, 2001.

Benamou, Georges-Marc. *Le dernier Mitterrand*. Paris: Plon, 1996.

Bozo, Frédéric. *La France et l'OTAN: De la guerre froide au nouvel ordre européen*. Paris: Masson, 1991.

———. *Two Strategies for Europe: De Gaulle, the United States, and the Atlantic Alliance*, translated by Susan Emanuel. Lanham, Md.: Rowman and Littlefield, 2001.

Brenner, Michael, and Guillaume Parmentier. *Reconcilable Differences: U.S.-French Relations in the New Era*. Washington, D.C.: Brookings Institution Press, 2002.

Brett, Jeanne M. *Negotiating Globally: How to Negotiate Deals, Resolve Disputes, and Make Decisions across Cultural Boundaries*. San Francisco: Jossey-Bass, 2001.

315

Bush, George, and Brent Scowcroft. *A World Transformed*. New York: Vintage Books, 1998.

Butler, Richard. *The Greatest Threat: Iraq, Weapons of Mass Destruction, and the Crisis of Global Security*. New York: Public Affairs, 2000.

Carpentier Jean, and François Lebrun, eds. *Histoire de France*. Paris: Seuil, 1987.

Chenu, Roselyne. *Paul Delouvrier ou la passion d'agir*. Paris: Seuil, 1994.

Cogan, Charles G. *Charles de Gaulle: A Brief Biography with Documents*. New York: St. Martin's Press, Bedford Books, 1996.

———. *Forced to Choose: France, the Atlantic Alliance, and NATO—Then and Now*. Westport, Conn.: Praeger, 1997.

———. *Oldest Allies, Guarded Friends: The United States and France since 1940*. Westport, Conn.: Praeger, 1994.

———. *The Third Option: The Emancipation of European Defense, 1989–2000*. Westport, Conn.: Praeger, 2001.

Cohen, Raymond. *Negotiating across Cultures: International Communication in an Interdependent World*. Washington, D.C.: United States Institute of Peace Press, 1997.

Cohen, Samy, ed. *Mitterrand et la sortie de la guerre froide*. Paris: Presses universitaires de France, 1998.

Cooper, Robert. *The Post-Modern State and the World Order*. London: Demos, 2002.

Debray, Régis. *Contretemps: Éloges des idéaux perdus*. Paris: Gallimard, 1992.

———. *Les empires contre l'Europe*. Paris: Gallimard, 1985.

Debré, Michel. *Entretiens avec le général de Gaulle, 1961–1969*. Paris: Albin Michel, 1993.

Delafon, Gilles, and Thomas Sancton. *Dear Jacques Cher Bill . . . Au coeur de l'Élysée et de la Maison Blanche, 1995–1999*. Paris: Plon, 1999.

Duroselle, Jean-Baptiste. *France and the United States: From the Beginnings to the Present*, translated by Derek Coltman. Chicago: University of Chicago Press, 1978.

Favier, Pierre, and Michel Martin-Roland. *La décennie Mitterrand*. Vol. 3, *Les défis (1988–1991)*. Paris: Seuil, 1996.

———. *La décennie Mitterrand*. Vol. 4, *Les déchirements (1991–1995)*. Paris: Seuil, 1996.

Freeman, Chas. W., Jr. *Arts of Power: Statecraft and Diplomacy*. Washington, D.C.: United States Institute of Peace Press, 1997.

Furet, François. *Le passé d'une illusion: Essai sur l'idée communiste au XXe siècle*. Paris: Robert Laffont/Calmann-Lévy, 1995.

Furet, François, Jacques Julliard, and Pierre Rosenvallon. *La République du centre: La fin de l'exception française*, 419. Paris: Calmann-Lévy, 1988.

Gaulle, Charles de. *The Complete War Memoirs of Charles de Gaulle*. Vol. 1, *The Call to Honor, 1940–1942*, translated by Jonathan Griffin. New York: Simon and Schuster, 1964.

———. *The Complete War Memoirs of Charles de Gaulle*. Vol. 2, *Unity, 1942–1944*, translated by Richard Howard. New York: Simon and Schuster, 1964.

———. *The Complete War Memoirs of Charles de Gaulle*. Vol. 3, *Salvation, 1944–1946*, translated by Richard Howard. New York: Simon and Schuster, 1964.

———. *Renewal, 1958–1962*. Part 1, *Memoirs of Hope: Renewal and Endeavor*, translated by Terence Kilmartin. New York: Simon and Schuster, 1971.

Gautier, Louis. *Mitterrand et son armée, 1990–1995*. Paris: Grasset, 1999.

Gnesotto, Nicole. *La puissance et l'Europe*. Paris: Presse de Sciences Po, 1998.

Godechot, Jacques, ed. *Les constitutions de la France depuis 1789*. Paris: Garnier-Flammarion, 1970.

Gordon, Philip H., and Sophie Meunier. *The French Challenge: Adapting to Globalization*. Washington, D.C.: Brookings Institution Press, 2001.

Grosser, Alfred. *Affaires extérieures: La politique de la France, 1944–1984*. Paris: Flammarion, 1984.

———. *The Western Alliance*. New York: Continuum, 1980.

Guéhenno, Jean-Marie. *La fin de la démocratie*. Paris: Flammarion, 1993.

Guerlain, Pierre. *Miroirs transtlantiques: La France et les États-Unis entre passions et indifferences*. Paris: L'Harmattan, 1996.

Hall, Edward T. *Beyond Culture*. New York: Anchor Books, 1976.

Ingersoll, K. A., A. J. Rayner, and R. C. Hine. *Agriculture in the Uruguay Round*. New York: St. Martin's Press, 1994.

Harrison, Lawrence E., and Samuel P. Huntington. *Culture Matters: How Values Shape Human Progress*. New York: Basic Books, 2000.

Holbrooke, Richard. *To End a War*. New York: Random House, 1998.

Josling, Timothy E., Stefan Tangermann, and T. K. Warley. *Agriculture in the GATT*. New York: St. Martin's Press, 1996.

Kissinger, Henry. *Diplomacy.* New York: Simon and Schuster, 1994.

Knapp, Andrew, and Vincent Wright. *The Government and Politics of France,* 4th ed., 202–203. London: Routledge, 2001.

Lacouture, Jean. *De Gaulle.* 3 vols. Paris: Seuil, 1984, 1985, 1986.

Landau, Alice. *Conflits et coopération dans les relations économiques internationales: Le cas de l'Uruguay Round.* Brussels: Bruylant, 1996.

Lanxade, Jacques. *Quand le monde a basculé.* Paris: NiL éditions, 2001.

Leites, Nathan. *Images of Power in French Politics.* Vol. 1. Santa Monica, Calif.: Rand Corporation, 1962.

——. *On the Game of Politics in France.* Stanford, Calif.: Stanford University Press, 1959.

——. *The Rules of the Game in Paris,* translated by Derek Coleman. Chicago: University of Chicago Press, 1966.

Lempereur, Alain. Preface to critical edition of François de Callières, *De la manière de négocier avec les souverains.* Geneva: Librairie Droz, 2002.

Livre blanc sur la défense nationale. Paris: CREST, 1972.

Malet, Albert, and Jules Isaac. *L'Histoire.* Paris: Hachette, 1961.

Mathy, Jean-Philippe. *French Resistance: The French-American Culture Wars.* Minneapolis: University of Minnesota Press, 2000.

Mazzucelli, Colette. *France and Germany at Maastricht.* New York: Garland, 1997.

Mead, Margaret, and Martha Wolfenstein, eds. *Childhood in Contemporary Cultures.* Chicago: University of Chicago Press, 1955.

Mearsheimer, John. *The Tragedy of Great Power Politics.* New York: W. W. Norton, 2001.

Mélandri, Pierre, and Justin Vaïsse. *L'Empire du milieu: Les États-Unis et le monde depuis la fin de la guerre froide.* Paris: Odile Jacob, 2001.

Michelet, Jules. *Le peuple.* Paris: Flammarion, Champ Historique, 1974.

Mignon, Ernest. *Les mots du général.* Paris: Fayard, 1962.

Mnookin, Robert H., Scott R. Peppet, and Andrew S. Tulumello. *Beyond Winning: Negotiating to Create Value in Deals and Disputes.* Cambridge, Mass.: Harvard University Press, 2000.

Monnet, Jean. *Memoirs,* translated by Richard Mayne. Garden City, N.Y.: Doubleday, 1978.

Nora, Pierre, ed. *Les lieux de mémoire.* 3 vols. Paris: Gallimard, 1997.

Paemen, Hugo, and Alexandra Bensch. *From the GATT to the WTO: The European Community in the Uruguay Round.* Leuven, Belgium: Leuven University Press, 1995.

Peyrefitte, Alain. *C'était de Gaulle.* 3 vols. Paris: Fayard, 1994.

Plantey, Alain. *La négociation internationale au XXIe siècle.* Paris: CNRS éditions, 2002.

The Political Testament of Cardinal Richelieu, translated by Henry Bertram Hill. Madison: University of Wisconsin Press, 1961.

Pratt, Polly. *French or Foe: Getting the Most out of Living and Working in France.* London: Culture Crossings, 1994.

Prost, Antoine. *Éducation, société et politiques: Une histoire de l'enseignement en France, de 1945 à nos jours.* Paris: Seuil, 1992.

Schecter, Jerrold L. *Russian Negotiating Behavior: Continuity and Transition.* Washington, D.C.: United States Institute of Peace Press, 1998.

Schnapper, Dominique. *La communauté des citoyens: Sur l'idée moderne de nation.* Paris: Gallimard, 1994.

Schrameck, Olivier. *Matignon Rive Gauche, 1997–2001.* Paris: Seuil, 2001.

Smyser, W. R. *How Germans Negotiate: Logical Goals, Practical Solutions.* Washington, D.C.: United States Institute of Peace Press, 2003.

Snyder, Scott. *Negotiating on the Edge: North Korean Negotiating Behavior.* Washington, D.C.: United States Institute of Peace Press, 1999.

Solomon, Richard H. *Chinese Negotiating Behavior: Pursuing Interests through "Old Friends."* Interpretive essay by Chas W. Freeman Jr. Washington, D.C.: United States Institute of Peace Press, 1999.

Suleiman, Ezra N. *Elites in French Society: The Politics of Survival.* Princeton, N.J.: Princeton University Press, 1978.

Trompenaars, Fons. *Riding the Waves of Culture.* London: Economist Books, 1993.

Utley, Rachel. *The French Defense Debate: Consensus and Continuity in the Mitterrand Era.* London: Macmillan, 2000.

Vahl, Remco. *Leadership in Disguise: The Role of the European Commission in EC Decision-Making on Agriculture in the Uruguay Round.* Aldershot, U.K.: Ashgate, 1997.

Vaïsse, Maurice. *La grandeur: Politique étrangère du général de Gaulle, 1958–1969.* Paris: Fayard, 1998.

Védrine, Hubert, *Les mondes de François Mitterrand: À l'Élysée, 1981–1995.*
Paris: Fayard, 1996.

Védrine, Hubert, with Dominique Moïsi. *France in an Age of Globalization,*
translated by Philip H. Gordon. Washington, D.C.: Brookings Institution
Press, 2001.

Watkins, Michael, and Susan Rosegrant. *Breakthrough International
Negotiation: How Great Negotiators Transformed the World's Toughest
Post–Cold War Conflicts.* San Francisco: Jossey-Bass, 2001.

Weber, Eugen. *Peasants into Frenchmen: The Modernization of Rural France,
1870–1914.* Stanford, Calif.: Stanford University Press, 1976.

World Trade Organization. *The Legal Texts: The Results of the Uruguay Round
of Multilateral Trade Negotiations.* Cambridge: Cambridge University
Press, 1999.

ARTICLES

Ash, Timothy Garton. "Odd Man Out," review of Oskar Lafonntaine, *The
Heart Beats on the Left,* translated by Ronald Taylor (London: Polity
Press, 2001). In *New York Review of Books,* November 1, 2001.

Azouvi, François. "Descartes." In *Les lieux de mémoire,* vol. 3, edited by
Pierre Nora, 4475–4519. Paris: Gallimard, 1997.

Beloff, Max. "Tocqueville and the Odd Couple: A Review of Franco-German
Relations." *National Interest,* no. 55 (spring 1999).

Bozo, Frédéric. "La France et l'Alliance atlantique depuis la fin de la guerre
froide: Le modèle gaullien en question." *Cahiers du Centre d'études
d'histoire de la Défense (1989–1999),* no. 17 (2001).

Brzezinski, Zbigniew. "Living with a New Europe." *National Interest* (summer 2000).

Casanova, Jean-Claude. "Présidentielle: L'État de la gauche." *Le Monde,*
March 22, 2002, 1, 20.

Charles, Christophe. "Les grands corps." In *Les lieux de mémoire,* vol. 3,
edited by Pierre Nora, 3199–3233. Paris: Gallimard, 1997.

Chartier, Roger. "La Ligne Saint-Malo-Genève." In *Les lieux de mémoire,*
vol. 2, edited by Pierre Nora, 2817–2850. Paris: Gallimard, 1997.

Christin, Olivier. "L'homme moderne et le sacré," review of Alain Tallon,
Conscience nationale et sentiment religieux en France au XVIe siècle
(Paris: Presses universitaires de France, 2002). In *Le Monde,* March 29,
2002.

Cooper, Robert. "The New Liberal Imperialism." *Observer*, April 7, 2002, 3.

——. "The Post-Modern State." In *Reordering the World: The Long-Term Implications of September 11*. London: Foreign Policy Centre, 2002.

Decherf, Dominique. "French Views of Religious Freedom." *U.S.-France Analysis*. Washington, D.C.: Center for the United States and France (July 2001): 2.

Droit, Roger-Pol. "Comment Descartes devint la France," review of François Azouvi, *Descartes et la France: Histoire d'une passion nationale* (Paris: Fayard, 2002). In *Le Monde des Livres*, March 15, 2002, 1.

Dumoulin, André. "Les ambitions de l'Europe: De l'après-Kosovo aux indicateurs de cohérence." *Politique Étrangère* (summer 2000).

Fontaine, André. "Les paradigms artificiels," in "1991–2001: Dix années qui ébranlèrent le monde." *La Revue Internationale et Stratégique*, special edition, edited by Pascal Boniface, no. 41 (spring 2001).

French Negotiating Style, United States Institute of Peace Special Report. Washington, D.C.: United States Institute of Peace, 2000.

Goulemot, Jean-Marie, and Éric Walter. "Les centenaires de Voltaire et de Rousseau." In *Les lieux de mémoire*, vol. 1, edited by Pierre Nora, 351–381. Paris: Gallimard, 1997.

Grant, R. P. "France's New Relationship with NATO." *Survival* 1, no. 38 (spring 1996).

Hélie, Jérôme. "Les armes." In *Les lieux de mémoire*, vol. 3, edited by Pierre Nora, 3235–3275. Paris: Gallimard, 1997.

Hoffmann, Stanley. "Clash of Globalizations." *Foreign Affairs* (July-August 2002).

——. "Deux universalismes en conflit." *La Revue Tocqueville* 21, no. 1 (2000).

——. "French Dilemmas and Strategies in the New Europe." In *After the Cold War: International Institutions and State Strategies in Europe, 1989–1991*, edited by Robert O. Keohane, Joseph S. Nye, and Stanley Hoffmann. Cambridge, Mass.: Harvard University Press, 1993.

——. "The Man Who Would Be France," review of Jean Lacouture, *De Gaulle*, vol. 1, *The Rebel, 1890–1944*, translated by Patrick O'Brian (London: Collins Harvill, 1990). In *New Republic*, December 17, 1990.

Howorth, Jolyon. "Défense européenne: Entre atlantisme et européisme." In *Ramses 2001*, edited by Thierry de Montbrial and Pierre Jacquet. Paris: Institut Français des Relations Internationales, 2000.

Isnard, Jacques. "La défense française et le modèle anglais." *Le Monde*, July 17, 2002, 1, 12.

Judt, Tony. "America and the War." *New York Review of Books*, November 15, 2001.

———. "Its Own Worst Enemy," review of Joseph S. Nye Jr., *The Paradox of American Power: Why the World's Only Superpower Can't Go It Alone* (Oxford: Oxford University Press, 2002). In *New York Review of Books*, August 15, 2002, 12–17.

Kagan, Robert. "L'Europe postmoderne." *Le Monde*, July 28–29, 2002, 8.

———. "Power and Weakness." *Policy Review* (June-July 2002): 3, 10–11.

Kauffmann, Sylvie. "Le nouvel unilatéralisme américain." *Le Monde*, January 2, 2002.

Krotz, Ulrich. "National Role Conceptions and Foreign Policies: France and Germany Compared." Harvard University, Center for European Studies Working Paper 02.1, 2002.

Lamy, Pascal, and Jean Pisani-Ferry. "L'Europe de nos volontés." *Les Notes de la Fondation Jean-Jaurès*, no. 27 (January 2002).

Langlois, Claude. "Catholics et laïcs." In *Les lieux de mémoire*, vol. 2, edited by Pierre Nora, 2327–2358. Paris: Gallimard, 1997.

Lempereur, Alain. "Negotiation and Mediation in France: The Challenge of Skill-Based Learning and Interdisciplinary Research in Legal Education." *Harvard Negotiation Law Review* 3 (spring 1998): 151–174.

Leparmentier, Arnaud. "Les relations entre la France et l'Allemagne connaissent de nouvelles tensions." *Le Monde*, November 29, 2000, 2.

Lequesne, Christian. "Une lecture décisionnelle de la politique européenne de François Mitterrand." In *Mitterrand et la sortie de la guerre froide*, edited by Samy Cohen. Paris: Presses universitaires de France, 1998.

"L'Europe-puissance: Entretien avec Javier Solana." *Politique Internationale* (summer 2001).

Lewis, Patricia. "From UNSCOM to UNMOVIC: The United Nations and Iraq." *Disarmament Forum* 2 (2001).

Montbrial, Thierry de. "La France est-elle 'l'ennemi numéro 1' des États-Unis?" *Le Figaro*, June 16, 1992.

Müllerson, Rein. *Jus ad bellum: Plus ça change (le Monde), plus c'est la même chose (le Droit)*, draft paper, Naval War College Conference on Terrorism, June 2002.

Nora, Pierre. "La génération." In *Les lieux de mémoire*, vol. 2, edited by Pierre Nora, 2975–3015. Paris: Gallimard, 1997.

———."La nation mémoire." In *Les lieux de mémoire*, vol. 2, edited by Pierre Nora, 2207–2216. Paris: Gallimard, 1997.

Nordman, Daniel. "Des limites d'état aux frontières nationales." In *Les lieux de mémoire*, vol. 1, edited by Pierre Nora, 1125–1146. Paris: Gallimard, 1997.

Ory, Pascal. "La gastronomie." In *Les lieux de mémoire*, vol. 3, edited by Pierre Nora, 3743–3769. Paris: Gallimard, 1997.

Pastoureau, Michel. "Le coq gaulois." In *Les lieux de mémoire*, vol. 3, edited by Pierre Nora, 4297–4319. Paris: Gallimard, 1997.

Revel, Jacques. "La cour." In *Les lieux de mémoire*, vol. 3, edited by Pierre Nora, 3141–3197. Paris: Gallimard, 1997.

Ryan, Alan. "Visions of Politics," review of Sheldon S. Wolin, *Tocqueville between Two Worlds: The Making of a Political and Theoretical Life.* (Princeton, N.J.: Princeton University Press, 2002). In *New York Review of Books*, June 27, 2002.

Starobinski, Jean. "Rousseau and Revolution." *New York Review of Books*, April 25, 2002, 55.

Thadden, Rudolph von. "Un équilibre difficile." *Zeitschrift für Kultur Austausch* 4 (2000): 12–13.

Wolfenstein, Martha. "French Parents Take Their Children to the Park." In *Childhood in Contemporary Cultures*, edited by Margaret Mead and Martha Wolfenstein. Chicago: University of Chicago Press, 1955.

Index

325

About the Author

Charles Cogan is a senior research associate at Harvard University's John F. Kennedy School of Government, as well as an affiliate at the John M. Olin Institute for Strategic Studies and the Center for European Studies. In 1992 he received from Harvard the degree of doctor of public administration. His doctoral thesis became his first book *(Oldest Allies, Guarded Friends: The United States and France since 1940)* and was followed by three others, dealing chiefly with France. A former military officer and a former journalist, he spent thirty-seven years in the CIA, twenty-three of them overseas. He was chief of the Near East South Asia Division in the Directorate of Operations (1979–84) and CIA chief in Paris (1984–89). He has lectured and written in English and French on history and foreign policy, focusing on French-American relations, the Middle East, and defense and intelligence issues.

FRENCH NEGOTIATING BEHAVIOR

This book is set in Bodoni Light; the display type is Bodoni Medium. Hasten Design Studio designed the book's cover; Mike Chase designed the interior and made up the pages. David Sweet copyedited the text, which was proofread by Karen Stough. The index was prepared by Sonsie Conroy. The book's editor was Nigel Quinney.